The Four World Cities Transport Study

Editor:	Caralampo Focas	London Research Centre
Project Directors:	Joseph Berthet	Paris - Institut d'Aménagement et d'Urbanisme de la Région d'Ile-de-France
	Caralampo Focas	London - London Research Centre
	John Keith	New York - Institute of Public Administration
	Hisatake Togo	Tokyo - Tokyo Institute for Municipal Research
Contributors:	Rosemary Dempster	London Research Centre
	Tetsuya Higuchi	Tokyo Institute for Municipal Research
	Brian Ketcham	Konheim and Ketcham, New York
	Carolyn Konheim	Konheim and Ketcham, New York
	Lesley Murray	London Research Centre
	Danièle Navarre	Institut d'Aménagement et d'Urbanisme de la Région d'Ile-de-France
	Louis Servant	Institut d'Aménagement et d'Urbanisme de la Région d'Ile-de-France
	Bill Shore	Institute of Public Administration
	Koichi Takagi	Tokyo Institute for Municipal Research
Assistance:	Andy Anderson	London Transport
	Regina Armstrong	Urbanomics
	Kozo Aoyama	Institute of Public Administration
	Patricia Broad	Office of National Statistics
	Mike Collop	Department of the Environment, Transport and the Regions
	Danielle Coupeaux	Institut d'Aménagement et d'Urbanisme de la Région d'Ile-de-France
	Maggie Ellwood	London Research Centre
	Aleyne Friesner	London Research Centre
	Michel Henin	Direction Régionale de l'Équipement d'Ile-de-France
	Kate Holgate	London Research Centre
	John Hollis	London Research Centre
	Chris Hyde	London Transport
	Kenshi Itaoka	Fuji Corporation
	Tomoya Kaji	Tokyo Institute for Municipal Research/ Institute of Public Administration
	Liz Kingsley	Institute of Public Administration
	Jun Kitamura	Tokyo Institute for Municipal Research
	Rachel Leeser	London Research Centre
	Makoto Mochizuki	Tokyo Institute for Municipal Research
	Fumihiko Numao	Tokyo Institute for Municipal Research
	Mami Oku	Tokyo Institute for Municipal Research
	Richard Smith	Government Office for London
	Dai Tamaru	Tokyo Institute for Municipal Research
	Miki Yasui	Tokyo Institute for Municipal Research

We wish to thank the following for financial assistance:

London:

- Department of the Environment, Transport and the Regions
- Government Office for London
- London Transport
- The London Boroughs

New York:

- United States Department of Transportation
- United States Federal Highway Administration
- United States Federal Transit Administration
- Bombardier
- David Rockefeller
- Heidrich & Struggles
- Konheim & Ketcham
- Rose Associates
- William S. Hack

Paris:

- Conseil Régionale Ile-de-France
- Prefecture d'Ile-de-France

Tokyo:

- Tokyo Metropolitan Government
- Tokyo Gas Corporation

The Four World Cities Transport Study

Fax (+44) 0171 787 5606
www.london-research.gov.uk

London: The Stationery Office

The question that now begins to gnaw at your mind is more anguished: outside the city does an outside exist? Or, no matter how far you go from the city, will you only pass from one limbo to another, never managing to leave it?

Italo Calvino, *Invisible Cities*

ISBN 0 11 702645 X

Copyright
London Research Centre
1998

81 Black Prince Road
London SE1 7SZ
Telephone 0171 787 5500
Fax 0171 787 5606

The views expressed in this book are those of the editor and do not necessarily reflect those of partners, sponsors or contributors.

Contents

Introduction

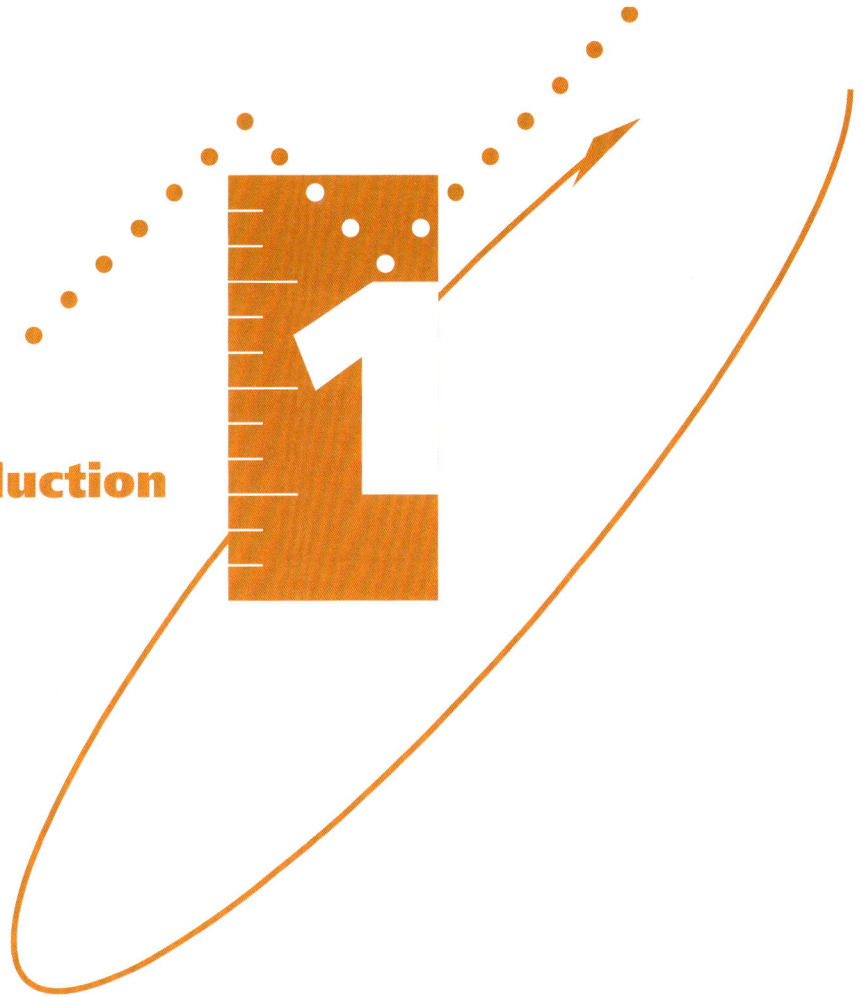

Content

1   Introduction

Increasingly the world's economies are becoming inter-linked. The world's leading metropolises are showing similar patterns of development, sprawl and environmental degradation. In cities, transport structures largely define development of the built environment, economic efficiency and quality of life.

This study focuses on the transport systems of - arguably - the four most advanced world cities - London, New York, Paris and Tokyo [1].

All four enjoy mature public transport systems and comprehensive road networks, historically spreading outwards. All four underwent suburbanisation well before the Second World War. All four are experiencing the same continuing post-war phenomenon - the dramatic growth of "exurbia", that is, the urbanisation of the hinterlands of their historic city areas. In each case, this exurbanisation, and its accelerating expansion, depends heavily on the car. In each case, sustainability and environmental quality are at risk.

The study reveals how the four world cities are responding to modern transport demands. Uniform measurements and indices reveal historical trends, and describe current conditions of socio-economic characteristics, travel behaviour and transport infrastructure.

Increasing use of the car

All the cities face different challenges, despite their common concerns arising from the post-war rise in car ownership and consequent road construction.

To varying degrees, all four cities have now concluded that further road building will not eliminate traffic congestion [2] and its consequences. Although some road construction is underway in Paris and Tokyo, it is mostly to build orbital links. It is shared wisdom that most new roads, in any event, appear to achieve only temporary relief from congestion - relief soon swamped by existing or potential suppressed demand.

Competitiveness

The perceived importance of transport systems to the quality of urban life and of economic competitiveness is well documented. (The Federal Transit Administration, for instance, has calculated that New York's public transport provides a $20 billion benefit to society at large, due to avoided congestion, energy use and emissions, and to the lower cost of social assistance [3].) However, all the cities, while acknowledging that they cannot build their way out of congestion, are tackling these issues differently, reflecting different settlement patterns.

---

1   London, New York, Paris and Tokyo are often recognised as being the world's "global cities", eg. in the *Four World Cities Study* (Llewelyn-Davies et al., 1996, p. i & pp. iii-iv). The authors of that report argue that these four cities are at the centre of a global system of production and information exchange.

2   The sustainability of accommodating increasing car use is being challenged by an increasing number of economists and environmental planners. Growing government concern was expressed, in particular, by the Commission of the European Union, which, in 1995, issued a *Green Paper, Fair and Efficient Pricing in Transport*, stating, "there is a growing realisation, that on current policies alone, transport trends are unsustainable" and that the reason for the unsustainability was, "increasing congestion, environmental consequences and accidents" (Commission of the European Communities, 1995, p.3). The European Commission's *Green Paper* claims that congestion costs the Union 2% of GDP every year, accidents another 1.5%, air pollution 0.4% (excluding global warming) and noise 10.2%; and that road transport accounts for over 90% of these costs. Other studies have suggested the combined costs of these externalities could be even higher; up to 5% of GDP has been estimated by the OECD (Commission of the European Communities, 1995, p.2).

3   Federal Transit Administration, 1996 b.

Paris and Tokyo have defined growth areas and promoted high density developments for both housing and employment. These high density developments encourage public transport and non-motorised trip making. Both cities are expanding their public transport rail and metro networks. London and New York are relying more on traffic management measures. Transport expenditure in New York and, to a lesser extent, in London, is mainly directed to restoring and upgrading existing systems after decades of neglect.

Regional governance

In Paris and Tokyo, strong regional governments have devised and are implementing long-term structure plans. The New York region, straddling three states, has no unified government, and thus no strong planning framework. Development is haphazard. London has had no city-wide government since 1985 (although this will change from 2000), and the strategic planning guidance offered by central government to the capital city cannot guarantee coherent regional development.

Mutual lessons

In 1992, the London Research Centre and the Institut d'Aménagement et d'Urbanisme de la Région d'Ile-de-France undertook jointly a detailed comparison [4] of the transport systems of London and Paris. The report identified strengths and weaknesses in both cities, and became a useful and much-quoted source for politicians and practitioners alike on both sides of the Channel.

The study showed London with a wide regional road network, and in the process of restoring planning and investment to a long-neglected public transport system. Paris was reported as continuing its steady investment

schedule, based on ambitious five-year plans for both roads and public transport. Where London had been seen as a model for development in the 1960s, by the early 1990s Paris seemed to lead the way.

Numerous recent studies have tried to compare major world cities, assessing perceived strengths and weaknesses in respect of global competition for trade and inward investment. The British Government commissioned one such recent report, the 1996 *London Comparative Study* [5]. This identified six common responses to current global economic forces:

- growth of the service economy

- expansion of economic and physical boundaries through improved transport and communications

- development of new "sunrise technologies" on peripheral, green-field sites

- decline and dispersal of manufacturing

- dispersal of "back office" functions to suburbs, regional hinterlands, other regions, even abroad

- economic contraction and consequent multiple deprivation in some parts of the cities

The present study updates and builds on the 1992 Paris-London comparison - adding New York and Tokyo - and extends the key transport analysis beyond that undertaken for the 1996 *London Comparative Study.* The intention is to learn from experience and best practice in similar settings.

The collaboration between non-profitmaking municipal research institutes in each of the four cities has brought

4   *Paris-London: a comparison of transport systems* (Focas & Navarre, 1992).

5   Llewelyn-Davies et al., 1996.

together a uniquely well-qualified international research team. The four institutes are:

- **London**   London Research Centre.

  The London Research Centre was established in 1987, by all the 33 London boroughs, after the abolition of the Greater London Council. Its remit is to collect, analyse and disseminate strategic information and research work of concern to London.

- **New York**   Institute of Public Administration and partners, Konheim & Ketcham.

  The Institute of Public Administration was established as a non-profit making independent body in 1907 to promote good practice in governance in the United States of America.

  Konheim & Ketcham is a private New York-based transport and environment consultancy.

- **Paris**   Institut d'Aménagement et d'Urbanisme de la Région d'Ile-de-France.

  The Institut d'Aménagement et d'Urbanisme de la Région d'Ile-de-France was created in 1960 as the research organisation for the Ile-de-France Regional Council. It provides the secretariat for Metropolis, a major world cities' organisation.

- **Tokyo**   Tokyo Institute for Municipal Research.

  The Tokyo Institute for Municipal Research was established in 1922 as a non-profitmaking independent body to undertake research on municipal policies and administration.

This study is also published in separate French and Japanese editions.

1.1   The contents of the study

The Four World Cities Transport Study is composed of three distinct sections, a description of government and the institutional organisation of transport in each city, an outline of the cities' socio-demographic structures and an analysis of their transport systems. The report is presented in five chapters.

1.   Introduction

This section presents the division of the cities into the zonal structures that form the backbone for the study's comparative analytical framework.

There is also provision of basic information and a description of each city, presented for each of the study's Zones.

2.   Institutional organisation of transport

The focus of this section is the management and organisation of transport, within a detailed analytical description of government organisation.

Offices in the City of London

Governing and decision-making for transport are of keen public interest in all four cities since urban administration crosses administrative and residential boundaries, and seems to require continuing change in institutional and managerial arrangements.

3. *Population, employment and social structures*

All four cities are still growing and expanding outwards.

This section outlines the population, employment and social structures of each city as they affect transport and travel. It examines trends in population growth; the cities' outward expansion; levels and densities of employment; the growth of car ownership.

4. *Transport structure*

This section forms a large part of the report. It provides a detailed description of the cities' transport structures (both public and private transport) and an outline of all new major transport infrastructure plans with secure funding.

A precise description of the physical characteristics of the transport systems, metros, regional railways, buses and motorways, is followed by an examination of the frequency of service on the metros and regional railways, as well as reliability (cancellations), punctuality, and overcrowding.

To obtain a dynamic picture of transport in each city, similar origin-destination matrices for each city and for each mode have been created. The travel analysis also includes trip making and commuting into the central areas, as well as all trips within the metropolitan areas. This is followed by a comparative analysis of the levels and trends of different types of traffic accident in each city.

The study investigates the international connectivity of each city by looking both at access to each city's airports, as well as the number of destinations which are served.

5. Conclusions

This section provides a broad analysis of the comparative data in the report. It also suggests that there are ways in which the cities can draw lessons from each other in order to improve their transport systems in ways that minimise environmental and economic cost.

The conclusions concentrate on two broad areas:

- greater integration of land-use and transport planning

- improved efficiency in transport systems

1.2   Defining the comparable Zones in the four metropolises

Since the cities vary in size and area, they have been divided into four comparable zones in order to be certain of measuring like with like.

The methodology presumes that all data must be expressed in uniform terms in order to be comparable.

Building on the methodological experience of the Paris-London study, zones sharing similar spatial and demographic characteristics [6] have been devised. All data are reported using common terms, eg kilometres/dollars, and common definitions have been created for system elements, such as length of railway systems. The geographical zones reflect historical patterns of urban development with broadly comparable population sizes. In each city, Zone 1 forms the central employment and cultural core of the metropolis. The three other zones can be seen as progressively larger rings [7]. The zones are compared both individually and cumulatively. The four zones are:

- **Zone 1** **The Central Area:** the central business area of the city, which contains between 180,000 and 600,000 inhabitants;

- **Zones 1 & 2** **The Metropolitan Area:** the densely built-up area of the city, which contains approximately 7 to 9 million inhabitants;

- **Zones 1, 2 & 3** **The Outer Metropolitan Area:** a commuter hinterland, which contains approximately 10 to 13 million inhabitants, and

- **Zones 1, 2, 3 & 4** **The Region:** the entire region, with at least 17 million inhabitants.

The terms: *Central Area, Metropolitan Area, Outer Metropolitan Area* and *Region* are used throughout the report to signify the Zones mentioned above.

It will be noted that Paris, being a denser and smaller metropolis, does not extend to Zone 4.

6   There has also been an effort to match some of the jurisdictional boundaries with the study's zonal structure to aid analysis; so for instance London's Zones 1 & 2 coincide with the Greater London boundary and Tokyo's Zones 1, 2 & 3 coincide with the boundary of the Tokyo Metropolitan Government.

7   As can be seen from map 1, not all the Zones are ring shaped, particularly Tokyo's Zone 3.

Map 1
Basic administrative structures - London - the entire region (Zones 1, 2, 3 & 4)

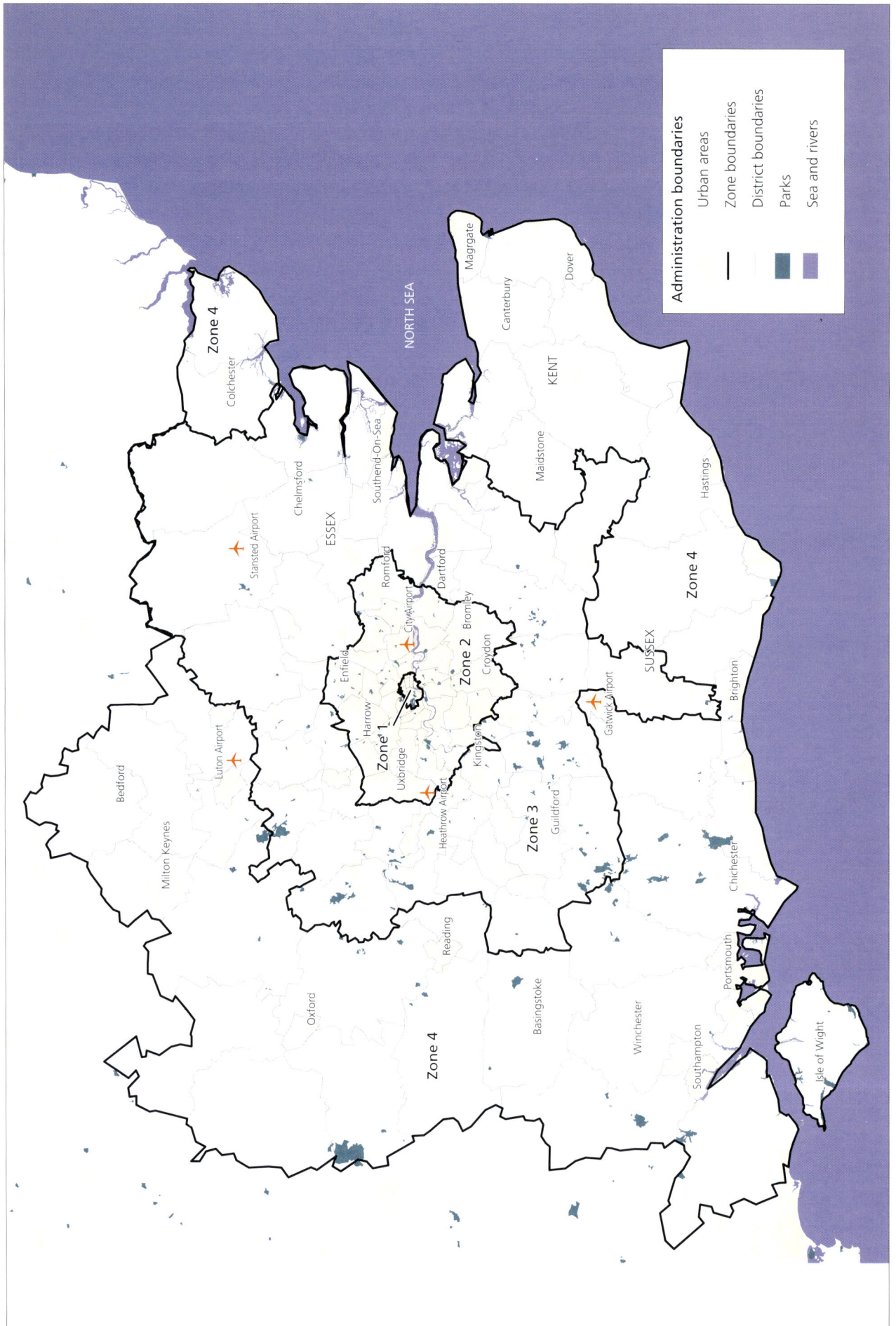

Administration boundaries

Urban areas
Zone boundaries
District boundaries
Parks
Sea and rivers

NORTH SEA

Zone 4
Colchester
Chelmsford
ESSEX
Southend-On-Sea
Stansted Airport

Margate
Canterbury
Dover
KENT
Maidstone
Hastings
Zone 4
SUSSEX
Brighton

Romford
City Airport
Dartford
Bromley
Zone 2
Croydon
Enfield
Zone 1
Harrow
Uxbridge
Kingston
Gatwick Airport
Heathrow Airport
Zone 3
Guildford

Luton Airport
Bedford
Milton Keynes
Reading
Oxford
Zone 4
Basingstoke
Winchester
Southampton
Portsmouth
Chichester
Isle of Wight

© Bartholomew's 1997; generated from Bartholomew's digital database: MM-1197-72

Scale 1cm = 14km

Map 1
Basic administrative structures - New York - the entire region (Zones 1, 2, 3 & 4)

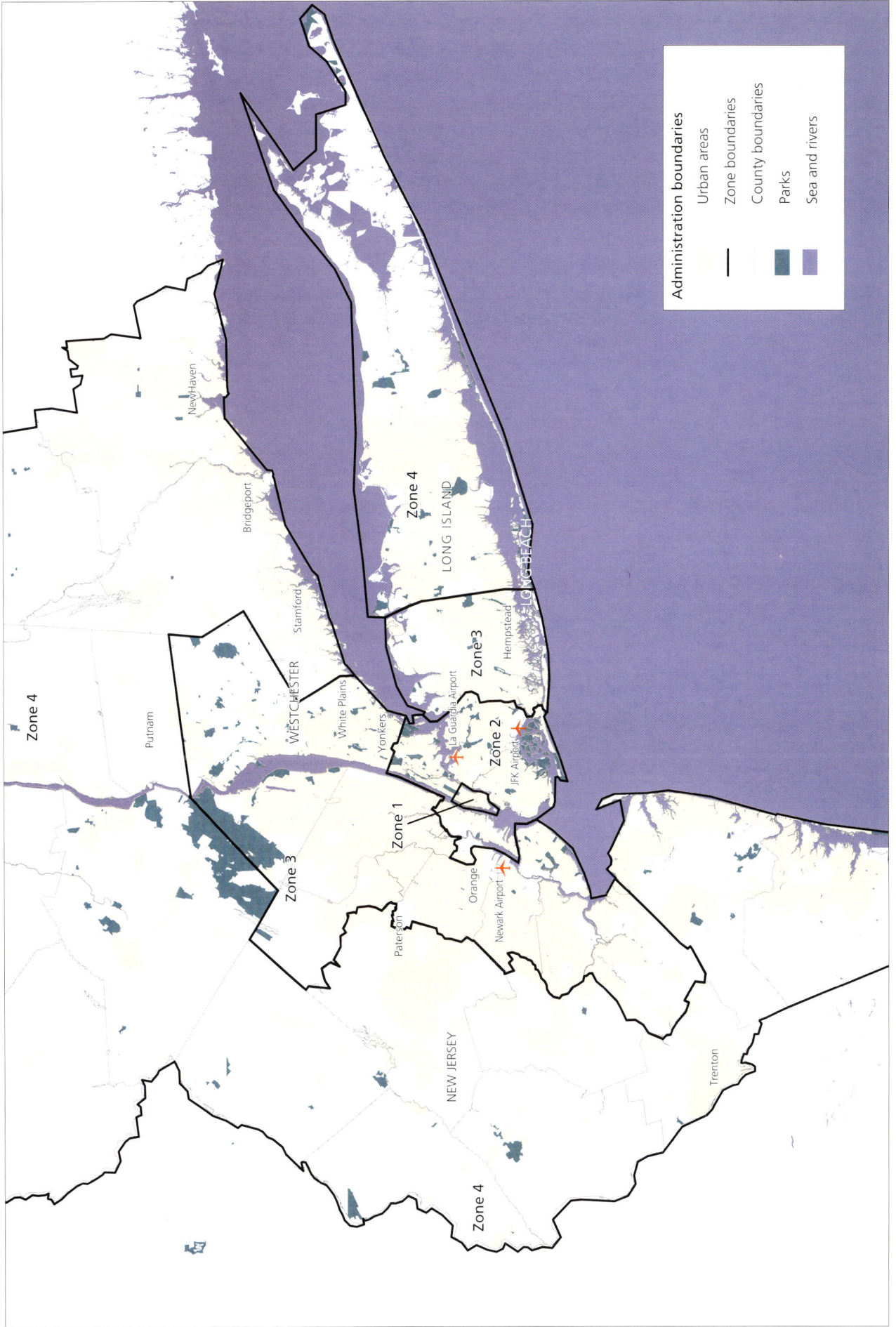

Administration boundaries

Administration boundaries		
Urban areas		
Zone boundaries		
County boundaries		
Parks		
Sea and rivers		

Zone 4

Zone 3

Zone 1

Zone 2

Zone 3

Zone 4

LONG ISLAND

LONG BEACH

WESTCHESTER

White Plains

Yonkers

La Guardia Airport

JFK Airport

Hempstead

Stamford

Bridgeport

New Haven

Putnam

Paterson

Orange

Newark Airport

NEW JERSEY

Trenton

Zone 4

Scale 1cm = 14km

Map 1
Basic administrative structures - Paris - the entire region (Zones 1, 2, 3 & 4)

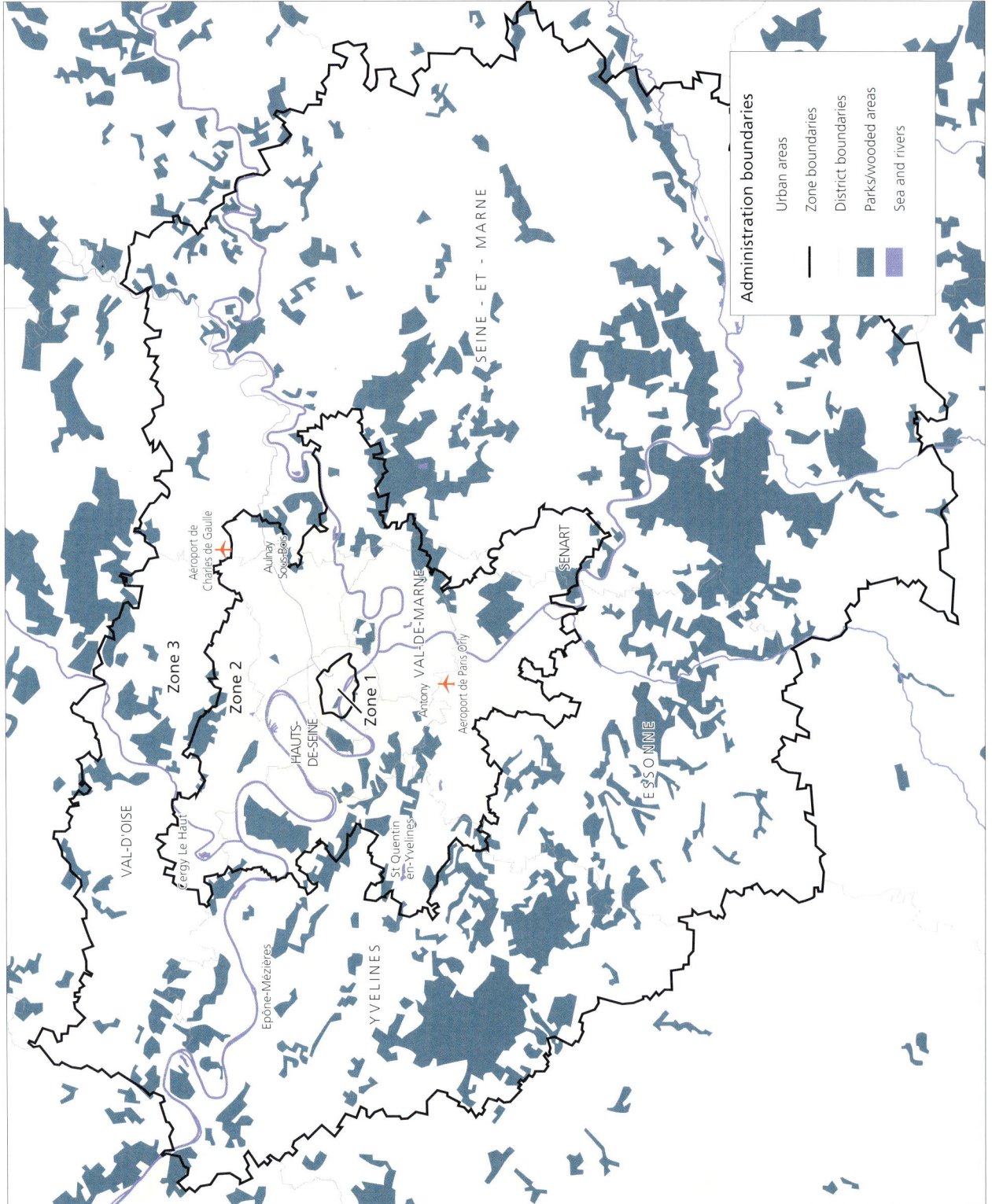

Scale 1cm = 8km

Administration boundaries

	Urban areas
	Zone boundaries
	District boundaries
	Parks/wooded areas
	Sea and rivers

VAL-D'OISE

Aéroport de Charles de Gaulle

Aulnay Sous-Bois

SEINE - ET - MARNE

Zone 3

Zone 2

HAUTS-DE-SEINE

Zone 1

SENART

Antony VAL-DE-MARNE

Aéroport de Paris Orly

Cergy Le Haut

St Quentin en-Yvelines

ESSONNE

Épône-Mézières

YVELINES

Map 1
Basic administrative structures - Tokyo - the entire region (Zones 1, 2, 3 & 4)

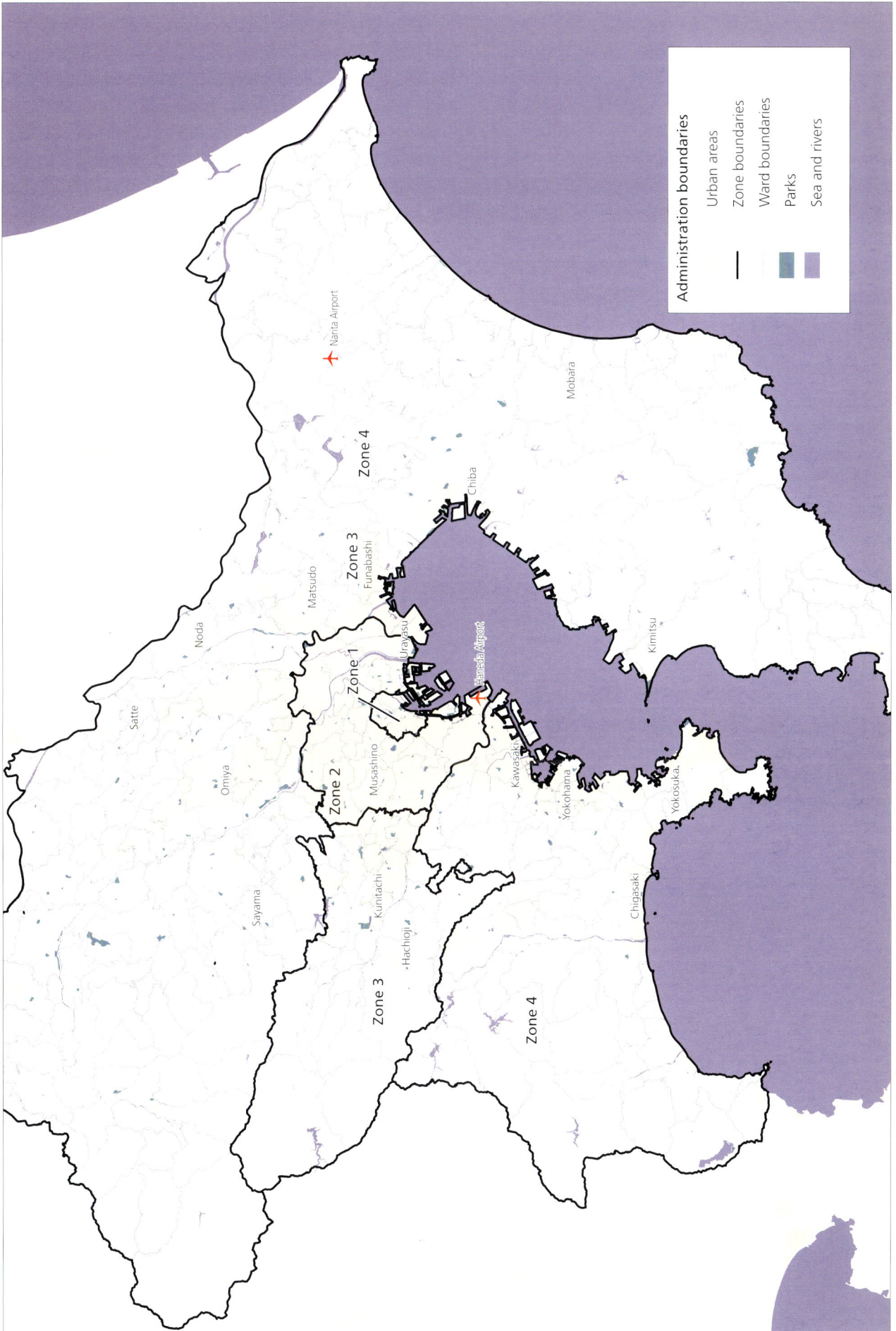

Scale 1cm = 9.5km

Administration boundaries

Urban areas
Zone boundaries
Ward boundaries
Parks
Sea and rivers

Narita Airport

Zone 4

Zone 3

Chiba

Mobara

Funabashi

Matsudo

Zone 1

Urayasu

Haneda Airport

Kimitsu

Noda

Zone 3

Kawasaki

Satte

Yokohama

Yokosuka

Omiya

Zone 2

Musashino

Kunitachi

Sayama

Chigasaki

Hachioji

Zone 3

Zone 4

Map 2
Basic administrative structures - London - the metropolitan area (Zones 1, & 2)

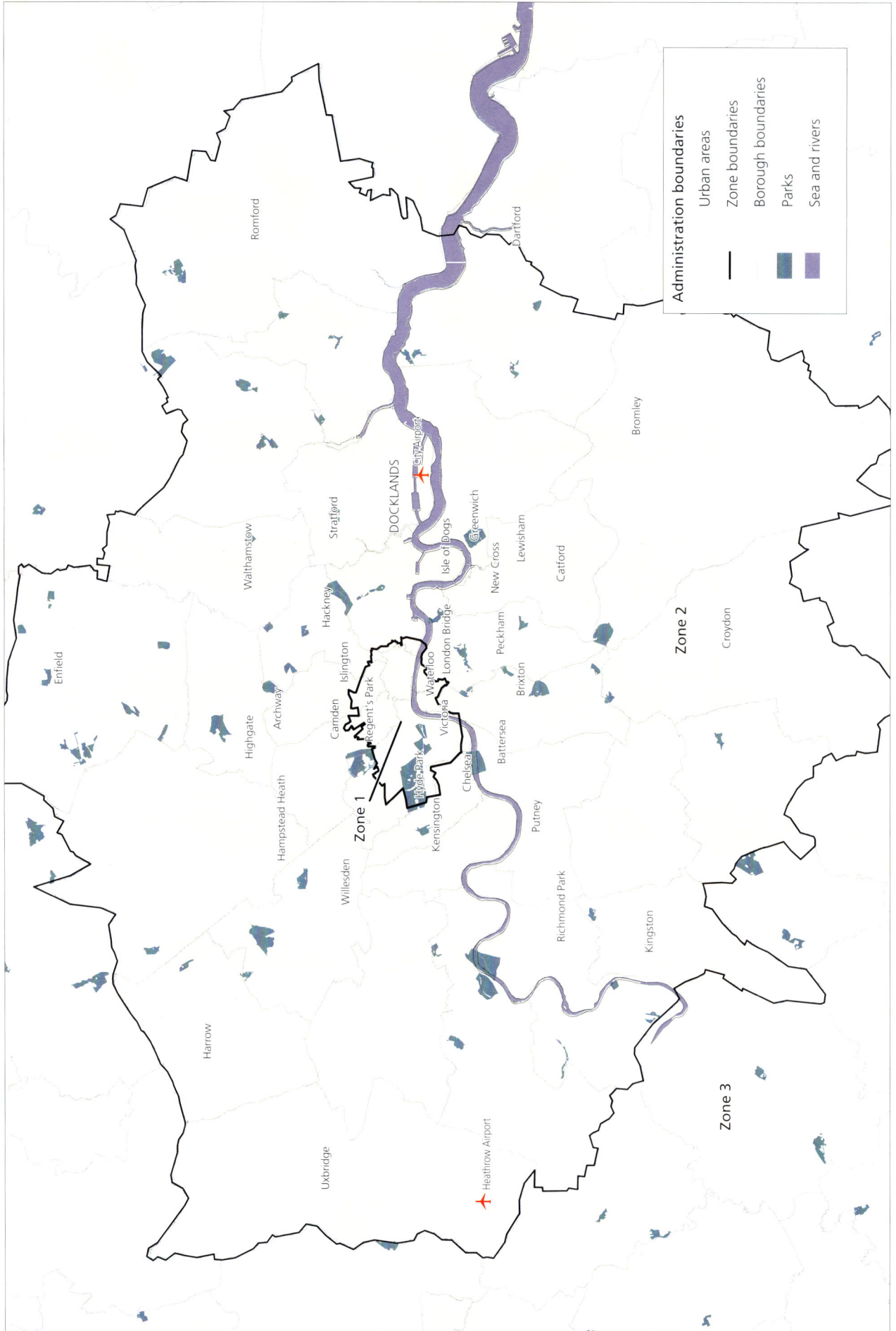

Zone 1

Zone 2

Zone 3

Romford

Dartford

Bromley

Croydon

Kingston

Richmond Park

Putney

Battersea

Brixton

Peckham

New Cross

Lewisham

Catford

Greenwich

Isle of Dogs

DOCKLANDS

City Airport

Stratford

Walthamstow

Hackney

Islington

Camden

Archway

Highgate

Enfield

Harrow

Uxbridge

Hampstead Heath

Willesden

Kensington

Chelsea

Hyde Park

Regent's Park

Victoria

Waterloo

London Bridge

Heathrow Airport

Administration boundaries

Urban areas

Zone boundaries

Borough boundaries

Parks

Sea and rivers

Scale 1cm = 3km

© Bartholomew's 1997; generated from Bartholomew's digital database: MM-1197-72

Map 2
Basic administrative structures - New York - the metropolitan area (Zones 1, & 2)

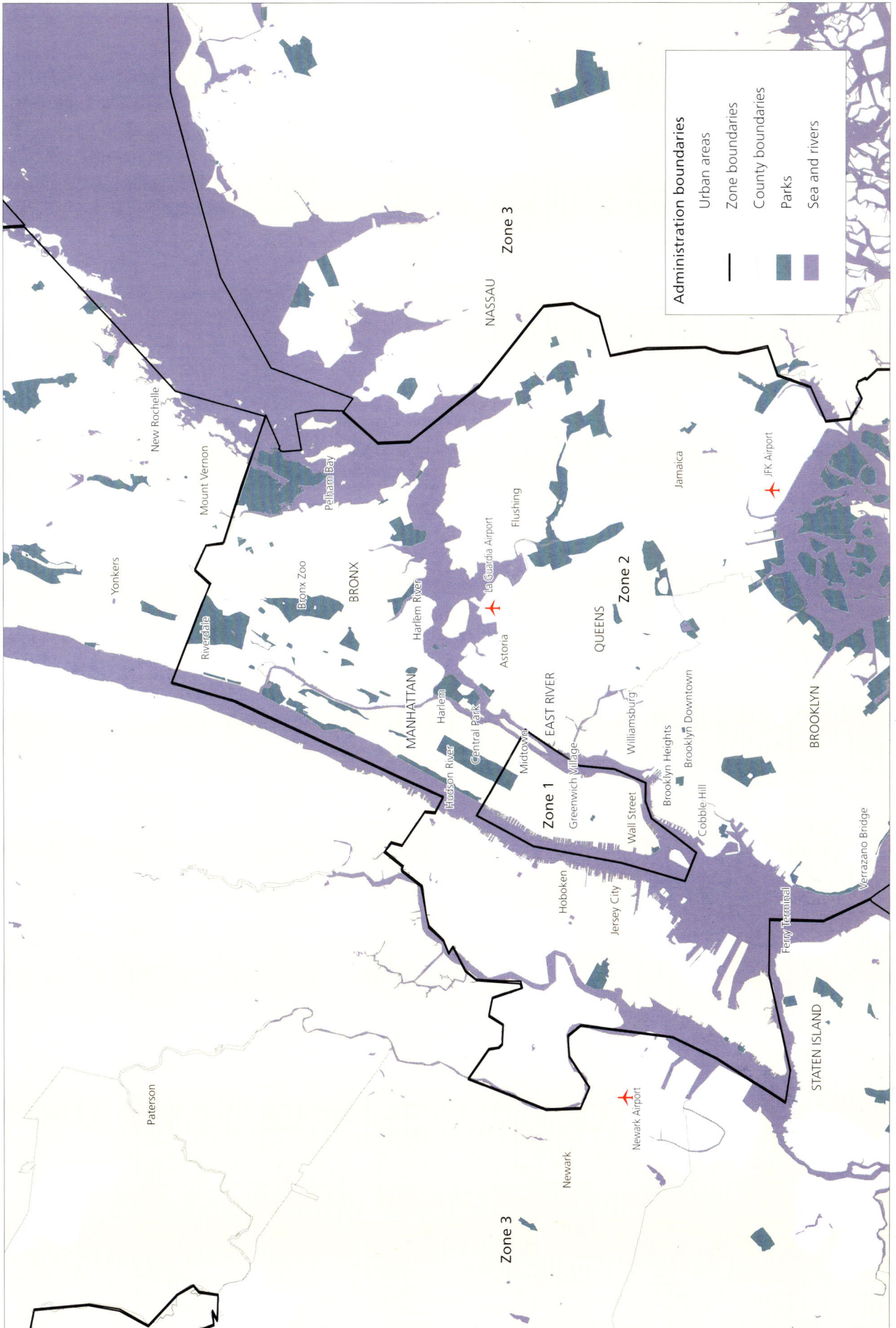

Scale 1cm = 3km

Administration boundaries

Urban areas
Zone boundaries
County boundaries
Parks
Sea and rivers

Zone 3

NASSAU

New Rochelle

Mount Vernon

Pelham Bay

Yonkers

Bronx Zoo

BRONX

Harlem River

Riverdale

La Guardia Airport

Astoria

Flushing

Jamaica

JFK Airport

Zone 2

QUEENS

MANHATTAN

Harlem

Central Park

Midtown

EAST RIVER

Greenwich Village

Williamsburg

Brooklyn Heights

Brooklyn Downtown

Hudson River

Zone 1

Wall Street

Cobble Hill

BROOKLYN

Hoboken

Jersey City

Ferry Terminal

Verrazano Bridge

STATEN ISLAND

Paterson

Newark Airport

Newark

Zone 3

Map 2
Basic administrative structures - Paris - the metropolitan area (Zones 1, & 2)

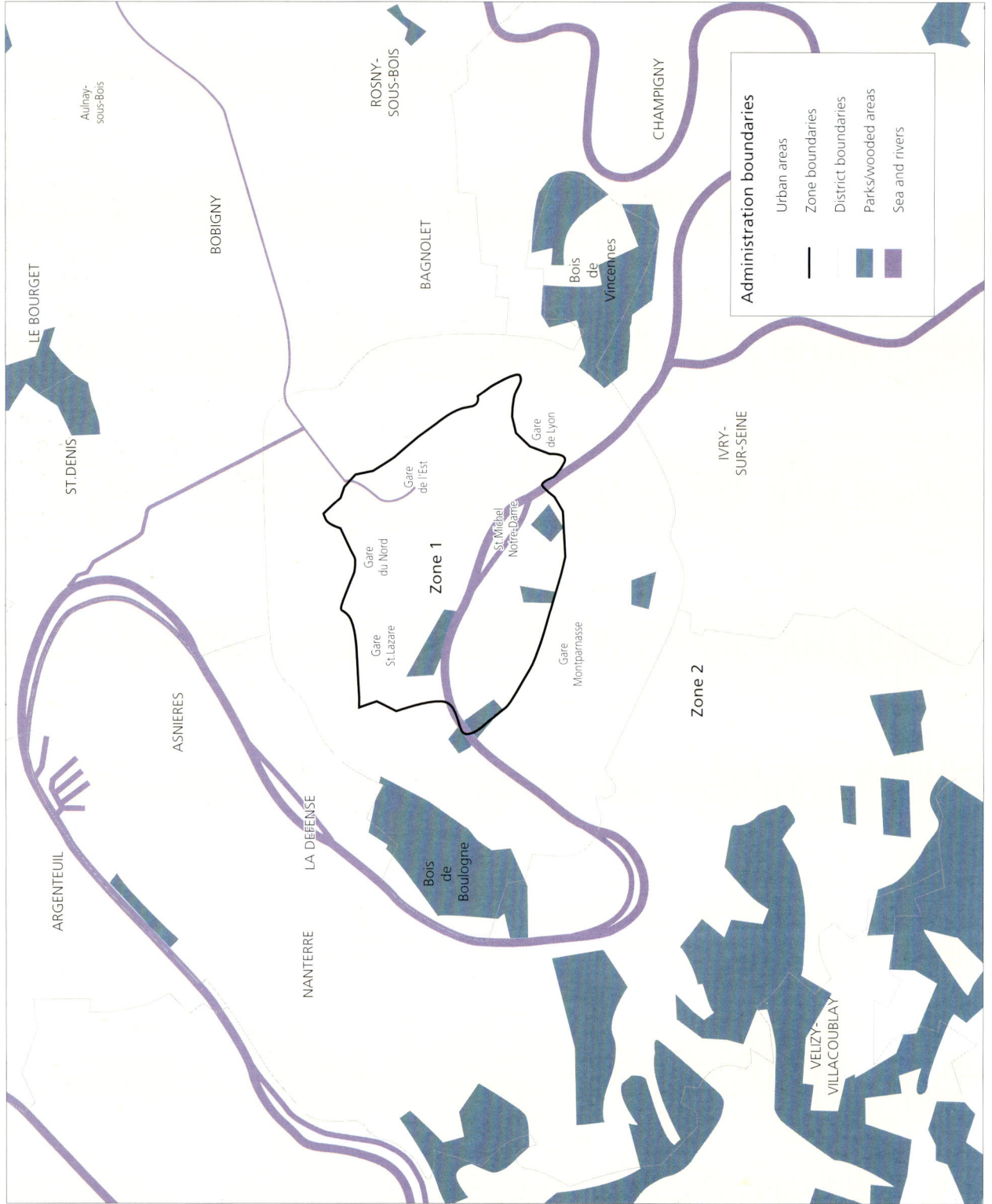

Scale 1cm = 1.3km

Administration boundaries

Urban areas

Zone boundaries

District boundaries

Parks/wooded areas

Sea and rivers

AULNAY-SOUS-BOIS

ROSNY-SOUS-BOIS

CHAMPIGNY

BOBIGNY

BAGNOLET

LE BOURGET

ST.DENIS

Bois de Vincennes

IVRY-SUR-SEINE

Gare de l'Est

Gare de Lyon

Gare du Nord

Zone 1

St.Michel Notre-Dame

Gare St.Lazare

Gare Montparnasse

Zone 2

ASNIERES

LA DEFENSE

ARGENTEUIL

NANTERRE

Bois de Boulogne

VELIZY-VILLACOUBLAY

Map 2
Basic administrative structures - Tokyo - the metropolitan area (Zones 1, & 2)

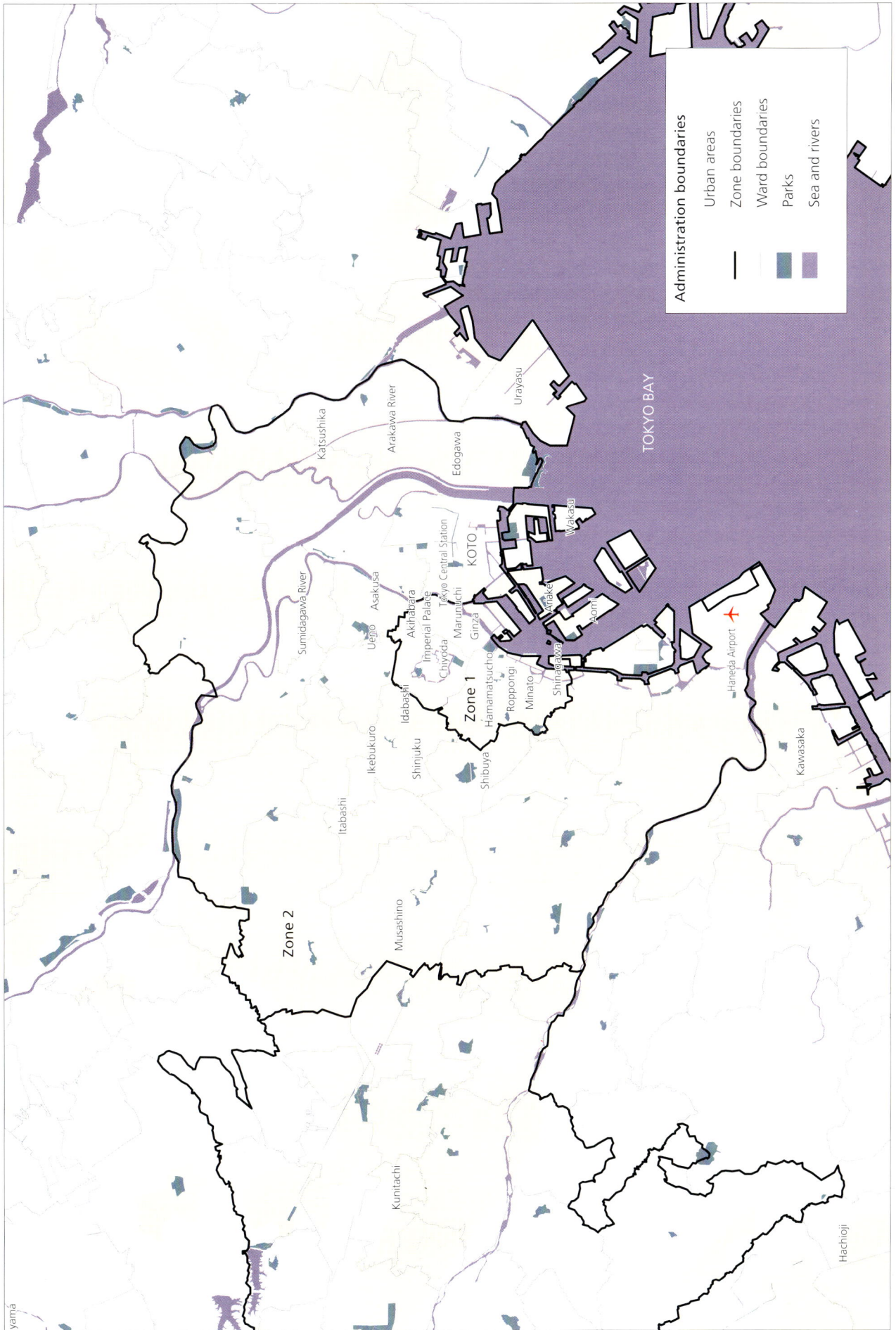

Administration boundaries

Urban areas

Zone boundaries

Ward boundaries

Parks

Sea and rivers

TOKYO BAY

Zone 1

Zone 2

Urayasu

Katsushika

Arakawa River

Edogawa

Wakasu

KOTO

Tokyo Central Station

Asakusa

Ueno

Akihabara

Imperial Palace

Chiyoda

Marunuchi

Ginza

Ariake

Aomi

Hamamatsucho

Roppongi

Minato

Shinagawa

Haneda Airport

Kawasaka

Shibuya

Idabashi

Shinjuku

Ikebukuro

Itabashi

Musashino

Sumidagawa River

Kunitachi

Hachioji

iyama

Scale 1cm = 3km

Introduction

Table 1
Summary description of Zones

	London	New York	Paris	Tokyo
Zone 1	Central London [8]	The southern half of Manhattan island (south of 60th street)	The centre of the Ville de Paris [9] (the commune of Paris)	Tokyo's three central wards of Chiyoda, Chuo and Minato
Zones 1 & 2	Greater London - an area encompassing the 33 London boroughs [10]	An area containing all of Manhattan, the boroughs of Queens, Brooklyn and The Bronx in the state of New York, and Hudson county in the state of New Jersey	The "built-up" area of Paris broadly defined as the area within the Francilienne orbital road	The ward area: this area is made up of 23 wards [11] (including Chiyoda, Chuo and Minato)
Zones 1, 2 & 3	A reduced south-east of England area - defined by districts in which at least 10% of residents commute to Greater London (Zones 1 & 2) [12]	An area containing the above plus Staten Island and the counties of Nassau, Richmond Westchester, Rockland in the state of New York, and the counties of Passiac, Bergen, Essex, Union and Middlesex in the state of New Jersey	The administrative region known as the Ile-de-France	The Tokyo Metropolis - the area administered by the Tokyo Metropolitan Government [13]
Zones 1, 2, 3 & 4	The region of the south-east of England [14]	A tri-state region within the states of New York, New Jersey and Connecticut containing New York City and 26 surrounding counties [15]	*Paris does not have a Zone 4*	The Tokyo metropolis and the 3 prefectures of Saitama, Chiba and Kanagawa

8   This geographical definition of central London is often referred to as the "central statistical area". It is an area that is bounded by the main London rail termini. It includes the whole of the Corporation of London and the following wards in the boroughs listed below:

- Camden   Bloomsbury, Brunswick, Holborn, Kings Cross, Somers Town
- Islington   Bunhill, Clerkenwell
- Kensington and Chelsea   Hans Town
- Lambeth   Bishops
- Southwark   Cathedral, Chaucer, Riverside
- Westminster   Baker Street, Belgrave, Cavendish, Churchill, Hyde Park, Knightsbridge, Millbank, St. Georges, St. James, Victoria

9   This is composed of 11 (numbers 1 to 11) of the Ville de Paris' 20 arrondissements.

10   Greater London is composed of the self-administering Corporation of London (the "City") and 32 boroughs which are listed below:

- Barking and Dagenham
- Barnet
- Bexley
- Brent
- Bromley
- Camden
- Croydon
- Ealing
- Enfield
- Greenwich
- Hackney
- Hammersmith and Fulham
- Haringey
- Harrow
- Havering
- Hillingdon
- Hounslow
- Islington
- Kensington and Chelsea
- Kingston upon Thames
- Lambeth
- Lewisham
- Merton
- Newham
- Redbridge
- Richmond upon Thames
- Southwark
- Sutton
- Tower Hamlets
- Waltham Forest
- Wandsworth
- Westminster

Housing in Brooklyn in New York's Zone 2

11   Other than the three central wards it includes the following wards:

- Adachi
- Arakawa
- Bunkyo
- Edogawa
- Itabashi
- Katsushika
- Kita
- Koto
- Meguro
- Nakano
- Nerima
- Ota
- Setagaya
- Shibuya
- Shinagawa
- Shinjuku
- Suginami
- Sumida
- Taito
- Toshima

12   It includes Greater London and the following districts in the counties listed below:

- Berkshire   Bracknell Forest, Slough, Windsor and Maidenhead
- Buckinghamshire Chiltern, South Bucks, Wycombe
- Essex   Basildon, Braintree, Brentwood, Castle Point, Chelmsford, Epping Forest, Harlow, Maldon, Rochford, Southend-on-Sea, Thurrock, Uttlesford
- Hampshire   Hart, Rushmoor
- Hertfordshire   Broxbourne, Dacorum, East Hertfordshire, Hertsmere, St. Albans, Three Rivers, Watford, Welwyn Hatfield
- Kent   Dartford, Gillingham, Gravesham, Rochester upon Medway, Sevenoaks, Tonbridge and Malling, Tunbridge Wells
- Surrey   Elmbridge, Epsom and Ewell, Guildford, Mole Valley, Reigate and Banstead, Runnymede, Spelthorne, Surrey Heath, Tandridge, Waverley, Woking
- West Sussex   Mid Sussex

This is similar to the "Functional Urban Area" concept used in a number of comparative studies, including the recent report on north-western European Metropolitan Regions (Group for European Metropolitan Area Comparative Analysis, 1996).

13   It includes the ward area (Zones 1 & 2) and Tama area (Zone 3 - which consists of 27 cities, 3 towns and 1 village) extending to the west of the ward area.

14   The region of the South East of England contains Greater London, and the following counties:

- Bedfordshire
- Berkshire
- Buckinghamshire
- East Sussex
- Essex
- Hampshire
- Hertfordshire
- Isle of Wight
- Kent
- Oxfordshire
- Surrey
- West Sussex

15   It includes the following counties in the states listed below:

- Connecticut   Fairfield, Litchfield, New Haven
- New Jersey   Bergen, Essex, Hudson, Hunterdon, Mercer, Middlesex, Monmouth, Morris, Ocean, Passaic, Somerset, Sussex, Union, Warren
- New York   Dutchess, Kings (Brooklyn), Nassau, New York (Manhattan), Orange, Putnam, Queens, Richmond (Staten Island), Rockland, Sullivan, Suffolk, The Bronx, Ulster, Westchester

1.3 A description of the cities

The distinct Zones of the four cities are described in a disaggregate fashion in order to acquaint readers with each cities' historical development, different social and economic composition, and current urban dimension.

1.3.1 London

London, the capital of the United Kingdom of Great Britain and Northern Ireland, is the largest and most populous city of Western Europe. London is situated in the south-east of the island of Britain, which is its wealthiest region. London is a historic city which developed much of its character in the 19th century. It has been expanding outwards throughout the 20th century.

The city grew on the banks of the river Thames and until the beginning of the 20th century it was one of the world's largest ports. London's growth has historically been based on manufacturing and commerce. Today, London's economic base has changed and most of the capital's economic activity is in the service sectors, with finance and tourism playing a major role. The port of London has moved down the river Thames to Zones 3 & 4 and the traditional dock areas in Zone 2 are being transformed, primarily into offices and housing. London's manufacturing sector has also largely disappeared from Zones 1 & 2.
London's growth started with its establishment as a world trade centre in the 17th century when it had a population of about half a million. By the 18th century the population had doubled. By 1881 its population had reached four and a half million. Until then, London was a compact city of high density. Its outwards spread commenced with the construction of its metropolitan railways, the first of which, built partly underground and steam driven, opened in 1863. The railways, especially after their electrification which started in the 1890s, and the construction of deep bore tunnels, led to the creation of London's distinct brick built Victorian suburbs.

If the railways caused the suburbs, the motorcar shaped London in its current form. The Abercrombie plan of 1940 tried to limit London's sprawl with a "green belt" and to channel further development into new and expanded towns, linking them together with new orbital highways. The green belt policy has been effective in creating a band of largely undeveloped land around metropolitan London. However, new developments have leap-frogged the green belt and proliferated in Zone 3 in towns such as Guildford and Aylesbury.

As planning waned, giving way to market forces in the 1980s and 1990s, developers created car dependent complexes containing housing, retail, leisure and office complexes in hitherto rural areas of the south-east.

Zone 1
is located almost entirely on the northern bank of the river Thames. It is an area roughly bounded by the Circle metro ("Underground") line and encompasses all the main-line railway stations. It contains in the east the self administrating Corporation of London (the "square mile" financial district) and the "West End", the entertainment area that is most visited by tourists. Within this central area are housed the Parliament, Buckingham Palace (the monarch's residence) and most of the national government offices and large company headquarters. It is also the location of most of the colleges of London University, such as the London School of Economics.

The population of the central area has been falling for most of the 20th century. The residential population of central London is now about 190,000, a reduction from about half a million at the beginning of the century. Most of the central area is now occupied by offices and shops.

Zone 2
(including Zone 1) is today known as Greater London, an area of 1,578 square kilometres (including Zone 1). It had its own local government until it was abolished in 1986 [16]. Currently local administrative and policy functions are carried out by 32 boroughs and the

Corporation of London. Many of the metropolis' functions, such as the fire service, are carried out by independent bodies, whose boards are either appointed by the boroughs or national government.

Zone 2 is roughly bounded by London's orbital motorway, the M25, and the "green belt" - an area in which new construction is heavily proscribed. Within Zone 2 are most of London's suburban and inner city neighbourhoods that developed in the second half of the 19th century and the first half of the 20th. The inner city neighbourhoods are composed mostly of two and three storey houses, the majority of which have now been subdivided into flats.

The outer London suburbs grew with the expansion of the metropolis' railways. Most of these date to the inter-war years and are typically two storey detached or semi-detached houses with gardens.

Parts of inner London, mostly in the east, were demolished and rebuilt after the Second World War, either because of war damage or to rid the city of poor quality housing, "slum clearance". The result has been the creation of large and often high-rise local authority-owned housing estates. Many of these have become foci of deprivation, social exclusion and crime.
The city north of the river Thames contains numerous metro lines, whilst the southern part is densely served by over-ground railways which have a lower frequency of service. The metro system (the "Underground") and the buses in Greater London are run or regulated by a nationalised company, London Transport. The regional and national railways are run as franchises by a number of private operators.

The wealthiest parts of Greater London are in the west and north, with poor areas concentrated in the old manufacturing and port areas of the east (the "East End") and north east (Lee Valley). There are also deep pockets of deprivation in many inner-city areas such as

Peckham (inner south-east) and Hackney (inner north-east).

London is one of the world's most cosmopolitan cities. Greater London contains over 1.6 million people from ethnic minority groups (37 ethnic groups have over 10,000 members each) [17]. The biggest ethnic group in Greater London is Irish (over a half million of London residents were born in Ireland). Other significant ethnic groups (with at least 50,000 people), are Bangladeshis, Cypriots, Indians, Jamaicans, Pakistanis, Scots and Welsh.

Zone 2 is also the area where the largest recent schemes of urban regeneration have taken place. These include the massive redevelopment of London Docklands where there are now major office, housing and retail complexes, and the new London City Airport.

Europe's premier airport, in terms of passenger throughput, London Heathrow, is also situated within Zone 2.

Zone 3
is not defined by an administrative structure, but is an area specially defined for the purpose of this study. This area of 8,807 square kilometres is composed of local authority districts from which at least 10% of residents commuted to the central area in 1991. It includes a number of large urban areas, such as Basildon, Hemel Hempstead, High Wycombe, Slough and Watford.

Zone 3 encompasses largely undeveloped green belt and semi-rural areas. It does not include the main cities of south-east England but includes many car oriented developments - large leisure and retail activities, such as out-of-town shopping centres, of which the largest is Lakeside in Essex. This attracts many drivers outwards from Zone 2 as well as from large parts of southern England.

16   Currently, the government is committed to creating an elected new local government structure for London in 2000.

17   Storkey et al., 1997

Zone 3 is served by a dense network of radial regional rail lines with frequent services, at least in the peak hours. Although local employment is growing, the Zone is characterised by heavy rail commuting to Zones 1 & 2.

Zone 3 contains two further major airports: London-Stansted (north-east), and London-Gatwick (south).

Zone 4

covers the rest of the south-east of England, with an area of 16,839 square kilometres. It includes major cities such as Bedford, Brighton, Colchester, Luton, Oxford, Portsmouth, Reading, Southampton and the 1960s new town of Milton Keynes. It also includes many smaller historic towns such as Canterbury, Chichester and Winchester and all the south-eastern coast of England. The coastal areas have been developed since the beginning of the century, attracting a high proportion of retired people.

The south-east of England (Zones 1, 2, 3 & 4) is the wealthiest part of the United Kingdom and contains a third of the nation's population. Zone 4 is an area with a continuously growing population and employment.

The car dominates transport, although the whole area is well served by regional rail. The main towns have extensive local bus networks.

Luton Airport, in the north-west, is in Zone 4.

1.3.2 New York

With New York City at its core, the New York region straddles parts of three states, Connecticut, New York and New Jersey.

The City of New York was founded in 1898. Prior to that the Boroughs of Brooklyn and Manhattan were municipalities in their own right and the other boroughs of what became the City (Queens, The Bronx, Staten Island) were the exurbia of that time.

Although New York City is not the national capital, it is the nation's largest and most densely developed city, as well as its financial capital. The tri-state region is composed of nearly 20 million people living in 33,000 square kilometres governed by over 2,000 units of government, including three states, 31 counties, and 780 municipalities.

The island that forms the region's core is Manhattan, located at the head of a well protected deep harbour and at the mouth of the wide Hudson River. It became a major port in the 18th century and the nation's principal maritime centre in the 19th century, when the Hudson was connected in 1824 to a canal built across New York State to the Great Lakes, forming a waterway 2,000 kms to the west. In the mid 19th and early 20th centuries, Manhattan was the primary portal for enormous waves of immigrants who swelled its residential population to a high point of 2.3 million in 1910 and provided the labour for a substantial manufacturing economy.

The overall patterns of growth have been shaped by the region's geography (an island at its core, river barriers and sea, alluvial plains and rocky terrain), and economic and social forces - such as the powerful magnetism of Manhattan which can be clearly seen in the development pattern, location decisions of corporations, and the real estate market, as much as by an overall plan.

Always the financial capital of the nation, lower Manhattan, constrained by its narrow streets laid out in the 17th century, the most notable being Wall Street, expanded vertically in the 1920s as steel construction and the deep bedrock foundation facilitated the building of skyscrapers. At the same time, high speed elevators, coupled with a rapid expansion of metro lines, enabled unprecedented densities of development. High-rise apartment houses were built along the major avenues the full length of the island. The dismantling of Manhattan's last elevated metro lines in the late 1950s made the upper east side more attractive for high-rise dwellings.

In the aftermath of the Second World War, the Manhattan central business district was transformed. Corporations, seeking signature buildings for their headquarters, spawned a boom of higher than ever skyscrapers, made possible by curtain-wall construction, the underlying deep bedrock, and a confluence of metro and regional rail lines. Industrial activities in Manhattan, including the port, declined gradually over a 30 year period. In post-war years the service sector grew, offsetting the decline in manufacturing.

The pattern of settlement of upper Manhattan and the surrounding counties was shaped in the first quarter of the 20th century by metro lines that were built by developers to spur migration and by a large network of motorways that fanned out into the region. In the 1930s, famed public works administrator, Robert Moses, built motorways both across New York City and into the farmland of Long Island, east of the city, using both bridge and tunnel tolls and national government anti-depression spending. He continued to build motorways after the Second World War, so that by 1960 the New York region had more kilometres of motorways than the entire state of California.

From 1950 to 1990, nearly 5 million people moved into the counties surrounding New York City. Until the Second World War, suburbs grew up around established towns located along rail lines. Following the War, large numbers of city residents took advantage of government subsidies and tax deductibility of mortgages for single family homes and relocated to new, large scale, largely car dependent, suburban housing developments.

Attracted by the sizeable educated work-force that could be found in the suburbs, corporations relocated further and further from the region's core. While, initially, business followed the labour force to the suburbs, by the 1980s, the growing availability of jobs outside the city, plus the relatively low cost of car travel, spurred residential development in ever more distant open spaces. Consequently, between 1962-92, the region's

Manhattan (Zone 1)

urbanised land increased by 60% with only a 13% increase in population.

In many areas within the older cities of the region, second generation European descendants were replaced by black and Hispanic residents. Little change occurred in suburban-type areas at the outer edges of the city, which retained their white, middle class population. By the 1970s, several "brownstone neighbourhoods" (districts where 19th century townhouses are under historic preservation designation) close to the central business district became "gentrified" by affluent white families. They paved the way for the conversion of former industrial areas into high rise developments on the waterfronts of Hudson and Queens counties.

In the 1990s, the region has received about 100,000 immigrants a year, two-thirds of them residing in New York City. Most of the new wave of European immigrants (Poles, Russians and Irish), and even more, those from Asia, the Middle East and Central and South America, settled in clusters, creating neighbourhoods of distinct ethnic character.

Zone 1,
the central business district of the New York region, is an area of 23 square kilometres in Manhattan south of 60th Street, containing 18% of the region's employment. The southern end of Manhattan contains the financial district, City Hall and municipal agencies and an increasing residential population, both in Chinatown and in new and converted luxury high-rise buildings.

The granite foundation of Lower Manhattan is separated from the deep rock formation underlying the rest of Manhattan by about 2 kilometres of boggy soil resulting from filled-in streams that restrained high-rise construction from the vicinity of Canal Street to 20th Street. This "valley" in the New York skyline is a less dense area of residences, including the historic Greenwich Village. The numbered street grid system in which Fifth Avenue is the spine that defines the East and West Sides of most of Manhattan, starts in the valley.

The West 30s became the centre of the garment industry, making Manhattan the fashion centre of the country. Just north of the garment centre lies the theatre district, adjacent to Times Square, which continues to be one of Manhattan's principal tourist attractions. In midtown, extending from the East 30s to the southern boundary of Central Park at 59th Street, are the corporate towers that dominate the midtown Manhattan skyline. In this area Fifth Avenue is the major shopping street.

Zone 2,
an area of 734 square kilometres, is New York City outside the Manhattan central business district,

(excluding Staten Island), and Hudson County in New Jersey.

Zone 2 has a predominantly residential nature, typified by closely spaced single family homes with mid-rise apartment houses near metro stations. Outlying areas, beyond the reach of metro lines, contain detached houses on larger plots.

Residents are largely car dependent or travel by bus to metro, or more recently, on commuter coaches, to the central business district. The residential areas that comprise most of Zone 2 are interspersed at regular intervals by main roads, served by local buses and lined with small shops. Each of these pedestrian accessible shopping streets serves as the core, and reflects the character of Zone 2's many distinct neighbourhoods.

Zone 2 also has two growing office districts in downtown Brooklyn and along the Jersey City waterfront in Hudson County. Local commerce and small industries, many located in older industrial buildings along the East River waterfront and adjacent areas of Brooklyn, Queens and the Bronx, produce 21% of the region's jobs.

Zone 2 is divided by the wide rivers that surround Manhattan. These areas are connected to the central business district by extensive radial metro lines. The limited number of vehicular crossings constitutes a major travel constraint in the region. The waterways are crossed by 16 bridges and four vehicular tunnels, but their limited capacity can contribute to major peak hour delays for car and lorry access to the core.

Two of the region's three major airports (John F. Kennedy and La Guardia) are within Zone 2, both in the Borough of Queens.

Zone 3,
an area of 5,036 square kilometres, contains those counties that are within relatively easy commuting distance of Manhattan. East of New York City, on Long

Island, Nassau and Suffolk counties are surrounded by the sea, an attraction as well as a barrier. The commuters travel by rail, car and commuter coaches from enclaves of mainly single family houses.

Most of the older towns in Zone 3 have a distinctive shopping street and town centre. Over the years, shopping centres, anchored by supermarkets, flanked by service shops built around vast parking areas, have replaced small stores on the older Main Streets for routine shopping needs. In the last decade, many of these shopping centres have not survived competition from new megastores.

The spread of housing and the scatter of non-residential facilities have created long distances between residences, shopping, schools, offices, and other places of personal business. The major routes between these locations became lined with drive-in businesses of all kinds, each vying for the attention of passing motorists with distinctive, often flashy signposts and structures. The resulting lack of cohesive development fostered "many-to-many" origin and destination trip patterns that have further reinforced car dependence.

The region's third major (Newark) airport is in Zone 3, in the county of Essex in New Jersey.

Zone 4,

an area of more than 27,000 square kilometres, contains the remaining counties of the region, extending some 125 kilometres from Manhattan. Although there are historic village centres and Connecticut has two cities of more than 100,000 people, Zone 4 is predominantly of very low density and contains most of the open space remaining in the region. Even more than in Zone 3, the Zone 4 work-force works within the same Zone (95% of workers). They go to the corporate and industrial "parks" within Zone 4 that provide about 31% of the entire region's employment. Most travel originating in a Zone 4 county remains within that county, nearly all of it car dependent due to the very dispersed development.

Retail stores outside villages in Zones 3 & 4 are located on arterial roads, making them accessible only by car, necessitating large parking areas, and leading to a proliferation of out of centre developments of all kinds. To further accommodate car-bound citizens, schools, libraries and post offices have also been relocated to fringe areas, where there is ample free parking. Consequently, for those people living more than 50 kilometres from Manhattan, all but about 2% of personal travel is by car. Public transport use that does occur is almost all commuter trains, buses and ferries to Manhattan.

1.3.3 *Paris*

The first town on the site of modern Paris appeared in 52 BC under the name of Lutèce. It developed on the island in the river Seine and flourished as a commercial centre based on river traffic throughout the period of the Roman occupation. Paris became the capital of the Gaulles from 500 onwards but developed very slowly over the next half millennium. By 1000, it had expanded from the island to the left bank of the Seine, where the first university was set up. Between 1500 and 1789 the city grew both economically and culturally with a concomitant rise in population. It was a densely built city reaching up to the limits of Zone 1. After the crisis of the 1789 revolution, the city experienced new-found prosperity with the growth of industrialisation and heavy immigration.

In the mid 19th century, the Government's prefect of Paris, Haussmann, undertook a series of major public works to avoid the "asphyxiation" of the centre. He built the grand north-south and east-west boulevards, the Champs Elysées and the Opera quarter. The first urban rail line to the western suburbs opened in 1837. The city began to expand outwards and from then on, factories began relocating from the centre to the suburbs and with them, the working classes. A great urban expansion took place within Zone 2, largely along the lines of the metro and railways. This pattern continued until the Second World War.

Between 1950 and 1970, largely unplanned urban expansion took place within Zone 2. The undeveloped areas between the railway lines quickly filled in. To control the galloping urbanisation, the state created in 1965 an urban development plan, the Schéma Directeur d'Aménagement et d'Urbanisme (finally implemented in 1976) which provided for the development of four "restructuring poles" in the near suburbs (in Zone 2): Créteil, La Défense, St. Denis and Vélizy-Villacoublay; and five new towns on the outskirts of the built-up area: Cergy Pontoise in the north-west, Evry and Sénart in the south-east, Marne-La-Vallée in the east, and St. Quentin at Yvelines in the south-west (in Zone 3). These new urban centres were created to avoid dispersion of population and employment throughout the region.

The creation of the "poles" and the new towns has had the effect of:

- slowing down the population loss of the centre, especially in Zone 1;

- significantly transferring jobs from Zone 1 to Zone 2 and, in particular, in the service sectors, from the 8th and 9th arrondissements to La Défense and the département of Hauts de Seine;

- moderating the growth of urbanisation in Zone 3, which has largely managed to keep its rural character despite high-rise developments in some of the smaller communes.

The Ile-de-France region extends over 12,000 square kilometres with a current population of over 11 million people, spread over eight départements. The Paris region is usually subdivided into the following centre and two rings (which in total correspond to about two thirds of our study area - the entire Ile-de-France region):

- Ville de Paris, with surface area of 105 square kilometres, which corresponds to the département de la Seine;

- "première couronne" three inner départements, with a surface area of about 200 square kilometres: the Hauts-de-Seine, the Seine-Saint-Denis and the Val-de-Marne;

- "grande couronne" four outer départements, of differing sizes: Essonne (1,804 square kilometres), Yvelines (2,284 square kilometres), Val d'Oise (1,245 square kilometres) and Seine-et-Marne which covers half the eastern part of the region with a surface area of 5,915 square kilometres.

The Ville de Paris (a single commune) is divided into 20 arrondissements whilst the other seven départements are divided into communes. There are 1,281 communes in the whole of the Ile-de-France region.

Being the capital of France, Paris is the centre for all of the country's political, financial, economic and cultural activities. With the decentralisation laws of March 1982, the state transferred parts of its duties to the régions, départements and communes. However, in the Région Ile-de-France it is still the state that holds most power. It is the state that has to approve the region's strategic plan ("schéma directeur d'aménagement et d'urbanisme"), it is the state which decides which are going to be the large public works ("grands projets") including transport, and it is the state which has overall control of the organisation that runs public transport.

Zone 1

corresponds to the 11 central arrondissements of Paris. It encompasses the principal administrative, financial, commercial and cultural sectors of the capital. It is crossed by the river Seine.

The "right" bank of the river Seine has most of the city's employment. This is mostly concentrated on the western side where are located government offices and the financial district. Housing predominates on the eastern side where housing prices are relatively affordable.

The "left" bank of the Seine is more residential than the "right" but house prices are very high, in particular in the 7th arrondissement. The western side is noted for the location of ministries and embassies, whilst the eastern side (the "quartier latin") is characterised by the "grandes écoles" (elite academic institutions) and universities, such as the Sorbonne. Although a large number of the "grandes écoles" have relocated to the suburbs (eg, the École Polytechnique), a number of faculties of prestigious colleges still remain.

The urban fabric is composed of older four to five storey buildings or of larger buildings of the Hausmann period (1850-1914) with six to seven storeys.

The centre of Paris contains a dense web of metro lines which extend radially into Zone 2. It also contains all Paris' main rail termini.

Zone 2

comprises the remaining nine arrondissements of Paris, the département of the Hauts de Seine, the near totality of the two other départements of the "première couronne" and even a small part of the four départements of the "grande couronne". This Zone is known as the "zone agglomérée" (built-up area) and includes the five new towns built at a distance of 25 to 30 kilometres from central Paris to concentrate what was otherwise seen by city planners as a "tache d'huile" (oil slick) of urban development that started in the 1960s.

The nine arrondissements in Zone 2 are largely residential, especially in the west (the 15th, 16th, and 17th arrondissements), with cheaper housing in the north and east. The suburbs close to the Ville de Paris display a mixed urban form of residential areas, such as those within the Ville de Paris, and areas of employment. The latter are composed of offices, artisanship, light industry and services, mostly concentrated in the north-east and south-east or in the département of the Hauts de Seine and the developmental "pôle" of La Défense in the west.

Further out, housing is in the form of large estates, the oldest of which were built in the 1960s.

Paris' new developments at La Défense

New developments are concentrated in the economically fast growing areas abutting the two international airports, Roissy (Charles de Gaulle) in the north and Orly in the south.

Further new developments are taking place in the Massy-Saclay area in the south, attracted by high technology industries, a university and the grandes écoles which relocated there in the last few decades.

The new towns also attract small scale commercial and service sector employment.

Zones 1 & 2 in Paris are characterised not only by a dense metro network but an expanding regional metro which rapidly crosses the city centre.

Zone 3
is still essentially rural. It includes the rest of the Région Ile-de-France, which forms the greatest part of the four départements of the "grande couronne". Urbanisation is concentrated in the valleys (Seine, Oise, Marne, and Yvette) and in some secondary centres. The majority of the surface area is agricultural land and forests.

Transport in Zone 3 is car dominated with some role for regional rail and buses linking the region's urban areas.

1.3.4 Tokyo

Tokyo has been the hub of Japan since 1604 when the first Tokugawa Shogun established the headquarters of his military regime in Edo (what is now Tokyo). After the fall of the shogunate in 1867, the new government remained in Tokyo. In the 1880s it took only about two hours to walk across the entire built-up area of the city.

The first railway initiated services in 1872. Tokyo's built-up area has expanded hand-in-glove with the development of its transport network, especially railways. After the Great Kanto Earthquake of 1923, as the reconstruction of Tokyo proceeded, much of the

population dispersed from the central area to the suburbs along the railways. Public transport within the Yamanote loop line was limited to city-operated buses and trams. Consequently, suburban commuters to the central area were obliged to transfer to the city-operated modes of transport at the stations along the Yamanote loop line. These transferring points evolved into the busiest parts of the metropolis. Before the Second World War many new residential areas were developed, and from 1930 broad streets lined with large buildings were built in the central business district.

Much of Tokyo was destroyed during the Second World War, but was quickly rebuilt. After the 1950s, owing to Japan's rapid economic growth, mass migration to Tokyo swelled the suburban residential areas. During the "bubble economy" period in the latter half of the 1980s, the central business district saw a dramatic growth pushing up land prices and rents, which further accelerated the efflux of the residential population. Many people moved to the suburbs where land was comparatively cheap (although land prices increased there too to some extent). Some commuters moved to areas even beyond Zone 4.

As the capital of Japan, the Tokyo Metropolis is the hub of the nation's political, economic and cultural activities. The jurisdictional area of the Tokyo Metropolitan Government consists of 23 wards, the Tama area (which includes 27 cities, three towns and one village), and a string of islands south of Tokyo Bay [18]. The mainland area stretches for about 90 kilometres from east to west and about 25 kilometres from north to south.

The Tokyo region, encompassing the Tokyo Metropolis and three prefectures (Kanagawa, Saitama and Chiba) is within a radius of about 50 kilometres of central Tokyo and forms an extended commuting area.

The Tokyo region is composed of about 32 million people living in 13,143 square kilometres (3.6% of the nation's land and 26% of its population). It is governed by 267 units of government, which include the Tokyo

Metropolitan Government and three prefectures, the 23 wards, 118 cities, 104 towns and 18 villages.

Due to the concentration of urban functions, Tokyo encounters various urban problems including a housing shortage, crowded commuting, and worsening traffic congestion. In the central three ward area of the Tokyo Metropolis, while the night-time population is decreasing, the day-time working population increased until 1995. The fundamental task the Metropolitan administration has set itself, is to fill the gap between the night-time population and the day-time working population in the central area of Tokyo and to transform Tokyo from a centralised urban structure into a multi-centred structure with mixed residential and employment functions.
Commuting from homes in the suburbs to the central area remains a major problem, with trains heavily overcrowded during the peak hours. In an effort to reduce congestion by having offices and residences close to one another, dispersion of offices to sub-centres in Zone 2 and business core cities in Zones 3 & 4 is being promoted. The construction of orbital transport networks has become a priority so as to start reorienting the city from having a centralised urban structure to having a multi-centred one.

More widely, in Japan, there are concerns about matters such as the excessive concentration of governmental, business and other functions in Tokyo. Furthermore, there is a concern regarding the adequacy of protection against disasters, especially earthquakes. These concerns have aroused interest in relocating the national capital to a new site and the national government set up a Deliberative Council on the Relocation of the Capital in December 1996. The selection of a candidate site for a new capital of Japan, away from Tokyo, is currently being undertaken.

Zone 1,

an area of 42 square kilometres (three central wards), is located in the centre of the 23 ward area which forms the built up area of the Tokyo Metropolis. Within this area are the National Diet, the national government offices, the supreme court and most foreign embassies, along with many headquarters of major corporations. Its daytime working population is 2.38 million (1990) which is equivalent to 33% of the total daytime working population in the 23 wards area (Zones 1 & 2). By contrast it has only just about a quarter of a million residents.

Zone 2,

an area of 575 square kilometres, is made up of 20 wards, excluding the central three wards. These form Tokyo's densely built-up area.

Broadly speaking, Zone 2 can be divided into two parts. One is the inner ward area surrounding the central three wards and the other is the outer ward area which is mainly residential. Among those wards on the outskirts, there are three (Adachi, Katsushika and Nerima) in which the population had increased until 1990. However, since 1995, the population has been decreasing in all the wards except the Nerima ward. In Zone 2, the population in total is decreasing, though the trend is not as pronounced as in Zone 1.

Therefore, just as in Zone 1, the restoration of night-time population has become an important policy goal, especially in the inner ward area. The Yamanote loop line operates in central Tokyo, and encompasses the main sub-centres such as Ikebukuro, Shibuya and Shinjuku. These sub-centres are currently developed to take on business functions, which otherwise would have located in the central area.

Zone 3,

an area of 1,160 square kilometres, is the suburban fringe of the 23 wards area (Zones 1 & 2). It is adjacent to the western side of the ward area and extends to the north west. The area is generally referred to as "Tama" and within it, it includes the "Tama New Town".

18   About 32,000 people live on the islands; but they are excluded from this study.

Zone 3 can be broadly divided into two parts. One is the urban area adjoining the ward area and the other is the hilly area stretching towards the prefecture's north western boundary.

Zone 3 consists of 27 cities, three towns and one village. It has been mainly developed as the residential area which took in the rapidly increasing population of Tokyo after the Second World War. For instance, Tama New Town has intentionally been developed as a dormitory city since the 1960s and is characterised by massive housing estates. With a revision in the planning law in 1986, new developments at Tama New Town (with an estimated population of 300,000) have boosted employment.

In order to prevent a further increase of commuters to the central area from the Tama area and to create a better mix of residential and employment areas, the Tokyo Metropolitan Government designated five cities, including Tachikawa, Hachioji and Machida, as the "core" cities of Zone 3. By doing so, the Tokyo Metropolitan Government is trying to induce businesses, commercial and cultural functions to relocate to these outer "core" cities. The policy of the Tokyo Metropolitan Government is to develop these cities and, at the same time, provide roads and public transport in order to link these cities with one another. Through such a policy, the Tokyo Metropolitan Government is trying to transform the Tama area as a

Housing in Tokyo's new towns

whole into a "self-sufficient urban region" which can act as a counter magnet to the ward area (Zones 1 & 2).

Zone 4,

an area of 11,366 square kilometres, is the area of three prefectures (Kanagawa, Saitama and Chiba) which surround the Tokyo Metropolis.

At the outset of the 20th century, most of Zone 4 was farmland, except for Yokohama (in the Kanagawa prefecture) which developed as a port. From the inter-war years, industry spread all along the coast between Tokyo and Yokohama.

After the Second World War, Zone 4 swiftly developed as a residential area with the outward migration from Tokyo, resulting from its economic development and relocation of industrial plants from the central area to the suburbs.

Cities like Yokohama, Chiba and Omiya are the commercial centres of their respective prefectures, but a large proportion of their residents still commute to central Tokyo. For example, the night-time population of Yokohama exceeds 3 million, but its day-time population is only about 90% of that, which shows that a substantial number of residents commute to central Tokyo.

While the population of the Tokyo Metropolis is decreasing, the population of these three prefectures is still increasing. In Saitama prefecture, the population increased by 5.5% between 1990 and 1995, and the growth rate of Chiba prefecture was 4.4%. The population increase in these adjoining prefectures (Zone 4) is a reflection of increased home ownership.

To counteract long-distance commuting, it is a national policy objective to create areas of mixed land-use. To implement this policy, the national government (through the National Land Agency) has drawn up the "National Capital Region Development Plan". For the Tokyo region, the National Land Agency is trying to develop seven "business core cities" such as Yokohama and Chiba in Zone 4, and two "business core cities", Tachikawa and Hachioji in Zone 3. This policy is being carried out in co-operation with the Tokyo Metropolitan Government and the adjacent three prefectures. These "business core cities" are each expected to become the centre of a self-sufficient urban area.

Institutional arrangements for transport

2

Content

2 Institutional arrangements for transport

Each of the four cities has different organisational structures that relate to the planning and provision of transport. These are either influenced by strong centralising tendencies of national government or by a strong sense of regionalism.

In London responsibilities are fragmented, with a number of non-government organisations involved. This has resulted in decision-making powers being concentrated at national level. The fragmentation of responsibilities has often meant that decisions are not being taken and, overall, the result has been a weakened planning system.

The New York region, too, is fragmented, between three States and numerous other jurisdictions, so no co-ordinated planning takes place. The lack of effective planning in both London and New York is leading to a growth of scattered low density developments, nearly always car-based, taking hold throughout the regions.

Paris and Tokyo have strong national planning frameworks. Paris is the exception to the rule in France in not having had transport powers decentralised from the centre to the regions. National government controls both the planning of transport and its operations through nationalised industries.

Tokyo's planning system is characterised by the seeking of a consensus. Planning is based on shared powers and responsibilities amongst the national ministries, the local governments and the private sector. The operation of transport is shared between the public and private sector.

Figures 1a to 1d show the organisations involved in transport in each of the four regions.

Figure 1a summarises the range of services managed by various organisations in London. Responsibility for some services is shared. Ultimate responsibility for strategic and local planning lies with the Secretary of State for the Environment, Transport and the Regions. A statutory joint committee of the London boroughs, the London Planning Advisory Committee, advises both the Secretary of State and the boroughs on strategic planning and transport issues and on major development proposals. Other organisations, such as London Transport, which currently manages the metro system and procures bus services in the capital, have boards directly appointed by national government.

In the New York region decision-making organisations and operators are concentrated at the State or sub-regional level. The United States Department of Transport is the main organisation with decision-making powers at national level, but planning and provision are decentralised to the States. There are no uniform structures for the planning or operation of transport. In New York the fragmentation of powers allows individual politicians to have a significant influence in the decision making process.

This contrasts with the geographical and political remit of major transport-related organisations in Paris (see figure 1c) where, although national government has a strong input through the Regional Prefect, transport provision is planned centrally at regional level, covering the whole of the Ile-de-France. Non-government organisations do not have a significant impact.

Tokyo has a centralised policy system (see figure 1d). Like Paris, non-government organisations have little impact.

Institutional arrangements for transport

Figure 1a
Organisations involved in transport planning and operations in London

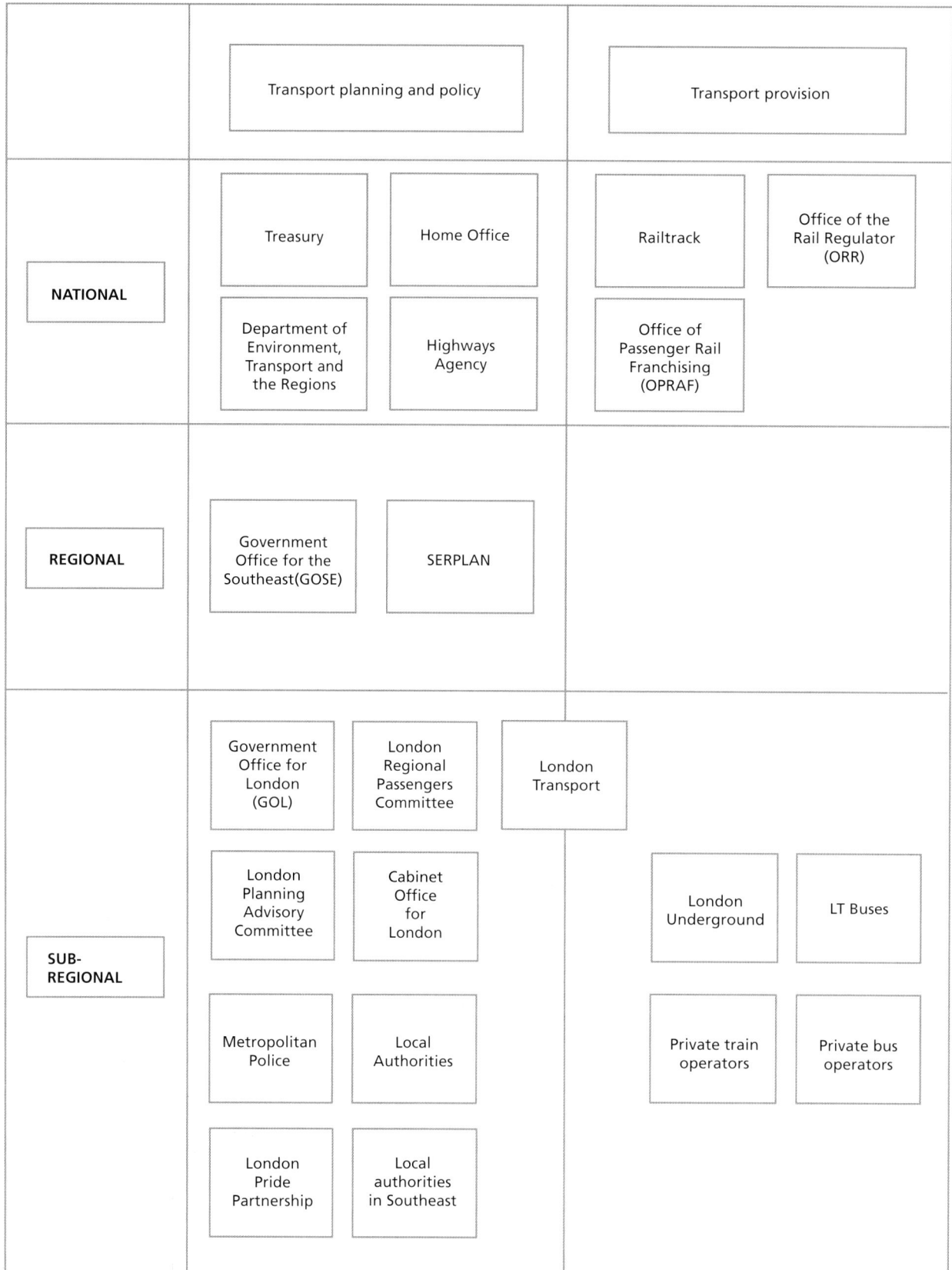

	Transport planning and policy	Transport provision
NATIONAL	Treasury / Home Office / Department of Environment, Transport and the Regions / Highways Agency	Railtrack / Office of the Rail Regulator (ORR) / Office of Passenger Rail Franchising (OPRAF)
REGIONAL	Government Office for the Southeast(GOSE) / SERPLAN	
SUB-REGIONAL	Government Office for London (GOL) / London Regional Passengers Committee / London Transport / London Planning Advisory Committee / Cabinet Office for London / Metropolitan Police / Local Authorities / London Pride Partnership / Local authorities in Southeast	London Underground / LT Buses / Private train operators / Private bus operators

Figure 1b
Organisations involved in transport planning and operations in New York

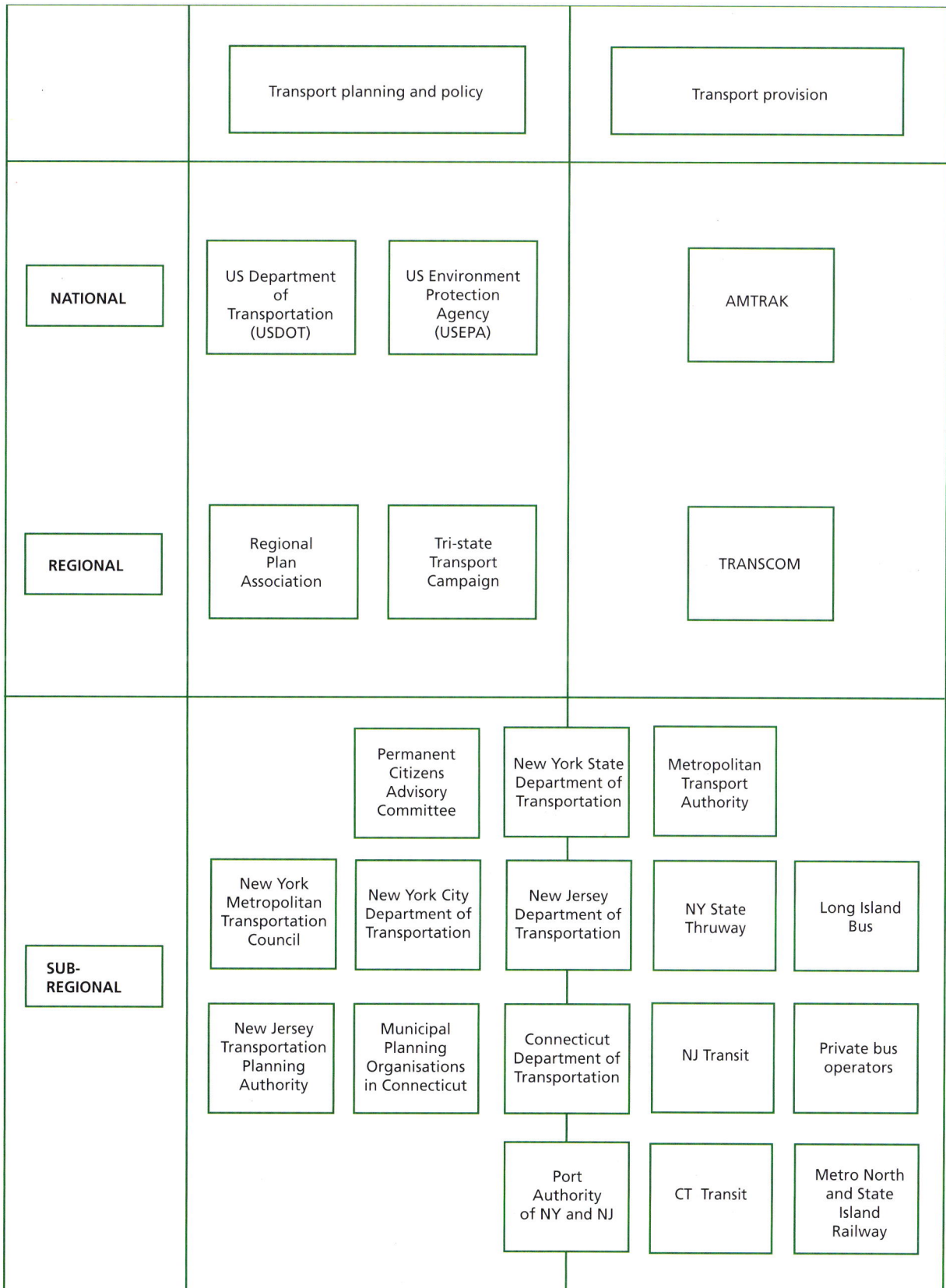

	Transport planning and policy	Transport provision
NATIONAL	US Department of Transportation (USDOT) / US Environment Protection Agency (USEPA)	AMTRAK
REGIONAL	Regional Plan Association / Tri-state Transport Campaign	TRANSCOM
SUB-REGIONAL	Permanent Citizens Advisory Committee / New York Metropolitan Transportation Council / New York City Department of Transportation / New Jersey Transportation Planning Authority / Municipal Planning Organisations in Connecticut / New York State Department of Transportation / New Jersey Department of Transportation / Connecticut Department of Transportation / Port Authority of NY and NJ	Metropolitan Transport Authority / NY State Thruway / NJ Transit / CT Transit / Long Island Bus / Private bus operators / Metro North and State Island Railway

Institutional arrangements for transport

Figure 1c
Organisations involved in transport planning and operations in Paris

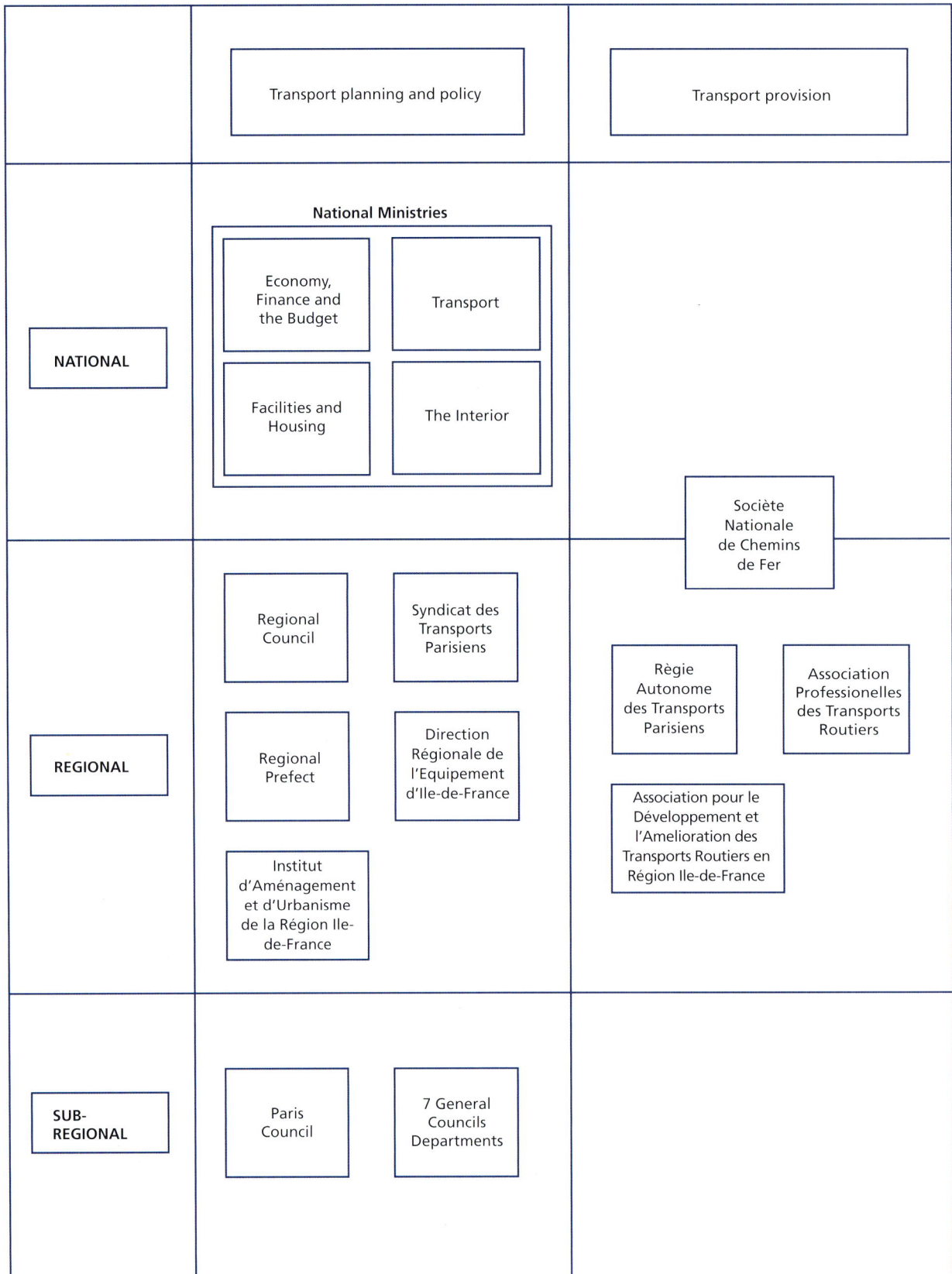

	Transport planning and policy	Transport provision
NATIONAL	**National Ministries** Economy, Finance and the Budget Transport Facilities and Housing The Interior	Sociète Nationale de Chemins de Fer
REGIONAL	Regional Council Syndicat des Transports Parisiens Regional Prefect Direction Régionale de l'Equipement d'Ile-de-France Institut d'Aménagement et d'Urbanisme de la Région Ile-de-France	Règie Autonome des Transports Parisiens Association Professionelles des Transports Routiers Association pour le Développement et l'Amelioration des Transports Routiers en Région Ile-de-France
SUB-REGIONAL	Paris Council 7 General Councils Departments	

Figure 1d
Organisations involved in transport planning and operations in Tokyo

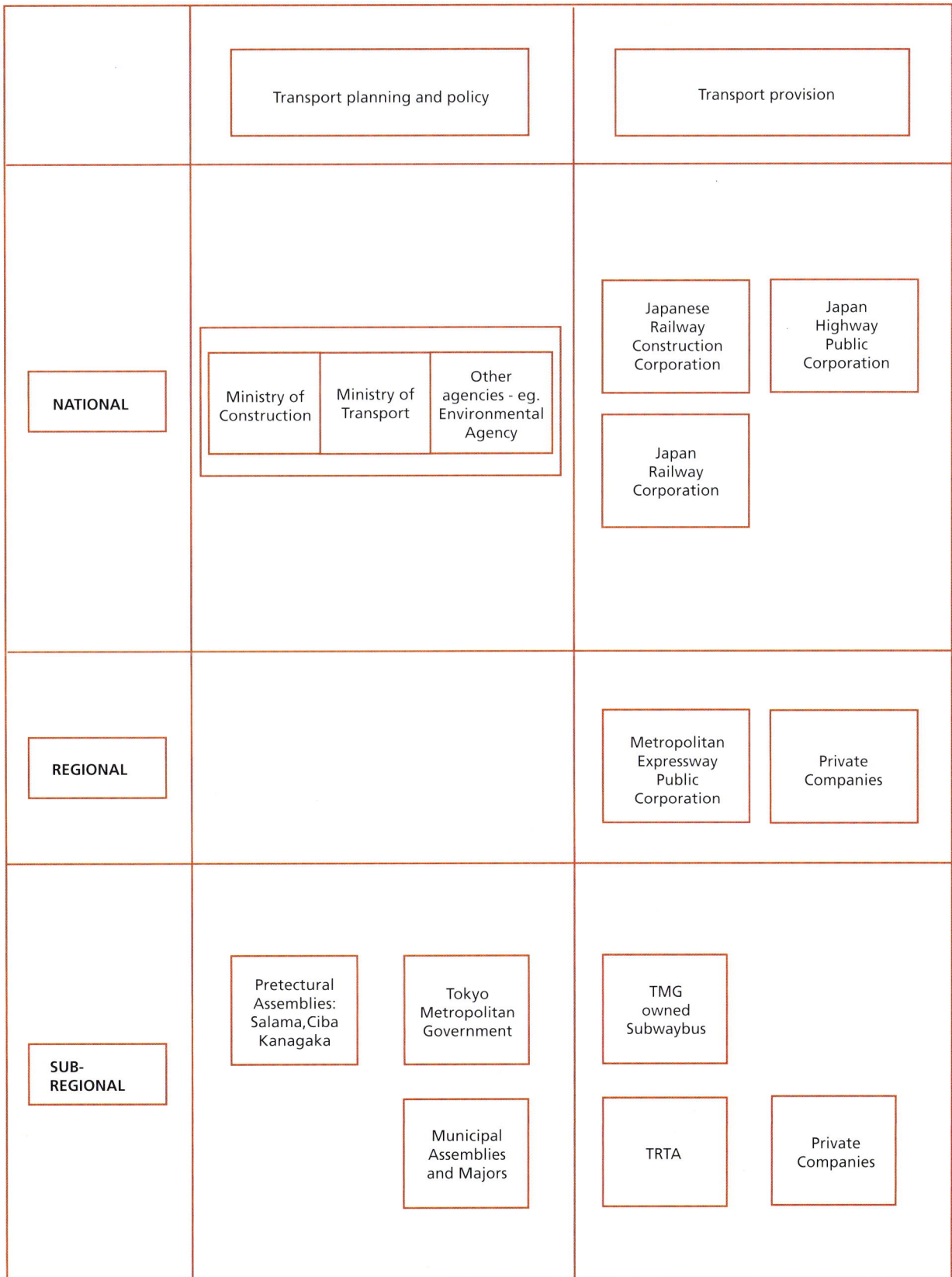

	Transport planning and policy	Transport provision
NATIONAL	Ministry of Construction / Ministry of Transport / Other agencies - eg. Environmental Agency	Japanese Railway Construction Corporation / Japan Highway Public Corporation / Japan Railway Corporation
REGIONAL		Metropolitan Expressway Public Corporation / Private Companies
SUB-REGIONAL	Pretectural Assemblies: Salama,Ciba Kanagaka / Tokyo Metropolitan Government / Municipal Assemblies and Majors	TMG owned Subwaybus / TRTA / Private Companies

2.1 London

2.1.1 The national context

The national government of the United Kingdom consists of two bodies: the House of Commons, with Members of Parliament, elected through their constituencies; and the House of Lords, to which members are either appointed or inherit their position. The Government, formed from the majority party or coalition in the House of Commons, forms a Cabinet with Ministers responsible for various departments. One of these is the Department of the Environment, Transport and the Regions, formed after the General Election in May 1997, through the merger of the Department of Transport and the Department of the Environment.

Outside London, local government boundaries and the division of responsibilities in some areas have been undergoing reorganisation under the Local Government Act of 1992. In these areas, the changes have led to the removal of some two tier county and district councils and their replacement by unitary authorities with responsibility for those functions, including planning and transport, previously divided between the two levels. In other areas county and district councils will be retained. Currently plans are being made for the creation of a new Greater London-wide strategic authority with an elected mayor.

Within the United Kingdom there are a number of Acts that have shaped transport and planning dating back to the Transport Act of 1555, which obligated parishioners to contribute towards maintenance of roads. Government intervention, however, was kept to a minimum until after the Second World War, with the nationalisation of the railways in 1947.

In the United Kingdom, whenever a major initiative is being taken, new primary legislation (an Act of Parliament) is required. The Department of the Environment, Transport and the Regions may also issue regulations under powers conferred by primary legislation, for example, in relation to lorry noise limits. It also provides advice on best practice without setting mandatory standards, such as the recent planning guidance note "*Planning and Policy Guidance 13*", which linked transport and land-use issues, seeking to reduce car travel through planning policy.

2.1.2 National government bodies involved in transport planning

Before the last General Election in May 1997, there were two main government departments with direct influence on transport: the Department of Transport and the Department of the Environment. These two departments have now been merged to form part of a new Department of the Environment, Transport and the Regions which is headed by a Secretary of State who is, at present, also the Deputy Prime Minister.

The national government's main functions in the field of transport planning are:

- to set national policy and take the lead in policy guidance for local authorities

- to set the regulatory framework to deal with safety and environmental matters

- to promote the provision of infrastructure - trunk roads and motorways, railways, ports and airports

- to determine the organisational framework within which public transport operators work.

The Department of the Environment, Transport and the Regions is responsible in England for all transport matters that are functions of national government. It is responsible throughout the United Kingdom for airports policy; railways; major ports; road traffic law and the Highway Code; the taxation, safety and testing of road vehicles; the licensing and testing of drivers; the licensing of lorry and bus operators and the registration of bus services; civil aviation (including international air service agreements) and vehicle licensing and registration. The Department is directly responsible for capital investment in motorways and other trunk roads and it provides financial support and exercises controls on investment in other public sector transport projects.

The Department of the Environment, Transport and the Regions has a number of executive agencies, including the Highways Agency, the Driving Standards Agency, the Driver and Vehicle Licensing Agency, the Vehicle Certification Agency and the Vehicle Inspectorate. The Department works closely with many other bodies - particularly local highway authorities that are responsible for all roads other than motorways and trunk roads, which are the responsibility of the Highways Agency.

The Highways Agency was set up in 1994 as an executive agency responsible for "managing a safe, reliable, efficient and environmentally acceptable" motorway and trunk road network on behalf of the Secretary of State for Environment, Transport and the Regions. In London this includes: the maintenance and enhancement of trunk roads and motorways; identifying and carrying out improvements to safety; reducing the visual impact of trunk roads through its landscape strategy; developing innovative solutions to road transport problems, which include enforcement cameras and introducing bus lanes on motorways.

The Government Office for London acts as the regional client of the Highways Agency for new road schemes in London. Apart from trunk roads and motorways, the London boroughs are (with minor exceptions) highway authorities for all roads in their area.

2.1.3 *Regional organisations involved in transport planning*

There are three main governmental organisations dealing with the entire region of the south-east of England.

- The Government Office for the South-East and the Government Office for London

  These bodies were set up in 1994 along with offices for each region of England, and together cover the region. The Government Office for London, however, is headed by a more senior civil servant and acts as a point of contact with the boroughs, voluntary organisations and the private sector. However, it has no control over many important aspects of public provision such as the health service, revenue grants to local authorities, funding of London Transport or the Highways Agency. Among the organisation's objectives is to "provide frameworks for sustainable land-use planning and transport policies and play a part in ensuring their effective implementation".

- The Standing Conference on London and South-East Regional Planning

  The Standing Conference on London and South-East Regional Planning is the only region-wide organisation with a direct remit for planning including transport, although this is in an advisory capacity only. For over 35 years, the Standing Conference on London and South-East Regional Planning and its predecessor have provided a forum for co-ordinating regional strategy and ensuring an adequate framework for development plans. It is composed of representatives from all local authorities in south-east England outside Greater London, and the London Planning Advisory Committee on behalf of the 33 London boroughs.

It provides advice to the government on regional strategy. The government, in turn, issues Regional Planning Guidance notes which guide local authorities in their planning functions.

2.1.4 Transport planning organisations in Greater London

The sub-regional local authorities of the south-east of England include the two tier system of county and district councils, unitary authorities, and the 33 local authorities within Greater London.

The local authorities throughout the region are responsible for planning within each of their areas, with the guidance of the Standing Conference on London and South-East Regional Planning, outside the Greater London area, and the London Planning Advisory Committee within Greater London.

Since the abolition of the Greater London Council in 1986, the London boroughs have evolved to meet the needs of a metropolis without a co-ordinating body. They are currently represented by the Association of London Government.

In transport matters there have evolved various statutory and non-statutory committees with specific roles and at times these committees operate in an uncoordinated manner. One of the main ones is the Transport Committee for London, which came into effect in 1998 through the merger of the London Boroughs Transport Committee, the London Committee on Accessible Transport, the Traffic Controls and Signals Unit, and the Parking Committee for London. In addition there are other organisations, such as the London Road Safety Advisory Group and the London Air Quality Network (joint-borough organisations).

In the past five years a number of governmental organisations and ministerial appointments have also been established at a London-wide level. These include the Government Office for London, the Transport Co-ordination Group, the Traffic Director for London and the Cabinet Sub-Committee for London. These organisations were set up to be co-ordinating bodies which would negate the need for one strategic body in the capital with a co-ordinating role. The new Government aims to rationalise the role of the plethora of transport organisations in London with the establishment of an elected mayor and a Greater London Authority, a new strategic government for London.

Until the new Greater London Authority is set up, numerous organisations have an important role in the provision and planning of transport within Greater London. The following are the most significant ones (this is not a comprehensive list):

- The Transport Co-ordination Group

  The Transport Co-ordination Group brings together the key organisations and individuals involved in transport in London. The group is chaired by the Regional Director of the Government Office for London and seeks to keep those interested in transport aware of developments.

- The Traffic Director for London

  The Traffic Director for London, appointed by the Secretary of State for Environment, Transport and the Regions, is now sponsored by the Government Office for London to co-ordinate implementation and improvements to the Priority ("Red") Route Network.

- The London Planning Advisory Committee

  The London Planning Advisory Committee was formed in 1986, under the Local Government Act of 1985 and is the London boroughs' statutory planning committee. Its responsibilities include giving advice to London boroughs on strategic transport planning issues and passing the collective view of the boroughs to the national government.

- Cabinet Sub-Committee for London

  The Cabinet Sub-Committee for London was established in 1992 and is chaired by the Secretary of State for the Environment, Transport and the Regions. Its membership comprises the Secretary of State for all departments with functional responsibilities in London. It has the aim of co-ordinating national government activities for the capital. The Sub-Committee meets three to four times per year but does not issue reports or statements.

Data for planning and policy issues are provided to the London boroughs and the London Planning Advisory Committee by the London Research Centre. The London Research Centre was set up by the boroughs, after the abolition of the Greater London Council, to provide transport information, and, in association with national government it has been responsible for carrying out the decennial London Area Transport Survey.

In addition, London-wide joint committees and 'partnerships' have emerged to fill the strategic vacuum in the capital left by the abolition of the Greater London Council. These have a variety of form and focus, some dealing with transport in specific areas and some with specific aspects of transport in the capital. London boroughs have joined the private sector in a number of organisations created to promote London as a 'world city'. The main private sector sponsored organisations are:

- The London Pride Partnership

  The London Pride Partnership is one of a number of 'City Pride' partnerships promoted by the Government to encourage joint public sector/private sector thinking on how particular cities should develop.

- London First

  London First is a private sector led consortium of nearly 300 businesses and other London organisations. It was initiated by the City of London, City of Westminster and the London Docklands Development Corporation to encourage inward investment.

National grant-giving bodies such as the Millennium Commission, one of the five National Lottery charities, also have an impact on London's development as do many other groupings and organisations in various geographical areas of London. Despite the myriad organisations within the capital, ultimate responsibility for transport policy issues in the capital falls to the national government.

A number of lobbying organisations are involved in campaigns to improve provisions for pedestrians and cyclists and improve/extend public transport services. These include groups, such as the London Walking Forum, the Pedestrians Association, and the London Cycling Campaign. Some of these organisations are represented on the London Transport Activists Roundtable, an umbrella group campaigning for sustainable transport in London. Furthermore, there are also business based organisations with strong lobbying power such as London Chambers of Commerce, the Freight Transport Association and the London branch of the Confederation of British Industry.

Since the 1997 parliamentary election, the new Labour Government has initiated plans to legislate for a strategic planning authority for the capital, controlling the funding for transport and regeneration schemes. Following the publication of the Government Green Paper, *New Leadership for London* in July 1997, the government has published a White Paper, *A Mayor and Assembly for London* (March 1998). A referendum took place in May 1998, in which the electors of London voted heavily in favour of the government's plans to create a mayor and an assembly in a new strategic authority for Greater London. It is proposed that the new authority have responsibility for a range of functions that come under the heading of sustainable development including land-use planning and transport. In particular the Paper proposes the creation of an authority with responsibility for transport matters, Transport for London. Until such organisations come into being, transport in London will still be influenced by numerous and disparate organisations.

2.1.5 Organisations involved in transport provision and regulation

Public transport provision in Greater London is co-ordinated by London Transport, which has a statutory duty to plan, provide and procure public passenger services for the capital, and the Office of Passenger Rail Franchising.

London Transport is a parent corporation with two wholly-owned subsidiaries: London Underground Limited and Victoria Coach Station. An important function of London Transport is the provision of integrated ticketing in the capital and the promotion of public transport through advertising, publicity and information services. Integrated and through-ticketing arrangements between the Underground and other rail services will continue following privatisation of the national and regional rail network, with London Transport entering into agreements with Railtrack, the

Table 2
Rail operating companies in the south-east of England

Rail Service	Name of parent company	Date of commencement of franchise	Length of franchise (yrs)
Thames Trains	Victoria Railways Holding	October 1996	7
Network South Central (now Connex South Central)	Connex Rail	May 1996	7
South West Trains	Stagecoach Holdings	February 1996	7
Network South East (now Connex South-Eastern)	Connex Rail	October 1996	15
London Tilbury and Southend	Prism Rail	May 1996	15
Great Eastern	Firstbus	January 1997	7.5
West Anglia Great Northern	Prism Rail	January 1997	7.25
Silverlink (previously North London Railways)	National Express Group	March 1997	7.5
Gatwick Express	National Express Group	March 1997	15 [19]
Thameslink	Govia	March 1997	7
Chiltern	M40 Trains	July 1996	7

19   The duration of this franchise will revert to seven years if planned rolling stock improvements are not implemented.

train operating companies and the Director of Passenger Rail Franchising.

The British Rail network providing rail services throughout England, Scotland and Wales was privatised under the Railways Act of 1993. The services previously provided by British Rail are now part of a fragmented network with rail infrastructure (including stations, signalling and power supply) now owned by Railtrack, a private company. Three rolling stock companies were created and sold and 25 train operating franchises granted. The franchising process is managed by the Office of Passenger Rail Franchising and began operation in 1997. The rail services in the south-east of England and their respective franchisees are shown in table 2, along with the date of commencement of the franchised service and the duration of the contract.

The system is regulated by the Office of the Rail Regulator. Following the change of government in May 1997, the Secretary of State for Environment, Transport and the Regions plans to strengthen the accountability of passenger franchise operators by setting up a National Rail Authority, which will include the existing Office of Passenger Rail Franchising. The train operating companies nationally have formed the Association of Train Operating Companies to co-ordinate participation in industry-wide schemes such as the Travelcard scheme and the London Concessionary Fares Scheme. The Rail Regulator oversees their activities.

Under the London Regional Transport Act of 1984, London Transport was given the duty to "tender activities and operations where appropriate". In 1994, London Transport Buses was established to co-ordinate bus related functions within London Transport. London Buses Limited, previously in London Transport ownership, was split into a number of bus operating companies, which were sold to the private sector in 1994. Since 1985, therefore, there has been progressive tendering of bus services and, since 1996, all bus services have been privatised. London Transport Buses is now responsible for route planning, service contract tendering and performance monitoring, while the privately owned bus operating companies are responsible for running services.

Outside Greater London, bus companies compete on the road, as any licensed operator can run services with 42 days' notice to the Traffic Commissioner. In addition, local authorities can procure "socially necessary" services.

Since the privatisation of bus services in Greater London, over half are now run by just three operators: Firstbus, Stagecoach and Arriva. Both Firstbus and Stagecoach also operate rail services in the region (as table 2 shows) and they both also have a significant share of the market nation-wide. The coach market is largely deregulated. A number of coach operators run commuter services into London, although this is on a limited scale.

Taxis in Central London

The Department of the Environment, Transport and the Regions has responsibility for overall policy on the regulations to be applied to taxis ("black cabs") and hire cars, (often referred to in London as "minicabs"). The regulations for London's 22,800 taxis are the responsibility of the Assistant Commissioner of the Metropolitan Police within Greater London and are administered on a day to day basis by the Public Carriage Office. Outside Greater London licences for taxis and hire cars are administered by local councils. London is the only city in the United Kingdom where hire cars do not need a licence to operate and therefore drivers are not vetted in any way. The main restriction on London's estimated 45,000-80,000 "minicabs" is that, unlike taxis, they are not allowed to ply for hire in the streets - they must be booked by telephone or by calling at the minicab office. They have a larger share of the market in the suburbs where "black cabs" are less common. Currently there are proposals to introduce some form of regulation in the "minicab" market.

2.1.6   Provision of accessible transport

There are a number of door-door services operating in Greater London for people with disabilities, such as "dial-a-ride", taxicard schemes and local authority transport. These are currently undergoing review by the Department of the Environment, Transport and the Regions following criticism of their incompatibility and under-funding. Thirty London authorities are in the London Taxicard Scheme, which is the responsibility of the London Committee for Accessible Transport. Although the scheme differs between authorities, users are allocated a certain number of trips by taxi (in two boroughs this is unlimited). In addition three authorities operate their own scheme.
London Transport has a Unit for Disabled Passengers, which deals with matters of accessibility on public transport generally, as well as administering the "dial-a-ride" scheme.

2.1.7   The transport planning process

Transport planning in the United Kingdom takes place within the overall development planning framework which comprises Structure Plans, Local Plans and in London and metropolitan authorities, Unitary Development Plans. Structure plans are prepared by county planning authorities and set out the policies and general proposals for the development and other use of land in the area including measures for improving the physical environment and the management of traffic. The plan is limited to policies and general proposals of structural importance. Structure plans deal with road proposals at the highest level of the hierarchy, the "primary" road network. Trunk roads are normally included as part of this network and all road schemes listed in the Department of the Environment, Transport and the Region's annual *Roads White Paper* will normally be included as proposals in structure plans.

Local Plans, produced by district authorities, should elaborate on the proposals for the improvement of the structure plan primary road network and indicate other proposed new roads and improvements.

Following the abolition of the Greater London Council, the system of local plans in London was superseded, each London borough being required to produce a Unitary Development Plan fulfilling the functions of structure and local plans. Unitary Development Plans must cover the whole area of a borough and adhere to the guidance set out in the Department of the Environment, Transport and the Region's Strategic Planning Guidance, which includes guidance on transport. Unitary Development Plans are composed of two parts:

- Part 1   contains general policies similar to a structure plan, and

- Part 2   contains site-specific proposals.

Following the adoption of Unitary Development Plans, local authorities must review plans and bring forward proposals for amendments that reflect strategic guidance and revised national Planning Policy Guidance Notes.

Local highway authorities in England (county councils, metropolitan district councils, London boroughs and the Corporation of London) must submit an annual Transport Policy and Programme document to the Department of the Environment, Transport and the Regions. The Transport Policy and Programme document serves both to outline policy and to bid for national funds to undertake local transport measures. The funds bid for come from the Transport Supplementary Grant, which is the Department of the Environment, Transport and the Region's main grant in relation to roads' capital expenditure. In 1993 the Government introduced the 'package approach' to national government support of local transport investment. Instead of bidding for funding for a specific project such as a new road development, local authorities are encouraged to take a more active strategic and multi-modal role in relation to transport in their areas. The package may therefore include plans for integration of pedestrian, cycling and public transport facilities.

The transport planning process is required to some degree and at all levels to incorporate public participation. The 1968 Town and Country Planning Act made public participation a statutory requirement in structure and local plans. In the main, participation involves lobbying, including direct action, and participation in the public inquiry process. The latter are held during major planning appeals, road proposals and less so for public transport developments. Major transport projects must show that they have consulted widely to gain funds from national government.

Furthermore, many local authorities have extended the concept of public participation through Local Agenda

21 projects. The United Nations conference on sustainable development, the "Earth Summit", in Rio de Janeiro in 1992 adopted in its final resolution as "Agenda 21" a policy on sustainability centred on local action by local authorities and interested individuals and groups. The Association of London Government has recently launched a London Agenda 21, dealing with sustainability issues at a London-wide level.

There is also a statutory body set up under the London Regional Transport Act of 1984, the London Regional Passengers Committee, to communicate passengers' views and monitor public transport operations in London. However, its members are appointed by the Department of the Environment, Transport and the Regions and the Committee is not allowed to comment on fares policies. Furthermore, there are numerous pressure groups in London that impact on the transport planning process, including those from the commercial sector.

2.1.8 The impact of land-use planning

After the abolition of the Greater London Council in 1986, national government became the strategic planning authority for the capital, issuing planning guidance, which sets the context for Unitary Development Plans. The boroughs make their input to the process through the London Planning Advisory Committee which has a statutory remit to advise the Government and the boroughs.

The first Regional Planning Guidance was issued in 1989 and set the strategic land-use planning context. It differed substantially from advice prepared by the London Planning Advisory Committee.

The second version of the Regional Planning Guidance was issued in May 1996 and gives guidance for the period up to 2006. It sets out a fourfold vision for

Car parks and new roads in London's Docklands

London: "a strong economy; a good quality of life; a sustainable future; and opportunities for all". With reference to transport and development the Guidance advocates that authorities:

- identify locations that generate less travel, promote increased public transport use and other non-car modes

- develop proposals which facilitate new public transport links and bring in financial contributions from the private sector

- allocate sites at public transport nodes

- plan for provision of high quality public transport

- ensure freight access to industrial developments

- carry out assessment of the transport impact of development proposals

- develop complementary land-use and transport policies

The Guidance for Greater London should be read in the context of the Regional Guidance for the South-East of England published by the government in 1994, which sets out three key objectives: "enhanced economic performance; sustainable development and environmental improvement; opportunity and choice".

National government exercises influence also through providing advice to local authority planning departments as to how they should carry out their policies. The main form of this advice is through planning guidance notes. Latterly these notes have been used to curtail the use of the private car through land-use planning. Two such notes, (Planning and Policy Guidance 6 and 13) emphasise the promotion of development of retailing in town centres rather than out-of-town shopping centres, and an overall reduction in the growth of motorised journeys, encouraging alternative means of travel.

In the United Kingdom, local authorities can gain "compensation" from developers in the form of contributions to public works, which is called "planning gain". For the past decade, the national government has encouraged the provision of new roads associated with particular developments and a means of introducing the private sector into public infrastructure projects. More recently, some local authorities in the region are applying this legislative provision to the adoption of "green transport plans" (whose aim is for companies to set out plans to encourage employees to adopt "sustainable" forms of travel).

2.1.9 Transport funding

Although there are a number of national government sources of finance for transport, the role of the private sector in capital projects is strongly encouraged in order to reduce government subsidy. The national railway, British Rail, has recently been privatised and the government has encouraged the private sector involvement in projects ranging from road building to development of light rail, as well as major non-transport related projects.

Car user taxes include car registration tax, fuel tax, and value-added tax, which are all processed through national government general accounts. Road construction and improvement funds are then allocated through the national budget. The Highways Authority is responsible for motorway and trunk roads, new roads being constructed through design, build, finance and operate programmes. Local roads are constructed and maintained by local authorities using grants from national government.

There is no national railway plan and little investment in new lines. Privatisation of British Rail was completed in 1997. There are no grants available from national government for new construction. However the regional railways in the south-east of England receive government subsidy for operations.

London Transport, which receives no government subsidy for running the metro system, receives funds for bus operations, new line construction and renovation of existing track, stations and rolling stock. The level of funding has been changing year by year depending on government finances and national spending priorities and for the past decade London Transport has not had a

stable funding regime. Since 1994, London Transport's overall investment including renewals, has been about $1,600 million per annum, which is more than double what it was in the 1980s. Currently, more than half of this sum goes towards the construction costs of the extension to the Jubilee metro line.

In the national government's 1998 White Paper on transport, road pricing and the introduction of office parking charges are raised as possibilities, but no measures have yet been taken.

The private sector has an increasingly important role in transport provision in the United Kingdom, directly through financing transport by "planning gain" and by forming public/private partnerships through the "private finance initiative". This scheme was launched in 1992, with the aim of increasing the element of private sector finance in the provision of services and infrastructure. It is based on the assumption that the private sector is better placed to manage large capital projects than the public sector. London Underground uses the "private finance initiative" as a way of transferring risk to the private sector and has recently used the initiative in acquiring new trains for the Northern line. The "private finance initiative" has also been important in road schemes in Britain with contractors entering design, build, finance and operate contracts. Only one of the eight successful schemes that have been completed so far has been part located in the London region.

2.2 New York

2.2.1 The national context

The government of the United States is a federal system, in which the states cede power to the national government, a tri-partite structure of the President, the Congress and the Judiciary. Congress is composed of two branches: the Senate, which has two members from each state, elected for six years, and the House of Representatives, whose numbers are proportional to population and are elected every two years. Each House of Congress has committees, which have specific jurisdiction over transport policy.

Until the early 1960s, the national government's participation in transport came solely through its powers to handle interstate and foreign commerce and provide post offices and post roads. There was no provision for contributing to public transport except by providing airports and their safety mechanisms. The states actually built the highways; national highway funds were granted to the states through the Department of Commerce.

The New York region covers parts of three of the nation's 50 states: New Jersey, New York and Connecticut. Each state has the same three branches of government as the national government: Governors negotiate state budgets, executive agencies report to the governor, and quasi-independent authorities are usually controlled by governors through appointment of a majority of their boards.

All three states of the New York region have delegated the power to regulate land-use to municipalities, though both New Jersey and Connecticut have state land-use plans that ought to guide local decisions. Other local governments include school districts, water and sewer districts and other independent administrative structures. Traffic enforcement is usually performed by local police within a municipality and by state police on state-operated motorways.

Municipalities also have elected executives and legislatures. New York City is comprised of five counties (called boroughs) and 59 Community Districts, which have advisory and service co-ordination functions.

The national legislation that establishes the framework for transport planning, financing and operations at all levels is the 1998 Transportation Equity Act for the 21st Century. "Equity" refers to several new guarantees:

- revenues from petrol and other motor vehicle related taxes, which are deposited into the Transportation Trust Fund, are dedicated for transport;

- expenditure of at least $198,000 million for transport over the next 6 years, of which a minimum of 17.3% will go to public transport;

- each state receives at least 90.5% of revenues it deposits into the Trust Fund.

The Transportation Equity Act for the 21st Century builds on the landmark 1991 Inter-modal Surface Transportation Efficiency Act which integrated the funding and planning of all surface transport modes and established planning and performance reporting requirements.

Transport policies are also influenced by the Clean Air Act Amendments of 1990, the National Environmental Policy Act of 1970 and the Americans with Disabilities Act of 1990. The Clean Air Act Amendments, as amended in 1996, influence transport policy by requiring states to demonstrate that their plans and applications for national funds conform to each state's plan to achieve national ambient air quality standards by 2007. The penalty for failure to demonstrate conformity is a countdown to the suspension of national highway and transit funding.

The National Environmental Policy Act of 1970 mandated that national agencies and recipients of national funds adequately and accurately consider the environmental consequences of their plans or actions.

2.2.2 National government bodies involved in transport

The United States Department of Transportation was created in 1967 to bring together under one umbrella numerous disparate transport missions and programmes, some of which were in existence since the 18th century. The Department employs about 100,000 people in ten operating administrations including the Federal Highway Administration, the Federal Aviation Administration, the Federal Transit Administration, and the Federal Railroad Administration.

The United States Department of Transportation administers the Transportation Equity Act for the 21st Century by establishing policy and regulations, administering the planning and funding process, monitoring performance of funded programmes, and sponsoring research. The Federal Highway Administration and the Federal Transit Administration maintain regional offices that oversee and provide financial and technical assistance to state and municipal projects. The Federal Highway Administration works with state transport departments, whereas the Federal Transit Administration generally works directly with public transport system operators.

Road and transport services are provided by state departments of transport, and state chartered public transport agencies and authorities, as well as by county and municipal agencies and private operators. All the agencies are eligible for national funding, requests for which are submitted by each state in a five-year "Transportation Improvement Program". To achieve the United States Department of Transportation approval, a Transportation Improvement Program, updated annually, must reflect the priorities of long-range transport plans. In actuality, state governors principally establish transport policies, based on plans developed, largely, by the state departments of transportation and the public transport operating agencies. However, under national law, planning is intended to be a bottom-up process in which regional priorities in urbanised areas are established by local agencies and operators that are the members of Metropolitan Planning Organisations.

The Federal Transit Administration prescribes detailed uniform reporting requirements for public transport agencies on financial and operating performance. Each year, the Federal Transit Administration prepares a national summary of the data from all public transport systems. All entities receiving financial assistance from the Federal Highway Administration or the Federal Transit Administration must demonstrate compliance with civil rights requirements and efforts to achieve the Inter-modal Surface Transportation Equity Act goal of 10% participation of Disadvantaged Business Enterprises (primarily minority and women-owned firms) in federally assisted surface transport projects.

2.2.3 Regional organisations involved in transport planning and provision

Since delivery of transport is organised along state lines in the United States, the principal agencies of each state of the three states in the New York region are described below. In the 1960s and early 1970s the Tri-State Region's highway agencies were changed to State Departments of Transportation.

The main transport operators are summarised in table 3.

2.2.3.1 Organisations in the State of New York

New York's Department of Transportation, established in 1967, is delegated the primary responsibility for planning and co-ordination of all transport modes in the state, including public transport, walking and cycling, regulation and rate-setting for motor carriers and for allocating state and national funds. In the New York City

Institutional arrangements for transport

Table 3
Transport providers in the New York region

Name of operator	Type of organisation	Service provided	Area served
New York City Transit	Authority	Metro and buses	New York City
Staten Island Railway	Authority	Regional rail	Staten Island
Port Authority of New York and New Jersey	Authority	Air and sea ports, bridges, tunnels, the Port Authority Trans Hudson metro system, and bus terminals	New York and New Jersey within 40 kilometre radius of mid-Manhattan
Long Island Railroad	Authority	Regional Rail	between Long Island and New York City
Metro North	Authority	Regional Rail	between Grand Central station in Manhattan and suburbs north of New York City in New York State and Connecticut
New Jersey Transit	Corporation	Regional rail, commuter coaches, local buses, special van services	New Jersey to the Hoboken terminal on the Hudson river, to Penn Station and the Port Authority bus termini in Manhattan
New York City Department of Transportation	City agency uses national funds to subsidise private companies	Commuter coaches, special van services	between outer areas of Zone 2 and Manhattan
Long Island Bus	the Metropolitan Transportation agency	Local bus	Nassau and Suffolk Counties
Bee-Line	Subsidised and supervised private corporations	Local bus	Westchester
Connecticut Transit	State agency	Local bus	Connecticut
Connecticut Transit districts	State subsidised agencies that franchise or operate services	Local bus, vans	towns in Connecticut
Private (some subsidised) bus companies	corporations	Inter-city and airport bus services	Inter-state and between urban centres and airports

metropolitan area of the State, project plans and decisions are made largely by three regional offices, which also provide staffing and direction to the Metropolitan Planning Organisations. The state-owned roadway network consists of about 14% of the state's total roads, by length, but handles almost 60% of the total traffic.

The Metropolitan Transportation Authority is a public corporation, which operates regional rail, metro and bus services. The state governor appoints the directors with the advice and consent of the State Senate, but seven are recommended by the chief executives of the suburban counties, four by the Mayor of New York. The governor names the chair and five directors on his own.

The Metropolitan Transportation Authority is one of the largest public transport providers in the world. Its system, just within the New York State portion of the region, carries about 19,000 million passenger-kilometres a year with 1,700 million rail and bus trips a year. The Metropolitan Transportation Authority agencies, New York City Transit, Long Island Rail Road, Long Island Bus, Metro-North Railroad, Bridges and Tunnels, serve a population of 13.2 million people in an area fanning out from New York City east and north, covering Long Island, south-eastern New York State and western Connecticut. The Authority also operates and maintains seven tolled bridges and two tolled tunnels. Its surplus toll and other revenues are divided roughly equally between New York City Transit and the regional rail systems, Metro North and the Long Island Railroad.

The counties and the major municipalities perform the principal transport functions that are apparent to the public: maintenance of local roads and bridges; traffic management, including traffic signals; and parking management.

The most prominent local agency is the New York City Department of Transportation which oversees about 5% of expressways and major arterial roads in the region as well as local streets, minor roads, bridges, traffic signals,

parking meters and municipally-owned garages. It develops city-wide plans, such as a Bicycle Master Plan, undertakes special studies, such as of goods' movement, and plans transport improvements in specific areas of the city that are implemented in partnership with operating agencies.

The New York Metropolitan Transportation Council is the Metropolitan Planning Organisation that covers 10 of the Tri-State Region's 14 New York counties. Since the New York Metropolitan Transportation Commission's funding comes through New York's Department of Transportation it is widely viewed as being influenced by state policies. Political priorities for budgeting are expressed through three Transportation Co-ordinating Committees, one for New York City, one for suburban Long Island, and one for the northern counties of Westchester, Rockland, and Putnam.

The New York State Thruway Authority is a public corporation that operates the 170 kilometres of roads that extend across the state north and south and east and west (the largest toll highway system in the United States). It also operates the Tappan Zee Bridge, a major Hudson River crossing into the metropolitan area; and the 140 km New York State Canal System. Its three directors are appointed by the governor, and it is funded by toll receipts.

In New York City there are over 12,000 yellow-painted taxis ("yellow-cabs") that are the only vehicles permitted to ply for hire. The number of yellow taxis is restricted by local law, which specifies a fixed number of medallions that can be sold to owners of yellow taxis. There are also more than 30,000 for-hire passenger car services, operating from about 600 bases. The vehicles are, for the most part, owned or leased by drivers. These include 6,000-8,000 premium radio dispatched services, which operate largely under contract to corporations. Both of these fleets operate primarily in Manhattan. Zone 2 is mostly served by about 20,000 licensed for-hire cars that operate as part of neighbourhood based radio-dispatched services.

There are also about 5,000 to 10,000 unlicensed "gypsy cabs" that roam the streets, particularly in the poorer neighbourhoods.

2.2.3.2 Organisations in the State of New Jersey

In 1966, New Jersey established its Department of Transportation, which was the first comprehensive transport agency in the nation, responsible for roads, rail, airports and seaports. Prior to 1966, the Department operated only as a highway agency.

New Jersey Transit, initiated in 1979, is the nation's third largest public transport agency. It is governed by a Board of Directors appointed by the governor, chaired by the State Commissioner of Transportation and includes the State Treasurer and a third state official representing the governor. Of the citizen directors, two are executives of large corporations, one of a smaller business and one of a road freight business. New Jersey Transit operates the State's regional rail and bus systems.

The New Jersey Turnpike Authority and the New Jersey Highway Authority each operate toll roads in the state; the first, principally north and south between Philadelphia and New York, the second from the New Jersey coast to the northern State line. These agencies are governed by boards of directors appointed by the governor.

In New Jersey, in addition to the New Jersey Department of Transportation, there are eleven independent transport agencies, operating toll roads and bridges, rail services and ports. Co-ordination is sought among the numerous New Jersey transport agencies through a Transportation Executive Council composed of the chairs of the agencies and authorities under the Transportation Commissioner. It is charged with preparing a capital investment plan and co-ordinating programme development consistent with the State land-use plan.

The North Jersey Transportation Planning Authority, the Metropolitan Planning Organisation in the New Jersey portion of the region, covers 13 of the region's 14 northern New Jersey counties.

2.2.3.3 Organisations in the State of Connecticut

In 1966, the Connecticut Department of Transportation was established and given authority to provide public transport and manage the State's road network. It also became the State's primary agency responsible for the planning and development of transport. In addition to highways, the Connecticut Department of Transportation oversees the State's airports, regional rail and para-transit systems. It is headed by the State's Commissioner of Transportation, who is appointed to a four-year term by the Governor, with approval from the state's legislature. The agency is organised into five bureaux: Engineering and Highway Operations, Finance and Administration, Policy and Planning, Public Transportation, and Aviation and Ports.

In 1976, the State of Connecticut established Connecticut Transit to operate, under contract, local bus services in Hartford, New Haven, and Stamford and commuter coaches to Hartford and New Haven. In the three counties of the metropolitan region there are 11 Transit Districts that also provide bus services, generally under contract, and regulate other transport services, such as taxis. The Connecticut Department of Transportation indirectly provides for a regional rail service between New Haven and New York City via the Metropolitan Transportation Authority's Metro-North Railroad, and contracts with Amtrak (the national private corporation that runs most inter-city trains) to operate a rail service east of New Haven to New London (Shore Line East).

The State of Connecticut has fifteen regional planning agencies - voluntary associations of municipalities. Of these, ten are designated as the Metropolitan Planning Organisations because they are located in metropolitan areas with greater than 50,000 population, where such organisations are required by national law. In the Connecticut portion of the New York region, the Metropolitan Planning Organisations are centred on: Greater Bridgeport, Danbury, New Haven and Stamford.

2.2.3.4 Region-wide agencies

The Port Authority of New York and New Jersey's jurisdiction includes a 17-county bi-state region generally within a 40 kilometre radius of the Statue of Liberty in New York harbour. Its mandate is to promote and protect the commerce of the bi-state port, both sea and air, and to carry out regional improvements not likely to be financed by private enterprise nor by either state alone. The governor of each state appoints six commissioners to the agency's Board of Commissioners, subject to the approval of the state senates. In recent years, Port Authority policy has been closely overseen by the New York and New Jersey governors; meanwhile the agency has sharply reduced its planning functions and is now examining privatisation of many of its facilities.

The Port Authority of New York and New Jersey owns and/or operates numerous inter-modal facilities: large marine terminals in New Jersey, Staten Island, and Brooklyn; the region's three main airports, Newark International, JFK International, and La Guardia; interstate bus terminals in mid-town and upper Manhattan; six toll crossings between New Jersey and New York; the World Trade Centre; and the Port Authority Trans Hudson metro system from New Jersey to the west side of Manhattan.

The Transportation Operations Co-ordinating Committee was created in 1986 to provide a co-operative, co-ordinated approach to regional transport management in the region. It is a coalition of 15 agencies [20], funded by its members and the Federal Highway Administration. It carries out three main functions on behalf of its member agencies:

- the Operations Information Centre collects and disseminates real-time information on traffic interference, eg accidents

- the Regional Construction Co-ordination Program helps member agencies co-ordinate construction schedules to facilitate traffic flow

- the Technology Development Program conducts operational tests and other technology applications to improve the quality, timeliness, and dissemination of transport information

2.2.3.5 Non-governmental organisations involved in transport

New York has a number of influential non-governmental organisations involved in transport planning and in lobbying. The main ones are:

- Regional Plan Association

  The Regional Plan Association was established by concerned citizens in 1929 to focus on what has grown to be the 31-county Tri-State Region. Funded by foundation and corporate contributions and government contracts, the Regional Plan Association recommends

---

20   The Transportation Operations Co-ordinating Committee s member agencies are the: The three State Departments of Transportation, Metropolitan Transportation Authority, the Metropolitan Transportation Authority Bridges and Tunnels, New Jersey Highway Authority, New Jersey Transit Corporation, New Jersey Turnpike Authority, New York City Department of Transportation, New York City Transit Authority, New York State Police, New York State Thruway Authority, Palisades Interstate Park Commission (which operates a parkway), Port Authority of New York and New Jersey, and Port Authority Trans-Hudson Corporation.

research-based policy improvements and investments, fosters co-operation among government and private organisations and involves the public in considering and shaping the region's own future. It attempts to influence decisions affecting the Tri-State Region at all levels of government based upon its research and planning.

In 1996, the Regional Plan Association completed its Third Regional Plan, with recommendations, including: improving mobility; concentrating growth in town centres; investing in a competitive work-force; and reforming governance. Furthermore, the Association has recommended substantial improvement and investment in the region's rail system including links to the city's airports.

• The Tri-State Transportation Campaign

The Campaign, established in 1993, is a non-profit, coalition of public interest groups, which engages the New York-New Jersey-Connecticut metropolitan region's transport agencies in policy dialogue and tries to influence transport decisions away from car dependence.

• The New Jersey Transit Advisory Committees

Public input also comes from official advisory groups that develop special knowledge of the agencies they review. New Jersey Transit has two passenger advisory councils, whose members are appointed by the governor, one for the northern part of the state and one for the area around Philadelphia.

• The Permanent Citizens Advisory Committee to the Metropolitan Transportation Authority and other passengers' groups

In 1977, the Metropolitan Transportation Authority board formed the Permanent Citizens Advisory Committee with 15 members appointed by New York City officials and 14 by officials from the seven suburban counties. In 1981, the New York State Legislature formally established three passenger councils for each of the three public transport agencies: New York City Transit, the Long Island Railroad, and Metro-North. The Councils monitor performance, such as the quality of the passenger environment and the regularity of bus service, initiate studies and advocate policies. In 1995, the Permanent Citizens Advisory Committee gained a non-voting seat on the Metropolitan Transportation Authority board.

Numerous private sector organisations, notably the Straphangers Campaign, also monitor the Metropolitan Transportation Authority's performance. In Connecticut, Metro-North and Shore Line East riders are represented by a commuter council modelled after the Permanent Citizens Advisory Committee to the Metropolitan Transportation Authority, which reports to the Connecticut Department of Transportation.

2.2.4   Provision of accessible transport

The Americans with Disabilities Act of 1990 prohibits discriminating against anyone with physical or mental disabilities in employment, public services, public accommodation and telecommunications. As a result, new public transport vehicles and new or rebuilt public transport facilities must be fully accessible for people with disabilities. New buses must be wheel-chair accessible, and when a subway station is substantially refurbished, lifts must be installed. Specialised transport services may also be provided, but they may not substitute for making all facilities accessible.

2.2.5   *The transport planning process*

The Transportation Equity Act for the 21st Century assigns the initial responsibility for planning to the Metropolitan Planning Organisations. However, the real impetus occurs outside the Metropolitan Planning Organisation framework. Traditionally, plans emerge from operating agencies that define practical needs.

In the last 15 years, these have been dominated in the New York region by programmes to repair the infrastructure after decades of under-investment. As these goals are being reached, agencies are examining ways to expand the transport system. Under the Transportation Equity Act for the 21st Century, any significant increase in capacity should be preceded by undertaking a Major Investment Study, which is a broad evaluation of all alternatives to meet transport needs in a travel corridor.

Increasingly, long-held agency plans are being overtaken by political forces, especially in the rejection of new motorway lanes. The most powerful impetus for a project is the personal interest of a governor, a member of Congress, or the mayor of New York City. The Transportation Equity Act for the 21st Century contains $1,000 million in specific projects for the region that were initiated by members of Congress at the behest of a particular constituency, rather than going through the Metropolitan Planning Organisation. More and more, lobby groups are able to rally political support for concepts they initiated outside the official planning process.

To qualify for national funds, states are required to prepare long-range transport plans to maximise the use of existing facilities, to implement congestion management strategies, and to affect land-use and urban development through transport policies. State plans are to be developed from regional elements prepared by the Metropolitan Planning Organisations based on input from local governments and the public. The

Metropolitan Planning Organisations must build and maintain a regional transport model to guide their principal products: the Long Range Regional Plan (a strategic plan to achieve goals and objectives developed with public input), the Transportation Improvement Program, (a five-year programme of planning, design, and construction of individual projects), and the Unified Planning Work Program (the annual planning budget). The Metropolitan Planning Organisations are responsible for negotiating a budget request that, ideally, reflects a consensus on regional priorities of both its member agencies and the public. Agencies that are armed with well-documented plans to address clearly defined needs make a strong case. Nevertheless, funds are also allocated to maintain equity among jurisdictions. Once the Transportation Improvement Program and other programmes are approved by the United States Department of Transportation, funds are committed based upon appropriations by Congress and state and local agencies.

State plans set categories of priorities. New York State's calls, for example, for returning existing facilities to a state of good repair and maintaining them better; maximising service from existing facilities; minimising expansion of travel capacity and giving priority to public transport over highways when capacity must be increased; improving management and increasing attention to the potential of new technology; and, promoting economic development and relating transport to land-use goals. The long-range plan of New York State's Metropolitan Planning Organisation (the New York Metropolitan Transportation Council) sets the same priorities as the State plan.

The Transportation Improvement Programs are supposed to follow these general priorities and set out projects that have reasonable prospects of being financed. However, Transportation Improvement Program projects often emerge from specific local and county government proposals, rather than being identified at the regional level as within the long-range priorities.

National law and regulations require public involvement in transport planning and decision making. Most meetings conducted by national agencies are required to be open to the public. Both the Metropolitan Planning Organisations and state Departments of Transportation are required to provide "reasonable opportunity to comment"; at the very least, public hearings are required for adoption of long range plans, Transportation Improvement Programs, fare and toll increases, and environmental impact statements.

Some agencies are sceptical about public participation, questioning whether the participants represent a true cross-section of the affected public. On controversial projects, decisions are ultimately made through the political process, ignoring the carefully produced plan and the priorities listed in the Transportation Improvement Programs. Many public-interest organisations, asserting that they represent the legitimate public perspective, bypass the formal mechanisms for seeking input, and turn, instead, to influence the media and to lobby politicians.

2.2.6   The impact of land-use planning

Land-use decisions are made principally by the region's 780 municipalities, through the issuance of building permits, zoning, and approval of large developments. New Jersey and Connecticut have state land-use plans, but have not enforced them on municipalities and even state agencies ignore them. Counties also have planning agencies that, in many cases, have adopted detailed land-use plans, which only have persuasive, not legal authority.

Housing in New York's Zone 3

Transport plans of a Metropolitan Planning Organisation, which must be shown to be consistent with land-use plans, generally assume the continuation of current land-use and demographic trends. Therefore, they tend to contradict transport priorities as both local land-use plans and trends are resulting in a spread and scatter of development that can only be served by motor vehicles. Even where states have adopted land-use plans, they have not significantly affected decisions on local land-use or on transport projects.

In New Jersey, that pattern may change with the recent strong directive of the Governor for compliance of state programmes with the state-wide redevelopment plan to curb urban sprawl. A preliminary State plan revision, strengthened in 1997, calls for:

- guiding growth to higher density centres near public transport stops, setting development boundaries

- transport policies to reduce vehicular travel, using parking management, new technology and market mechanisms to promote use of high occupancy vehicles, walking and cycling

- commercial and housing policies to support downtown and neighbourhood revitalisation

- preservation of open spaces and natural resources.

New York has no land-use plan, and Connecticut's is limited to state projects and has sometimes been ignored by State agencies. Most transport investment is made in response to demands of residents and businesses that result from uncoordinated real estate development approved by individual municipalities based on local zoning codes. While private sector or municipal projects that are at variance with local zoning are subject to elaborate environmental review, state agencies are generally exempt from municipal ordinances. State agencies are, however, subject to development controls

mandated by state and national laws that protect coastal areas, wetlands and habitats of endangered species.

2.2.7 Transport funding

The law that establishes the national transport policy, the Transportation Equity Act for the 21st Century of 1998, continues the funding principles first enacted by Congress in 1991, by providing flexible use of Transportation Trust Fund revenues among all transport modes, rather than by employing the former method of segregating the financing of highways, public transport, and planning.

Of a total $25,600 million in Trust Fund revenues in 1996, 60% came from a $0.048 per litre tax on petrol, 23% from a $0.064 per litre tax on diesel fuels, and the balance from other motor vehicle related fees and taxes.

The Transportation Equity Act for the 21st Century of 1998 guarantees a minimum fund of $198,000 million, authorised for the next six years, of which a minimum of $34,000 million is for public transport. The allocation among the states, historically based on a formula that accounts for both population and extent of the road network, has been adjusted to ensure that every state will receive at least 90.5% of the tax on petrol the state pays into the Highway Trust Fund. New York will get 114% of its contributions, New Jersey 94% and Connecticut 90.5%.

Of the national total Transportation Equity Act for the 21st Century funds, the three states in the region will receive 9.3%, amounting to $2,400 million a year over the six year authorisation period. This represents an increase of $555,000 million or 30% over 1992-97 funding levels, which were subject to annual appropriations by Congress.

The Transportation Equity Act for the 21st Century establishes an Infrastructure Bank which can extend either loans or a credit line to be repaid by project revenues. The Act also allows employers to give $65 per month in non-taxable public transport fare and car-pooling benefits (a companion of the existing cap of $155 on parking benefits) increasing to $100 per month by 2002.

National funds represent only a portion of total transport funding on a state level. State funding, from vehicle-related taxes and tolls, is matched by local contributions, generated by property and sales taxes and parking fees and fines. Each of the three states in the New York region has a dedicated source of transport funds, generated primarily by state petrol taxes and motor-vehicle related fees. Except for Connecticut, tolls are an important source of revenues. However, the levels of taxation are quite different, as are the sources and reliability of supplementary funds.

New York State contributes approximately $2,800 million per year, 40% of which goes into a highway and bridge trust fund and 60% to a public transport operating fund, derived from:

- motor fuel taxes ($0.02 per litre for petrol)

- 17.7% tax on all petroleum products that are refined, imported or sold in the state

- a weight/distance tax on lorries

- vehicle registration and license fees

- toll revenues ($0.02 per kilometre and $3.50 at most bridges and tunnels for autos; lorries are charged much more)

The New Jersey Transportation Trust Fund receives approximately $700 million a year in backing for highway and public transport programmes and aid to localities from a variety of sources including petrol taxes, and tolls on bridges and tunnels. New Jersey has also established several means of "innovative financing," attracting private sector funds.

Connecticut's Transportation Fund receives about $850 million a year from petrol taxes and other motor vehicle-related fees, but it has eliminated tolls on motorways in the state. Connecticut's petrol tax has, historically, been the highest in the region, $0.1 per litre. It was first reduced to $0.09 in 1997, and to $0.08 in 1998.

Capital funds are typically leveraged by the states as backing for bonds that generate an up-front infusion of secure financing of long term projects.

Public transport operations and capital investment are subsidised in all three states, but the levels of subsidy differ greatly, from one system to another.

In New York the Metropolitan Transportation Authority's $1,300 million operating deficit is met with a plethora of subsidies, that include:

- national funds account for about 1.6% of subsidies

- about 16% is met by surplus tolls on the Metropolitan Transportation Authority's bridges and tunnels

- approximately 14% is from State operating assistance funds, with matching funds from New York City and suburban counties

- the largest share, 65%, is raised through a patchwork of taxes:

  - a 0.025% tax on retail sales in the Metropolitan Transportation Authority region

  - a 17% surcharge on business taxes paid in the Metropolitan Transportation Authority region

- 34% of the tax on petroleum products

- a portion of a tax on telecommunication lines

- taxes on high-end mortgages and property sales in New York City

New Jersey Transit operations, which cost about $800 million a year, are paid by passenger fares (50%), state subsidies (45%) and national subsidies (5%). The Transportation Trust Fund contributes about a third of New Jersey's $630 million annual capital funds, with two-thirds financed by national funds.

Connecticut public transport operating subsidies of about $123 million a year from the Transportation Fund account for about two-thirds of bus system costs, 27% of the Metro North operations and 84% of Shore Line East costs.

The two airport access programmes are funded primarily by a $3.00 Passenger Facility Fee, levied on passengers at the three airports, supplemented by funds from the Port Authority of New York and New Jersey's capital programme. In the case of the link to John F. Kennedy airport, the Port Authority will contribute $300 million in capital funds toward the $1,550 million project.

2.3   Paris

2.3.1   The national context

The National Government is made up of two bodies: the National Assembly (Assemblée Nationale), with directly elected deputies, and the Senate (Sénat), with members elected indirectly through local authorities. At regional level, functions are divided between three levels of authority: regions (régions), departments (départements), and municipalities (communes). There are 26 regions, each governed by a Regional Council (Conseil Régional); 100 departments, each governed by a General Council (Conseil General); and more than 37,000 municipalities, with a Municipal Council (Conseil Municipal).

The Regional Council (Ile-de-France for the Paris region) is composed of directly elected members, each elected for a period of six years and who elect the President of the Regional Council (President du Conseil Régional). The Council is consulted on the preparation of the national plan; and makes decisions to encourage regional development.

The General Council of a department acts under the authority of its President who is elected by members of the council. The eight departments of the Ile-de-France are the Ville de Paris (which is uniquely both a department and a municipality), Hauts-de-Seine, Val-de-Marne, Yvelines, Val d'Oise, Seine-et-Marne, and Essonne.

Each Municipal Council elects a mayor from amongst its members. Since 1973, municipalities have been strongly encouraged to form associations, which are organisations of a group of municipalities or a mixed association of municipalities, departments, and other organisations. In areas outside the Ile-de-France, these associations can play a major role in transport planning as the "organising authority". Responsibility for urban public transport rests with municipalities or associations of municipalities wherever an "urban transport perimeter" has been set; they then become the organising authority. In the Paris region the set up is significantly different with the national government taking a direct organisational and managerial role.

The decentralisation laws of 1982 redefined the powers of French local authorities, transferring some national government responsibilities to a more local level. Planning is a joint activity undertaken by both national government and local authorities. The law on internal transport (Loi d'Orientation des Transport Intérieurs) states:

"that the preparation and implementation of overall transport policy are provided jointly by the state and the local authorities within the terms of the European Community rules set out by the Treaty of Rome".

The 1995 Framework Law for Town and Country Planning and Development stipulates that the regional planning and development programmes should be prepared by the regions in association with the national government. Final approval powers, however, lie with the Council of State. In the Ile-de-France, the structure plan (Schema Directeur de la Region d'Ile-de-France) is planned by local agencies of the national government in association with the regional government.

There are also a number of laws and decrees that stipulate the powers and responsibilities of public transport organisers and operators in particular, the responsibilities of the main rail providers in the Ile-de-France, the Régie Autonome des Transports Parisiens and the Société Nationale des Chemins de fer Français.

2.3.2 *National government bodies involved in transport planning*

In the Ile-de-France, in contrast to other regions in France, organisation of the transport system is centralised at national level, although functions are carried out by regional organisations. National government through the Ministry of Finance and the Ministry of Transport has responsibility for:

- the regulation of transport activities

- general policy framework for urban and non-urban passenger services

- national and regional passenger transport projects

- the supervision and organisation of public transport on a national scale

- trusteeship of national companies (the Régie Autonome des Transport Parisiens and the Société Nationale des Chemins de fer Français).

- definition and implementation of state financing for provincial public transport

- preparation of a national transport master plan

- initiation and approval of regional town plans

- promotion of research studies and innovative transport programmes

- promotion of public transport network development and inter-modality through grants to local authorities

- placing contracts for the national road network.

The French system seeks to avoid overlapping jurisdictions. National government, therefore, has sole regulatory authority and can impose obligations on the regions, departments and municipalities. Main roads are the responsibility of the national government, which therefore acts as contracting authority, through the Direction Départementale de l'Équipement (a national government technical service operating at departmental level).

National government is represented at local level by the regional prefect, and the departmental prefects. In the Ile-de-France the regional prefect is also the prefect of Paris. In contrast with the other French regions, overall authority for enforcement of traffic law rests with the Director of Police (Préfet de Police), rather than the mayor or the president of the Regional Council.

2.3.3 Region-wide organisations involved in transport planning

In all provinces in France except the Ile-de-France, transport planning functions are decentralised to the region or sub-regional bodies. Responsibilities and functions are divided between the three tiers of government: regions, departments, and municipalities. As stated previously, however, in contrast with other regions, the Ile-de France has a special status in the field of transport as the law on internal transport (Loi d'Orientation des Transports Intérieurs) does not apply to the Ile-de-France and national government oversees the organisation of pubic transport.

In the Ile-de-France, the regional government has no direct responsibility for organising and operating passenger transport. It therefore owns neither the road network nor the public transport network. Moreover, it is not represented within the Syndicat des Transports Parisiens, the authority with sole responsibility for organising public transport within the region. This situation is an inheritance from the past, when the national government had sole authority over transport policy in Ile-de-France. This does not mean that the Region has no powers in this field, as it is the government's main partner in selecting and jointly funding transport infrastructure. The regional council's current policy calls for the creation of a Regional Transport Agency for Ile-de-France in order that the region be given the same responsibility as other regional governments.

The Ile-de-France region and national government are jointly responsible for town and country planning, financing transport infrastructure, road safety and co-financing of the departmental roads of regional importance.

Overall responsibility for traffic police lies with the government appointed regional prefect, within a framework defined by special orders issued jointly by the three supervisory Ministers (the Interior, Defence

and Transport). Functions are divided between the various police forces in the region (the gendarmerie, the compagnies républicaines de securité, and the urban police). There is also the Service Interdépartemental d'Exploitation Routière, an organisation founded in 1988 to manage traffic on motorways in the Ile-de-France. This service is attached to the Direction Régionale de l'Équipement d'Ile-de-France (itself a regional administration under the authority of the ministry of urban and rural planning, facilities and transport). The Service Interdépartemental d'Exploitation Routière is introducing an integrated regulation and user-information system which enables traffic to be constantly monitored and analysed in order to adapt operational measures in real time, informing and guiding drivers, particularly by means of variable message panels.

Police powers depend on the administrative level of the roads: national motorways and national highways (belonging to the government), departmental (roads governed by the departments), municipal (other roads attributed to municipalities); the amount of traffic; and whether or not the road belongs to an urban area, as defined in the Highway Code.

The departments have functions relating to rural planning and the departmental road networks.

The municipalities' functions are in relation to town planning policy, land-use plans, and municipal roads.

2.3.4 Organisations involved in transport provision and regulation

Unlike road traffic, the organisation of public transport is based on a single authority: the Syndicat des Transports Parisiens. Founded in 1959, the Syndicat des Transports Parisiens is responsible for organising public transport within an area referred to as the Parisian Transport Region (Région des Transports Parisiens), which since 1991, has covered the whole of the

Ile-de-France region. The syndicat is controlled by a board of directors with 12 representatives of the departments (five for Paris and one for each of the seven others) and 12 appointed by the government. The board of directors is chaired by the regional prefect, who has a casting vote, giving national government ultimate control (a situation inherited from before the decentralisation laws of 1982). Neither the Region nor the municipal authorities are represented on the board of the Syndicat des Transports Parisiens. The syndicat has responsibility for the choice of public transport routes; the choice of transport operator; the transport operation mode; fares policy; and approval and management of transport operator budgets.

In Paris, transport operators fall into three categories:

- the Régie Autonome des Transports Parisiens, provider of metro and bus services

- the Société Nationale des Chemins de fer Français (the national railway company), provider of regional rail services

- private bus companies

Founded in 1948, the Régie Autonome des Transport Parisiens is the region's main provider of public transport, carrying 75% of overall passenger traffic. It operates the Paris Metro, part of the Réseau Express Régional and buses. Although it operates solely within the Ile-de-France region it is a national company supervised exclusively by the government. Its board of directors has 27 members: nine government representatives, nine representatives of Règie Autonome des Transport Parisiens employees, and nine people representing the company's immediate environment (five local elected officials, three "passenger representatives" and one "transport specialist"). The chairperson and managing director is appointed by Prime Ministerial decree on the proposal of the Minister of Transport.

A "contract plan" between the government and the Société Nationale des Chemins de fer Français determines the objectives assigned to the latter as part of the national master plan. There have been three such "contract plans" agreed to date: for 1985-90, 1990-94 and 1994-1998.

Founded in 1938, the Société Nationale des Chemins de fer Français is the second-largest provider of public transport in the Ile-de-France (17% of passenger traffic) where it operates the regional rail network and part of the Réseau Express Régional. It is a state-owned company, which operates throughout France and is under the authority of the national government (Ministry of Transport), its President being appointed by Prime Ministerial decree. In 1989 it founded a "regional passenger services department: Ile-de-France".

Paris' Réseau Express Régional

The regional services in Ile-de-France are 22% of the Société Nationale des Chemins de fer Français total passenger traffic.

The Syndicat des Transports Parisiens signed an agreement with the Société Nationale des Chemins de Fer in 1981. It differs from the Régie Autonome des Transports Parisiens agreement, as the Syndicat des Transports Parisiens does not approve the Société Nationale des Chemins de fer Français accounts or draft infrastructure projects (it simply issues its opinion).

Carrying 8% of passenger traffic, the private bus companies are represented by two professional associations: the Association Professionnelle des Transporteurs Routiers de voyageurs en Ile-de-France (55 corporations) and the Association pour le Développement et l'Amélioration des Transports en Région Ile-de-France (35 corporations). They operate regular lines, mainly on the outskirts of the Ile-de-France Region, and are monitored by the Syndicat des Transports Parisiens.

Taxi transport in Ile-de-France is based on two different systems, the Taxis Parisiens and the municipal taxis.

Parisian taxis serve most areas within Zones 1 & 2. Their operational area includes the Ville de Paris itself, adjoining municipalities and the approaches to the two airports Charles-de-Gaulle and Orly. They may ply for hire within their operational area. In other suburban municipalities, they may only be booked by telephone. They are supervised by the police chief of Paris, in co-operation with the prefects of the three departments of Hauts-de-Seine, Seine-Saint-Denis and Val-de-Marne. However, their prices are fixed by the Ministry of the Economy, Finance and the Budget. Access to the profession has been restricted since 1937, and is fixed by the supervisory authority. In 1996, the fleet of Taxis Parisiens reached 14,900 vehicles, including 57% belonging to self-employed drivers.

Municipal taxis are registered with municipalities outside the operational area of the Taxis Parisiens, and are only allowed to ply for hire within their own municipality. The mayor regulates their operations and gives them permits to use taxi ranks and ply for hire. Access to the profession is unrestricted. In 1992, there were 2,000 municipal taxis.

2.3.5 Provision of accessible transport

There is an overall national policy to support people with reduced mobility. Within various laws, regulations and decrees, there is a broad definition of people with reduced mobility, which includes older people, and those with children. A law of 1975 stipulates that public transport should be made accessible for people with disabilities. The "Loi d'orientation des transports intérieurs" contains specific measures to aid people with reduced mobility including the right to have information on services offered. Further laws and government decrees strengthen the obligation to make public transport accessible, especially for new projects. Regulations are included in the Urban Code (Code d'Urbanisme) and Construction Code (Code de Construction).

Organisations involved in the planning and provision of transport for those with impaired mobility include the Committee for Liaison for the Transport of People with Disabilities (Comité de Liaison pour le Transport des Personnes Handicapées) at national level; and at departmental level, the Departmental Consultative Commission for Security and Accessibility (Commission Consultative Départmentale de la Sécurité et l'Accessibilité), set up in 1995. There is a working party of the Committee for Liaison for the Transport of People with Disabilities in the Ile-de-France Region. Within the Syndicat des Transports Parisiens, there is a working group that brings together the Committee for Liaison for the Transport of People with Disabilities, administrators, and politicians to make decisions on accessibility issues. There is also specialised transport within the region for disabled people, with the Syndicat des Transports Parisiens and the Region committing funds for development. The Regional Council helps manage a scheme which allows people with disabilities to use taxis. The contract plan of 1994-98 provides for $66 million to be spent on improvements to rail accessibility. There has also been significant investment in low-floor buses.

2.3.6   The transport planning process

Until 1995, the national government was responsible for preparation of the Ile-de-France Region structure plan (the Schéma Directeur de la Région Ile-de-France). The relationship between transport and land-use is specified within the structure plan. The regional planning and development programme, approved in 1994, is the long term planning document, covering a period of 25 years to 2015. Since 1995, this function has passed to the Ile-de-France regional council.

The structure plan outlines the future regional development strategy and includes the long-term transport infrastructure plan (consistent with the region's development objectives). The latest version of the structure plan states that its aims are

- To develop the transport system to be able to handle a significant increase in mobility and cover all types of travel. It will follow a comprehensive strategy strengthening inter-modal transfers.

- To improve the public transport network, including further extensions of the railway system, creation of an orbital light rail system in the outer suburbs; and the development of feeder public transport systems based on dedicated rights of way.

Local authorities and public corporations must adhere to the plan when drawing up land-use plans and any other local plans. Land-use plans are prepared by municipalities in co-operation with the national government, the region and the department. Data for the structure plan and other planning and policy issues is provided by the Institut d'Aménagement et d'Urbanisme de la Région Ile-de-France. It is the Regional Council's research and planning body.

Public participation in the planning process takes place through elected representatives at the departmental and municipal level where they are formally invited to comment on the regional structure plan. Departments comment on issues that are of departmental level, whilst the municipalities comment on very local issues. The public is invited to comment directly at the stage of the public inquiry when the local planning documents are presented. This is the case for all structure plans, new infrastructures and all large projects. Large plans and the schema directeur generate information and consultation well above the legal requirements. Environmental impact studies are usually also carried out.

The region has also a permanent Economic and Social Committee of 110 members appointed by various organisations such as corporations and trades unions. This organisation contributes to the structure plan, although it has no powers of veto. The approval of the structure plan lies solely with the national government (although it has to be within the region's budgetary guidelines).

2.3.7   Transport funding

There are a number of different mechanisms in France to fund transport, based on users, employers, local authorities and national government. Unlike other regions in France, the Syndicat des Transports Parisiens shares responsibility for major public transport capital investments with an inter-ministry body, the Economic and Social Development Fund (Fond de Developpement Économique et Social), in co-ordination with the Region.

Much of the Syndicat des Transports Parisiens' budget comes from a hypothecated employers' tax, the "versement de transport". This payment is made by employers with 10 or more salaried employees within the Ile-de-France. It varies in different areas of the region but is 2.2% of the payroll. 85% of the "versement de transport" goes to subsidise the loss public transport operators make on "carte orange" season tickets. Furthermore, since 1983, employers in the Ile-de-France are also obliged by law to reimburse their employees half of the cost of their season tickets within the Ile-de-France (Zones 1, 2 & 3).

A "planning contract" is made between the national government and the region concerning public transport and road capital investment. A similar "planning contract" is made for the provision of public transport in Paris with the Syndicat des Transports Parisiens. These "planning contracts" last the entire term of the 5 year National Plan (in France, nation-wide planning is based on five-year plans).

The current "planning contract" covers the period from 1994 to 1998, and represents commitments totalling $5,700 million. The development of transport networks accounts for most of this sum: $3,700 million; of this $1,700 million is dedicated for roads and $2,000 million for public transport.

As part of the "planning contract", the Ile-de-France region contributes between 75% and 80% of the funding and subsidies for public transport and road programmes. It thus contributes far more than the national government to the funding of major regional transport infrastructures and the running of the public transport system, yet has little control.

2.4 Tokyo

2.4.1 The national context

The national government of Japan, the Diet, consists of the House of Councillors (the Upper House with 252 seats) and the House of Representatives (the Lower House with 511 seats). The term for members of the House of Representatives is four years although, on average, the House has been dissolved for elections every two and a half years. The term for members of the House of Councillors is six years with half the members elected every three years. The Prime Minister is designated by the Diet from amongst its members. The Prime Minister appoints the Ministers of State responsible for the various departments of government and together they constitute the Cabinet in which executive power is vested. A majority of the Ministers of State must be chosen from among the members of the Diet. The Emperor is, in the words of the Constitution, the symbol of the state and of the unity of the people. The Emperor appoints the Prime Minister as designated by the Diet and the Chief Judge of the Supreme Court as designated by the Cabinet.

The Japanese constitution applies the principle of autonomy to local government. A special law, applicable to only one local government area, cannot be enacted by the Diet without the consent of the majority of the voters in the area. The country is divided into 47 Prefectures. Prefectural governors, mayors of cities, towns and villages and assembly members are all directly elected.

The Tokyo region consists of the Tokyo Metropolis and three neighbouring prefectures, Saitama, Kanagawa and Chiba. Together they account for 26% of Japan's total population. The Tokyo Metropolis is a self-governing unit (the Tokyo Metropolitan Government) at the prefectural level consisting of 23 special wards, the Tama area and a string of islands in the Tokyo bay.

The Metropolitan Government of Tokyo is divided between the legislature (Tokyo Metropolitan Assembly) and the executive (Governor, administrative commissions and commissioners). The Tokyo Metropolitan Assembly has 128 members directly elected to serve for four years. The Governor, who is also directly elected to serve for four years, is responsible for metropolitan administration. The Tokyo Metropolitan Assembly oversees the administration, sets the budget and approves the accounts. It also enacts, amends and repeals local ordinances.

The 23 special wards are local self-governing municipal bodies found only in Tokyo. Services such as water supply, sewage treatment, refuse disposal and fire services are normally the responsibility of the city level of government under Japanese law but in the 23 special ward area of Tokyo they are administered at the prefectural level by Tokyo Metropolitan Government. The chief executive of each ward is directly elected. Due to a change in the Local Authority Law, from 2000, the 23 special wards will become responsible for some of these services.

2.4.2 National government bodies involved in transport planning

In Japan, national government has a strong influence on regional transport planning and policy. Transport policy is formulated and implemented by various national government agencies particularly by the Ministry of Transport and the Ministry of Construction. Policies are usually formulated and implemented with reference to the policies of a number of ministries. For example, for road transport, in addition to the Ministry of Transport, which has jurisdiction over registration, inspection and maintenance of vehicles, and the Ministry of Construction, which has jurisdiction over construction and maintenance of roads, the National Police Agency has jurisdiction over road traffic, the Ministry of Labour over administration of professional drivers, the Ministry

of International Trade and Industry over manufacturing of vehicles and the Ministry of Finance over vehicle tax.

In 1997, at the national Administrative Reform Conference, the Government decided to restructure central ministries. By January 2001, therefore, the number of ministries will be cut by half and be composed of the Prime Minister's Office and twelve ministries. A new Ministry of National Land and Transport will be formed from the Ministry of Transport, the Ministry of Construction, the National Land Agency, the Hokkaido Development Agency, and the Okinawa Development Agency.

Currently, the Ministry of Transport has jurisdiction over not only transport including railways, private cars, and aviation, but tourism and development of harbour districts. It monitors transport systems, through various laws including the Railway Operations Law and the Road Transportation Law.

The aims of the Ministry of Construction are to aid new developments, to balance developments between different areas, and to tackle urban and housing problems. The Ministry of Construction is also responsible for managing most of the toll and national roads (within designated sections, that constitute the main arterial routes).

2.4.3 Regional bodies involved in transport planning

The Tokyo Metropolitan Government is heavily involved in both planning transport, operating public transport and constructing new transport infrastructures. It is responsible for improving and building new roads. It also has a role in co-ordinating with the national government the management and improvement of national roads within the Tokyo Metropolis (Zones 1, 2 & 3). Furthermore it supports the upgrading of roads owned by the governments of cities, wards, towns and villages. Its responsibilities on railways are to construct new government-owned metro lines and stations, invest in private sector transport companies, and support new transport systems. All transport policies carried out by the Tokyo Metropolitan Government are restricted by national government guidelines, decrees and laws.

Within the Tokyo Metropolitan Government, the Bureaux of Transport, of Construction, and of City Planning are responsible for affairs related to transport planning, policy and operations in the metropolis.

The Tokyo Metropolitan Government Bureau of Transport is responsible for carrying out improvements to and the operation of government-owned transport systems. The Tokyo Metropolitan Government Bureau of Construction maintains roads and rivers. It also manages urban redevelopment and other infrastructure related tasks.

However, within the Tokyo Metropolitan Government, it is the Bureau of City Planning that formulates plans for transport. It plays a key role as it co-ordinates the various programmes of the different bureaux and also co-ordinates transport planning and operations between the Tokyo Metropolitan Government and the wards, cities, towns and villages in the metropolitan area. In addition, its responsibilities include co-ordination with the national government and other cities, the promotion of national plans, including the National Capital Region Development Plan, that affect the region.

The Tokyo Metropolitan Government Bureau of City Planning establishes urban development plans, approves city plans and enacts building control guidelines and checks their implementation. The Bureau's main obligations in planning are:

- to establish basic plans of urban and regional developments regarding urban structure, land-use and transport facilities,

- to create urban redevelopment programmes, and

- to guide the private sector so that their developments conform to the law and to regional policies.

The Tokyo Metropolitan Government has two basic aims in its planning policy:

- to create a disaster-resistant city, and

- to decentralise activities in Tokyo, through the establishment of a multi-centre urban structure.

The 23 special wards in Tokyo are responsible for all local functions except those that require co-ordination between two or more authorities. They carry out tasks that need a degree of flexibility according to regional conditions such as welfare funding; operating and maintaining regional public facilities such as parks; and the provision of local services. Thus, they do not have a significant role in either transport planning or provision.

The roads that are managed mainly by local authorities or bodies belonging to them, include national roads (outside designated sections), prefectural, local city, town, and village roads. Local government bodies have limited scope in making decisions on improvements to road infrastructure, hence they must always negotiate with the Ministry of Construction and other government agencies. This can restrict the autonomy of local city planning.

Local authorities have their transport projects based on the plans of various national councils, such as the Transport Policy Council (responsible to the Ministry of Transport). Therefore, the extent to which regional governments can influence transport plans is limited. The same applies to other local authorities. However, one of their main tasks is to reflect their residents' needs for urban transport in their particular projects.

2.4.4 Transport provision and regulation

There are two metro operators in the Tokyo metropolis: the Teito Rapid Transit Authority, which runs eight lines, and the Bureau of Transport of the Tokyo Metropolitan Government, which runs four lines and Tokyo's only tram line. The Teito Rapid Transit Authority is a special corporation regulated under a specific law.

There are numerous private railway operators in the Tokyo region, but only Japan Railways operates regional services in the central area of the Tokyo Metropolis (within the circular Yamanote line). However, several private operators and Japan Railways have arrangements to operate through-train service on metro line tracks of both the Teito Rapid Transit Authority and the Tokyo Metropolitan Government Bureau of Transport.

Within the Tokyo metropolis the Tokyo Metropolitan Government Bureau of Transport operates 117 bus lines of its own; the rest are run by private operators. There is tight regulation of bus routes and there is no competition between the private operators or the Tokyo Metropolitan Government operations.

The ratio of ownership of transport infrastructure in the Tokyo Metropolis, based on mileage in 1994, is:

- Metro   30 % by the Tokyo Metropolitan Government, and 70% by the TeitoRapid Transit Authority

- Regional rail   50% by Japan Railways, and 50% by other private railway companies

- Bus   10% by the Tokyo Metropolitan Government, and 90% by private bus and railway companies

Various laws and regulations control the operation of public transport systems and provide for the establishment of service standards. There are two major pieces of legislation to regulate regional railways: the Railway Operation Law, and the Railway Business Law.

The Railway Operation Law lays down the procedure and powers of national government in establishing or changing basic plans of railway operation. It also enables the national government to monitor the day-to-day operations of regional railways, and to carry out on-the-spot inspections. The railway companies have to have their fares approved by the Minister of Transportation.

Crowds on Tokyo's rail system

The Railway Business Law stipulates regulations for railway operations, equipment and fares. It establishes service standards, qualifications, and requirements for railway employees and penalties for those who disturb railway operations.

In the case of metro services, there is the specific Teito Rapid Transit Authority Law that regulates the metro lines owned by Teito Rapid Transit Authority. It establishes the service standards, procedures for monitoring, reporting, on-the-spot inspections and requirements for employees.

2.4.5   Provision of accessible transport

The Tokyo Metropolitan Government currently undertakes various programmes to make the whole of Tokyo a "welfare city". These programmes are carried out on the basis of the 1996 "Tokyo Ordinance for making the Welfare City", which aims at enabling all citizens to freely move about and participate in social activities. The Tokyo Metropolitan Government has set up a programme setting out the overall direction for the promotion of the new "welfare city". The clauses in the welfare programme relating to transport are:

- Improvement of public transport facilities. The main measures are: building lifts and escalators in railway stations, introducing new low-floor buses, and installing lifts for wheelchairs on buses.

- Improvement of roads. The main measures relate to pedestrians and are actuated by levelling roads and pavements at pedestrian crossings, and establishing accessible signalling.

These projects are targeted in areas in which welfare facilities, hospitals or stations are located, since older and disabled people are more likely to use them.

Most transport operators have discount fares for disabled people. Some local authorities also have a programme of subsidising taxi journeys for disabled, and operate special taxi services for those with low mobility.

2.4.6   The transport planning process

Japan has an overall long-term land-use structure plan, the Comprehensive National Development Plan. It is developed by the National Land Agency on the basis of the Comprehensive National Development Law. The first plan was promulgated in 1962 and it has been superseded by three subsequent plans. In 1998, the fifth Comprehensive National Development Plan, under discussion for more than three years in the National Land Council, was officially endorsed by the Cabinet. The national government will now begin laying out guidelines to promote strategies under the "grand national design for the 21st century plan".

The National Development Plan proposes the establishment of "four development corridors" in Japan: the north-east; the Sea of Japan coast; the Pacific coast; and, western Japan. It is hoped that this will ease the concentration of Japan's population and industries along a narrow Pacific coast corridor which begins at Tokyo. The plan also advances the concept of "residential areas situated in lush greenery", with the establishment and enhancement of medium and small scale cities; as well as farming, forestry and fishing villages that would serve as a new kind of living space in the coming century.

Road planning takes the form of the Long Term Plan for Road Improvement, formulated on the basis of the Road Improvement Emergency Measures Law. The New Five Year Road Improvement Plan, drafted on the basis of proposals by the Roads Council and the Long Term Plan for Road Improvement, includes targets for 2010-2015. It has formed the basic national policy of road improvements and backbone of the 1998-2003 Road Improvement Plan.

Railway improvement plans are proposed by the Transport Policy Council, under the control of the Ministry of Transport.

Railway and road improvement projects must be determined as part of a city-wide plan. City Plans laid by governors and mayors must be consistent with various other plans, including the Comprehensive National Development Plan.

The Tokyo Metropolitan Government draws up a general planning framework, which includes future direction, improvement goals, and means for securing new investment. Improvement plans are then implemented within the guidelines of the frameworks.

Plans for transport facilities, such as railways and roads, are implemented through decisions regarding civic designs made according to the City Planning Law. In the process of making these decisions, several measures are taken to ensure that the opinions of residents are taken into account. Such measures include public hearings, the submission of comments, etc. As well as the measures taken in line with the City Planning Law, other systems exist whereby residents can be interrogated in advance on the effects of various city plans.

In Tokyo transport policies are also tested against environmental criteria. The Tokyo Metropolitan Government formulated its Environmental Assessment Ordinance to conduct environmental assessments when making decisions on its regional plans. To ensure that the opinions of residents concerning the environment are reflected in regional planning, various procedures are followed, and proposed plans and the results of environmental assessments are made public.

One of the main elements of the planning system in Tokyo is the policy of having local government,

transport operators and private developers work together. This is best expressed in the land-use policies by which developers who wish to build on newly developed railways land, are required to pay for part of the railway project. The national government currently promotes housing development in line with the new railways or station development in the areas where current accessibility from Tokyo is poor.

2.4.7 Transport funding

The level of funding of transport schemes is decided annually by the Tokyo Metropolitan Government as part of its annual budget process. Then, decisions on specific new projects and allocations of funds are made.

Transport funding also comes from taxes on petrol, private car acquisition, and a petrol delivery tax. Moneys raised from these taxes go to local authorities. In addition there is an extensive toll road system encompassing all expressways, some general roads, tunnels and bridges. In Tokyo, the Metropolitan Express Public Corporation has authority for toll roads within the region, working within the basic plan provided by the Ministry of Construction. Toll roads themselves are financed through guaranteed government bonds, public enterprise bonds and private placement bonds.

Infrastructure investment for the metro comes from a variety of bonds, local government, national government and, in the case of the Teito Rapid Transit Authority, also from zero-interest loans from the Railway Construction Fund.

One of the more interesting and innovative aspects of transport infrastructure funding in Tokyo is the involvement of the private sector. Both for the construction of new roads and railways there is a substantial financial input from private developers.

For new road construction there is a new method to achieve private sector investment and to absorb profits from development projects. This method was used for the Trans-Tokyo Bay Highway project. The construction cost (about $9,000 million) was financed through loans from the Road Development Fund, government guaranteed bonds, and private investments.

Private developers are also involved in the funding of new railways. The metro improvement subsidy system covers public sector bodies that operate subways, the Teito Rapid Transit Authority and private sector companies. This system requires the national government to grant a subsidy covering 35% of the construction costs of new railways. Local governments are also required to cover the construction costs at the same rate as national government. There are also further subsidies that companies building new railways can draw on for their schemes, if they develop both housing and improve railways in the suburbs.

To encourage the construction of new railways, a new system was established whereby the Japan Railways Construction Corporation is requested to build new

railways or extend tracks and then transfer them to private operators at a low long-term interest rate (over 25 years, or 15 years for new-town railways). Under this system, national government and the local authorities concerned must cover any interest that exceeds the 5%.

Currently, there is no system in which profits arising from railway development projects are returned to operators, but there is a system in which beneficiaries or developers are required to pay for part of projects. Examples of this include the new-town developer cost-sharing system. In this system, developers are required to pay for part of construction and land purchase costs incurred when railway companies (both private or public) build railways between the centre of Tokyo and areas where these new towns are situated. The national government subsidises 18% of railway construction costs. A further 18% is paid by local authorities who also provide 10% of the capital to the private sector companies. This system was first applied to the New Joban line project.

Population, employment and car ownership

Content

3 Population, Employment and Car Ownership

While the world class status of the four cities is attributable to their commercial and cultural importance, the four cities are also among the most populated in the economically developed world.

Tokyo is the most populous region with over 32 million inhabitants. The populations of the metropolitan areas (Zones 1 & 2) of the four cities is roughly similar; the lowest being 6.9 million for London and the highest 8.8 million for Paris.

At over 33,000 square kilometres, the New York regional area is the largest region under consideration. Yet, New York also has the smallest and most concentrated central area.

Overall, Tokyo is the most densely populated city, except in the central area. Tokyo's central area by contrast has the highest number of employed, 2.4 million, with only a quarter of a million inhabitants.

All four cities have seen a spreading out effect, with a loss of residential population in their central and inner areas and a strong expansion of the suburbs and the periphery. For instance between 1970 and 1994, London's Zone 4 population increased by 1 million, New York's by 1.3 million and Tokyo's by 7.9 million. By contrast the populations of the cities' metropolitan areas (Zones 1 & 2), during the same period, decreased in London by 0.5 million, in New York by 0.7 million, and in Tokyo by 0.8 million.

Car ownership has also been growing in all four cities. Tokyo's level of car ownership is well below that of the other three cities. The highest levels of car ownership in all four cities are in their outer areas, with New York having the highest at 1.86 cars per household in Zone 4.

3.1 Zonal areas

Population, employment and other social data are presented both individually and cumulatively for each Zone.

Table 4a
**Zonal areas (square kilometres)
(disaggregated Zones)**

	London	New York	Paris	Tokyo
Zone 1	27	23	29	42
Zone 2	1,551	734	2,031	575
Zone 3	8,807	5,036	9,951	1,160
Zone 4	16,839	27,372	-	11,366

Table 4b
**Zonal areas (square kilometres)
(aggregated Zones)**

	London	New York	Paris	Tokyo
Zone 1	27	23	29	42
Zones 1 & 2	1,578	757	2,060	617
Zones 1, 2 & 3	10,385	5,793	12,011	1,777
Zones 1, 2, 3 & 4	27,224	33,165	-	13,143

3.2 Population

Paris has the largest number of residents in its centre, while New York's central area has approximately 100,000 fewer residents. London has the fewest number of residents in its central area, at less than 200,000. Tokyo's residential population in the central area represents less than 1% of the region's total. Tokyo's central area has a night-time population of 0.3 million and a day-time population of about 2.4 million.

Except for Tokyo, where the largest number of people is in Zone 4, the greatest numbers of residents of the three cities are in Zone 2. The distinct differences among the cities occur in their outer rings. All the cities, except Paris, have more people living in Zones 3 & 4 than in Zones 1 & 2.

Table 5a
Population 1990/91 (disaggregated Zones)

	London	New York	Paris	Tokyo
Zone 1	177,000	543,000	622,000	266,000
Zone 2	6,676,000	6,954,000	8,169,000	7,898,000
Zone 3	4,753,000	6,029,000	1,870,000	3,692,000
Zone 4	5,944,000	6,317,000	-	19,941,000

Table 5b
Population 1990/91 (aggregated Zones)

	London	New York	Paris	Tokyo
Zone 1	177,000	543,000	622,000	266,000
Zones 1 & 2	6,852,000	7,497,000	8,791,000	8,164,000
Zones 1, 2 & 3	11,606,000	13,526,000	10,661,000	11,856,000
Zones 1, 2, 3 & 4	17,549,000	19,843,000	-	31,797,000

Table 5c
Population estimates for 1995/96 (aggregated Zones)

	London	New York	Paris	Tokyo
Zone 1	189,000	544,000	622,000	244,000
Zones 1 & 2	7,074,000	7,533,000	n/a	7,968,000
Zones 1, 2 & 3	11,957,000	13,673,000	11,027,000	11,774,000
Zones 1, 2, 3 & 4	18,120,000	20,197,000	-	32,577,000

Tokyo's regional population far exceeds the other three cities - Tokyo is perhaps currently the most populous metropolis in the world.

In Tokyo about two thirds of the region's population reside in Zone 4. Paris is the most concentrated city and its population in Zone 3 is less than 2 million (Paris does not extend to Zone 4).

Figure 2
Population 1990/91 (aggregated Zones)
Millions

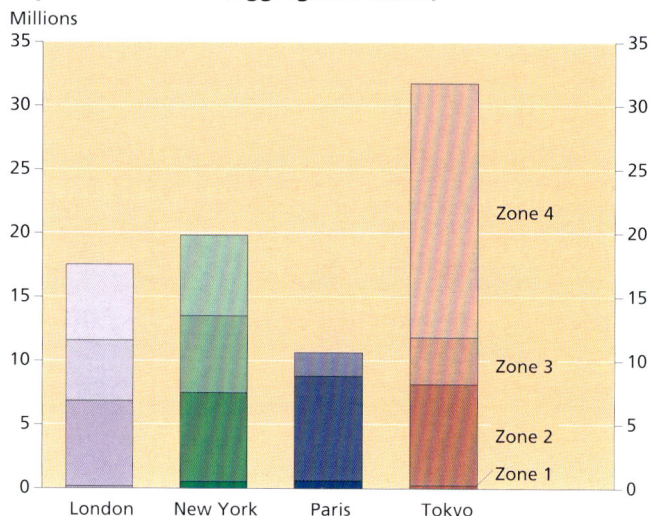

3.3 Population density

The cores of New York, Manhattan below Central Park, and Paris have retained a considerable part of their residential populations, while London and Tokyo have seen a profound hollowing out effect in their central areas, which are now mainly offices and other business; although in the 1990s London has seen some population growth in the central area.

The population density of New York's central area, at 23,610 persons per square kilometre, is the highest of the four cities. It is slightly higher than that for Paris, 21,450, and both are strikingly higher than the densities in London and Tokyo. New York has achieved these densities in Manhattan by developing vertically, in quite dramatic fashion in the lower end and the middle of the island. Overall, central London has been steadily losing population throughout the 20th century. In 1901 London's Zone 1 had a residential population density close to 18,000 persons per square kilometre and a population of about 480,000. By 1991 London's Zone 1 population had fallen to under 180,000 with a density of less than 7,000 persons per square kilometre (however, most recent estimates show a growth of about 10,000 since 1991). The centre of Tokyo has also hollowed out with a majority of its resident population

Housing in Tokyo's Zone 2

having disappeared over the past 40 years. Now Tokyo's population density in Zone 1 (the central three wards) is less than half of that in Zone 2 (the outer 20 wards) due to the marked loss of residential population in the

central area. Tokyo's hollowed out centre is characterised by a massive daily inflow of workers and a continual loss of residents. The loss of population is now extending to the rest of the metropolitan areas

Table 6a [21]
Population (residential) density 1990/91 (persons per square kilometre per Zone) (disaggregated Zones)

	London	New York	Paris	Tokyo
Zone 1	6,940	23,610	21,450	6,330
Zone 2	4,300	9,470	4,020	13,740
Zone 3	540	1,200	190	3,180
Zone 4	350	230	-	1,750

Table 6b [22]
Population (residential) density 1990/91 (persons per square kilometre per Zone) (aggregated Zones)

	London	New York	Paris	Tokyo
Zone 1	6,940	23,610	21,450	6,330
Zones 1 & 2	4,340	9,900	4,270	13,230
Zones 1, 2 & 3	1,120	2,330	890	6,670
Zones 1, 2, 3 & 4	640	600	-	2,420

21   This table has been constructed by dividing the figures of Table 5a by the figures of Table 4a.

22   This table has been constructed by dividing the figures of Table 5b by the figures of Table 4b.

Population, employment and car ownership

Map 3
Population density - the metropolitan area (Zones 1,2,3&4)

London

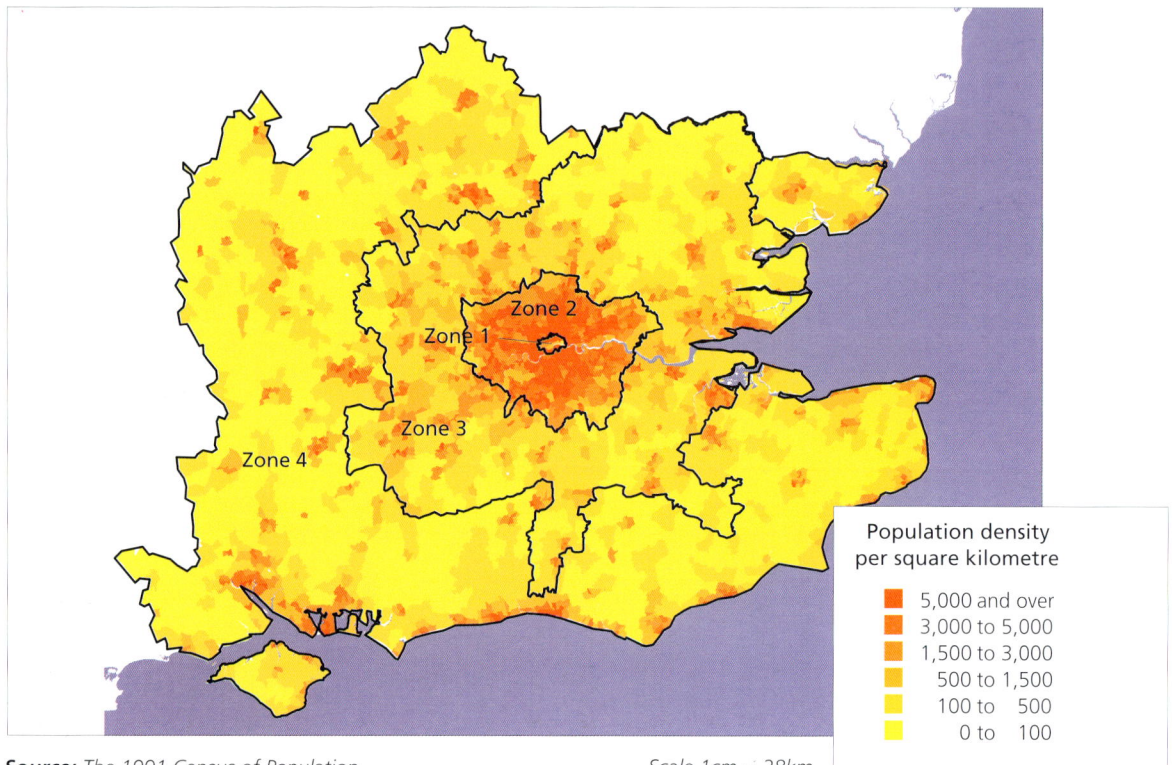

Source: *The 1991 Census of Population*   *Scale 1cm = 28km*

Population density
per square kilometre

- 5,000 and over
- 3,000 to 5,000
- 1,500 to 3,000
- 500 to 1,500
- 100 to   500
- 0 to   100

New York

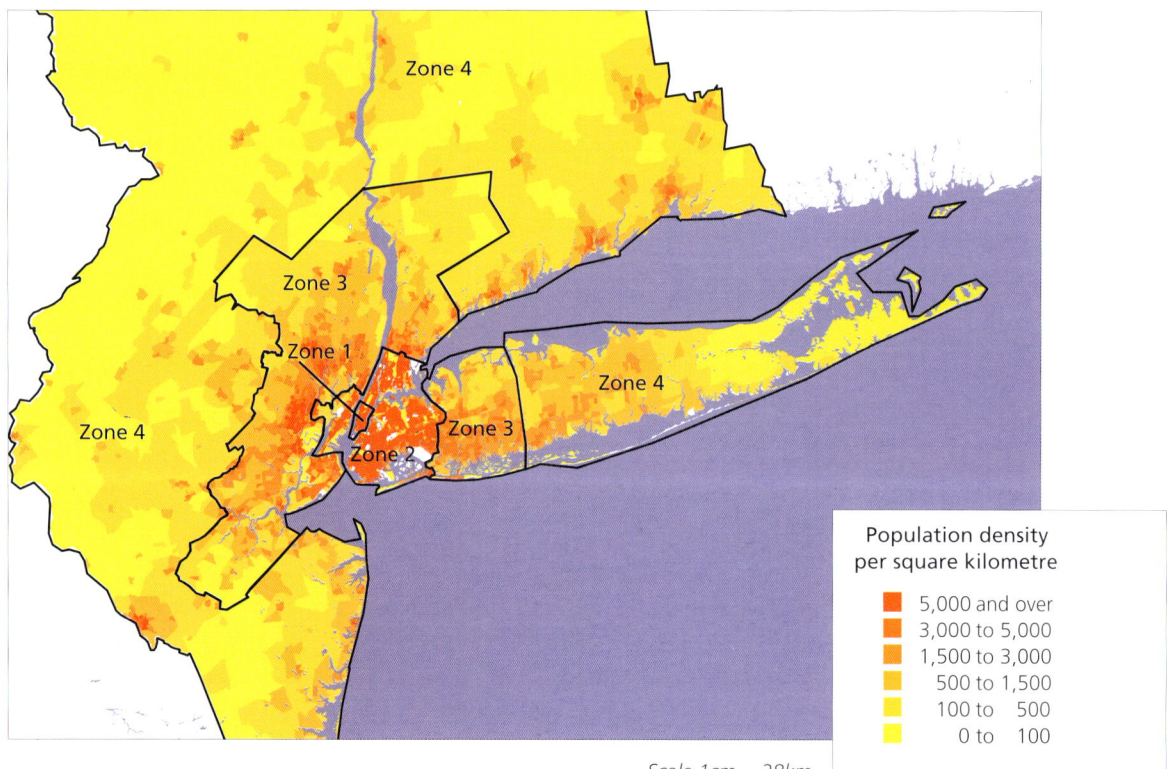

Scale 1cm = 28km

Population density
per square kilometre

- 5,000 and over
- 3,000 to 5,000
- 1,500 to 3,000
- 500 to 1,500
- 100 to   500
- 0 to   100

Map 3
Population density - the metropolitan area (Zones 1,2,3&4)

Paris

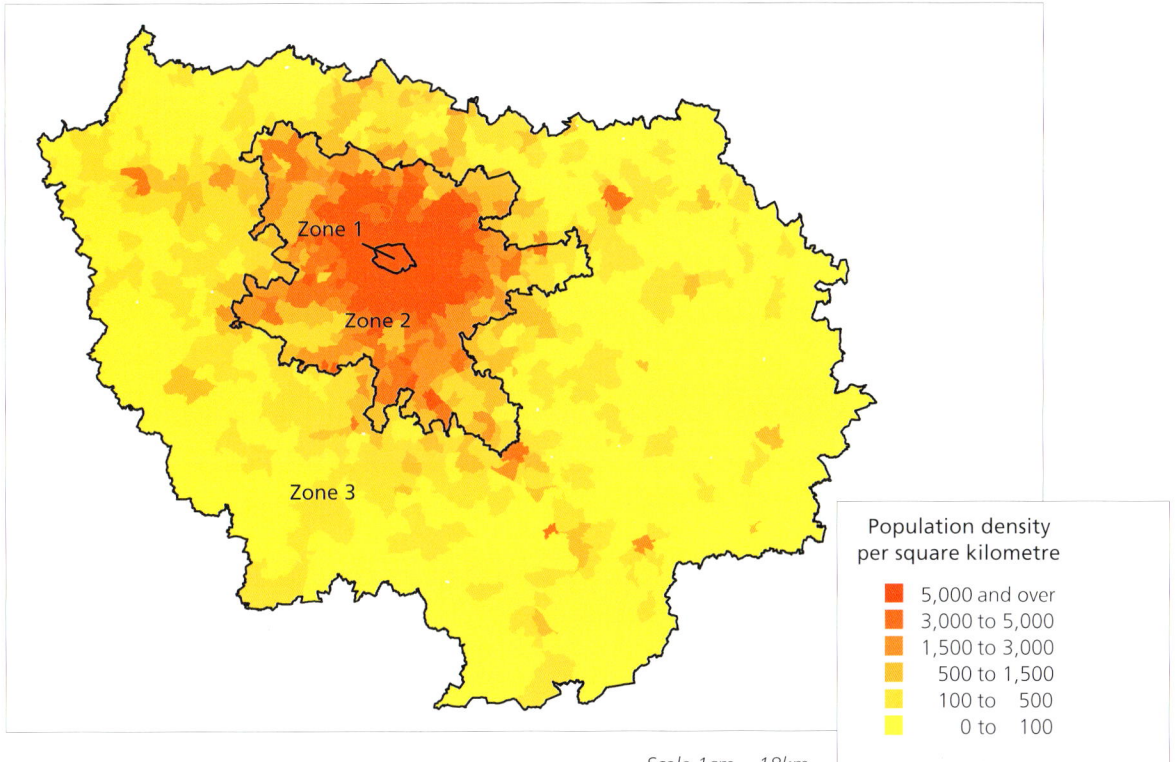

Population density
per square kilometre

5,000 and over
3,000 to 5,000
1,500 to 3,000
500 to 1,500
100 to 500
0 to 100

Scale 1cm = 18km

Tokyo

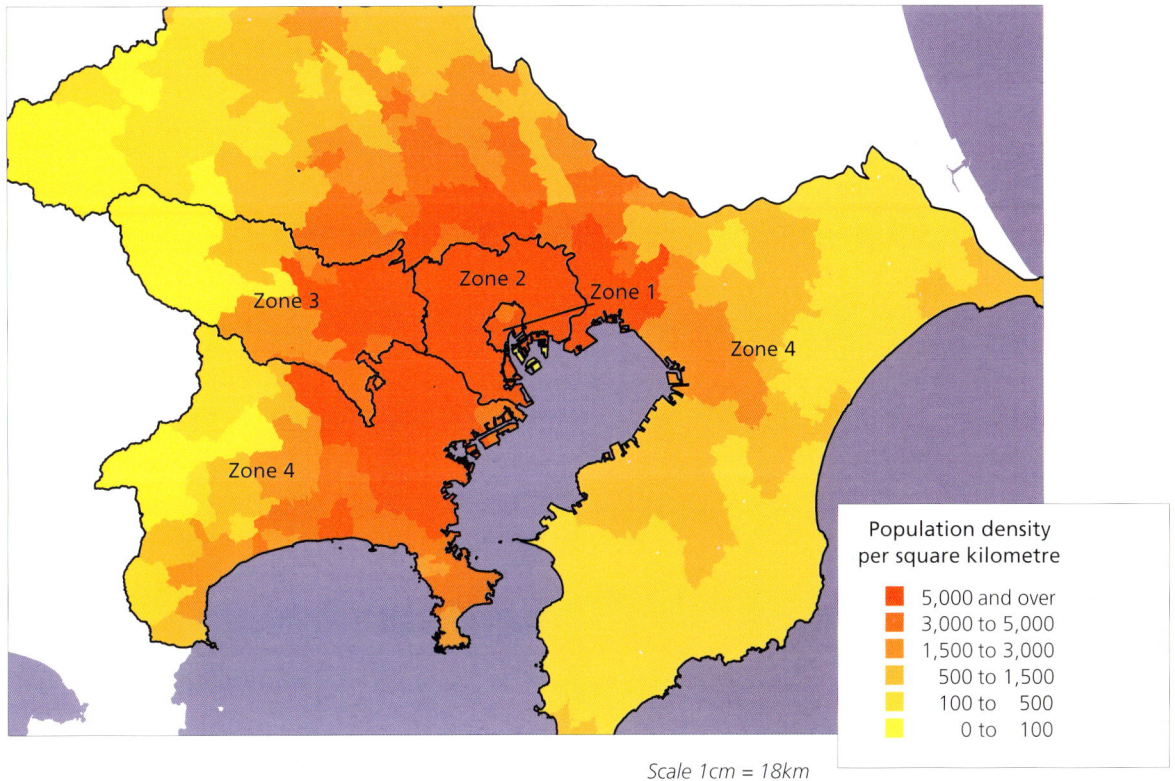

Population density
per square kilometre

5,000 and over
3,000 to 5,000
1,500 to 3,000
500 to 1,500
100 to 500
0 to 100

Scale 1cm = 18km

Population, employment and car ownership

Map 4
Population density - metropolitan area (Zones 1 & 2)

London

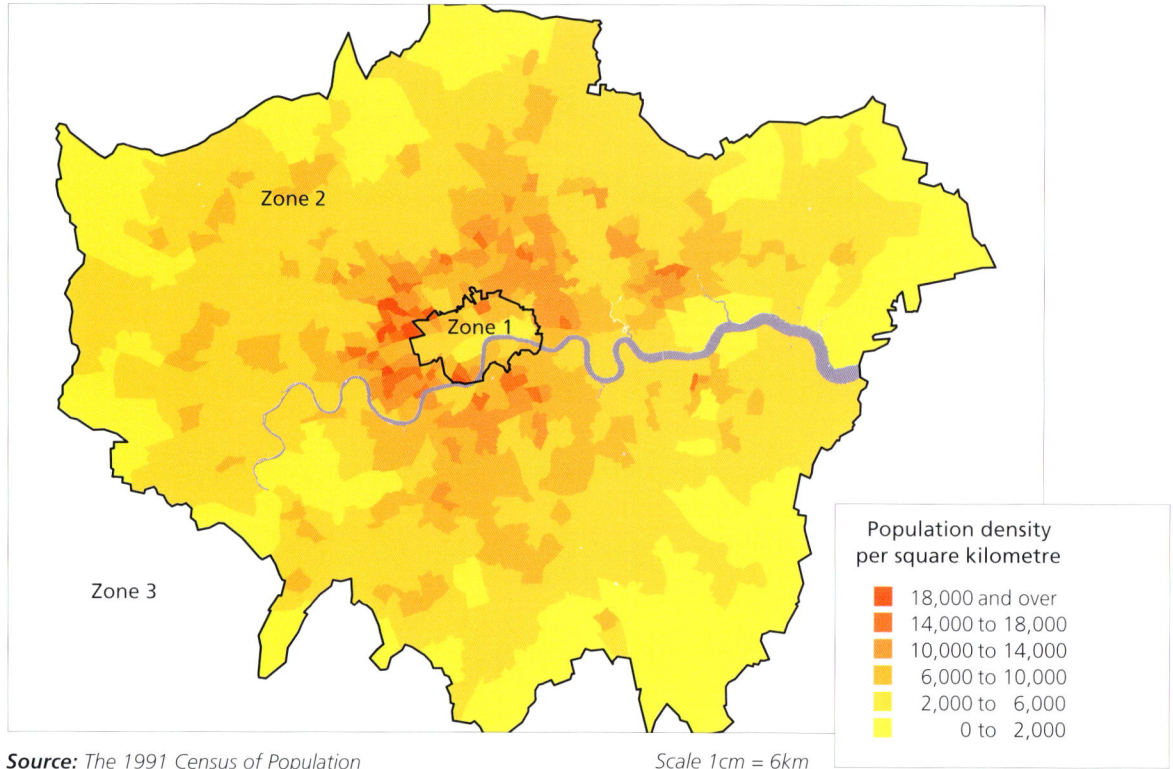

**Population density
per square kilometre**

- 18,000 and over
- 14,000 to 18,000
- 10,000 to 14,000
- 6,000 to 10,000
- 2,000 to 6,000
- 0 to 2,000

Source: The 1991 Census of Population

Scale 1cm = 6km

New York

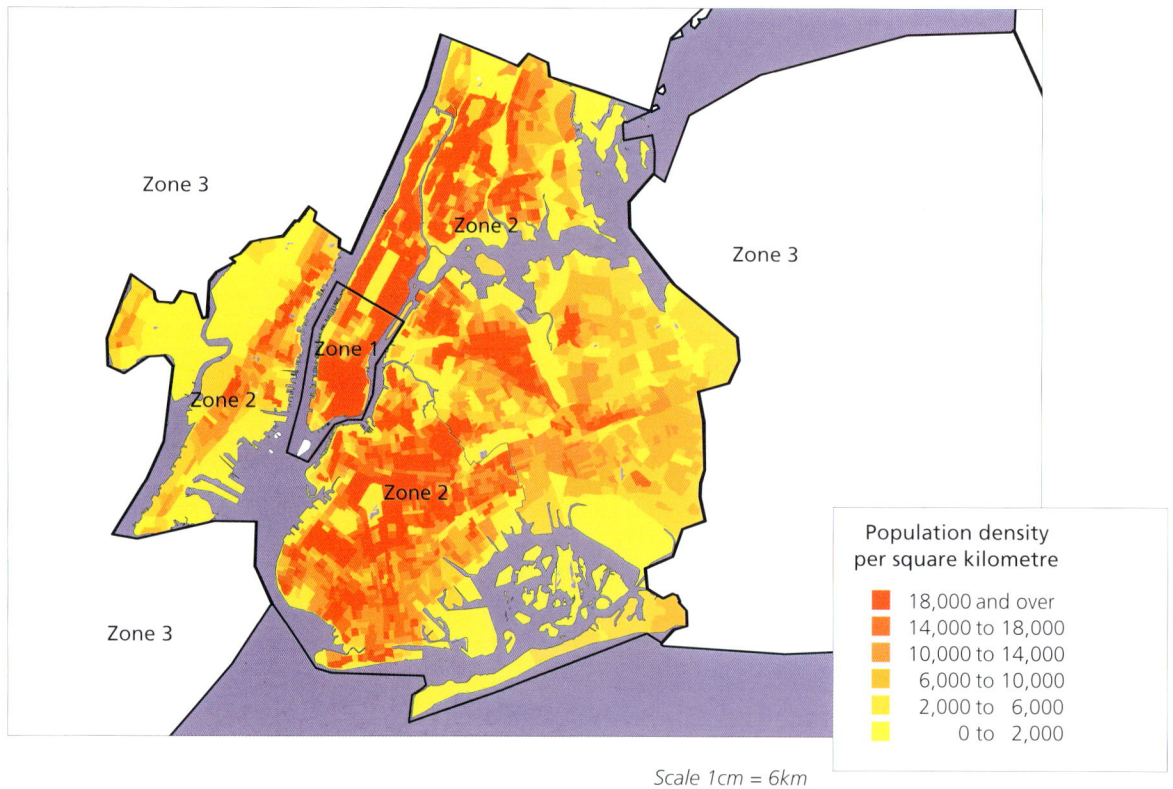

**Population density
per square kilometre**

- 18,000 and over
- 14,000 to 18,000
- 10,000 to 14,000
- 6,000 to 10,000
- 2,000 to 6,000
- 0 to 2,000

Scale 1cm = 6km

Map 4
Population density - metropolitan area (Zones 1 & 2)

Paris

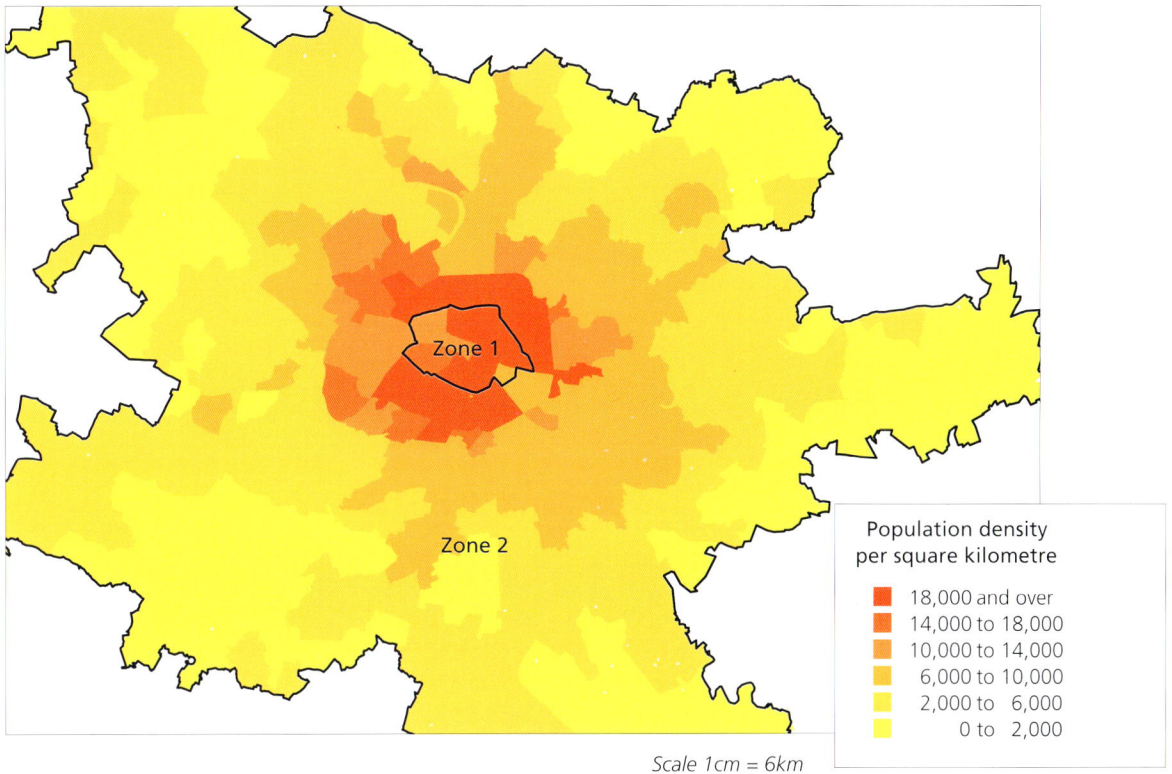

Population density
per square kilometre

- 18,000 and over
- 14,000 to 18,000
- 10,000 to 14,000
- 6,000 to 10,000
- 2,000 to 6,000
- 0 to 2,000

Scale 1cm = 6km

Tokyo

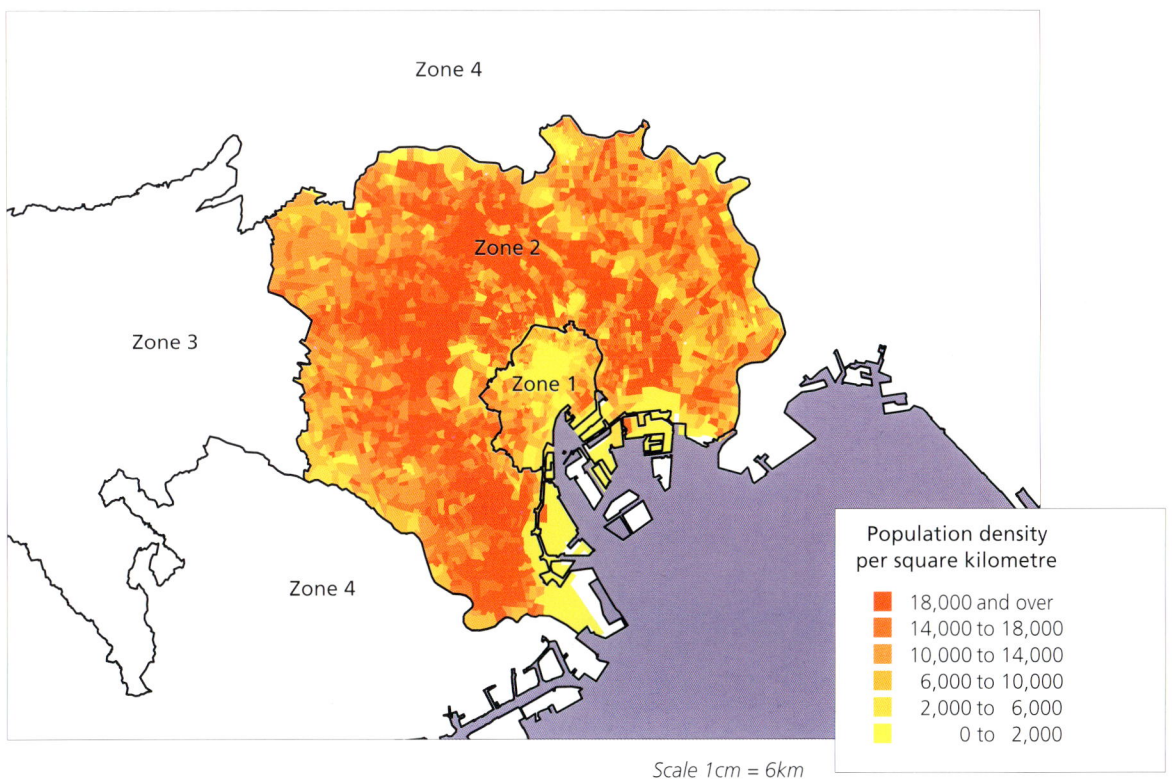

Population density
per square kilometre

- 18,000 and over
- 14,000 to 18,000
- 10,000 to 14,000
- 6,000 to 10,000
- 2,000 to 6,000
- 0 to 2,000

Scale 1cm = 6km

(Zone 2) which has the effect of further increasing the length of commuting trips to the city centre.

In Zone 2, New York and Tokyo are characterised by dense urban neighbourhoods while London and Paris are characterised by suburban developments with densities less than half of the other cities.

Population densities fall rapidly with distance from the city centre in all the four cities. New York's Zone 4 has the lowest population density, at 230 persons per square kilometre. In London, New York and Paris, population density diminishes with distance from the core. Tokyo differs slightly from the three other cities in that the greatest density is found in Zone 2, due to the severe hollowing out of the city centre. By contrast, Tokyo's population density in Zone 4 is substantially higher than the other cities. The population of Zone 4 is not spread throughout the region (as is largely the case in New York), but is concentrated in the urban areas of each prefecture. In Saitama prefecture, and in Chiba prefecture, 83.7% and 85% respectively of the population is living in city areas. For example, the density of population in the city of Koshigaya (Saitama prefecture) is 14,121 people per square kilometre and in the city of Kawasaki (Kanagawa prefecture), 8,448 people per square kilometre.

As shown by the example of Tokyo's Zone 4, average density does not tell the whole story from the perspective of travel. Of equal importance is whether the settlement pattern is a concentrated mix of land-uses, which fosters walking trips and public transport use, as is characteristic of nearly all of Tokyo, most of Paris, and Zone 1 and much of Zone 2 in London and New York. Paris has kept its high-density

neighbourhoods in Zone 2 and Tokyo has high density settlements throughout the region. Paris' structure plans have encouraged the development of high density towns and cities in Zones 2 & 3.

If, on the other hand, development patterns are dispersed, land-uses segregated, typical of Zones 3 & 4 in New York, and somewhat less in London, walking is almost impossible for most needs and public transport is uneconomical for all but a small proportion of trips.

3.4   Trends in population

All four cities have seen population shrink in their inner core since the 1950s, with the change being most marked in London, Paris and Tokyo. In London, New York and Paris the population seems to have somewhat stabilised or shown small signs of growth since the 1980s - but in Tokyo it is still decreasing.

Figure 3a[23]
Trends in population since 1950 (Zone 1)

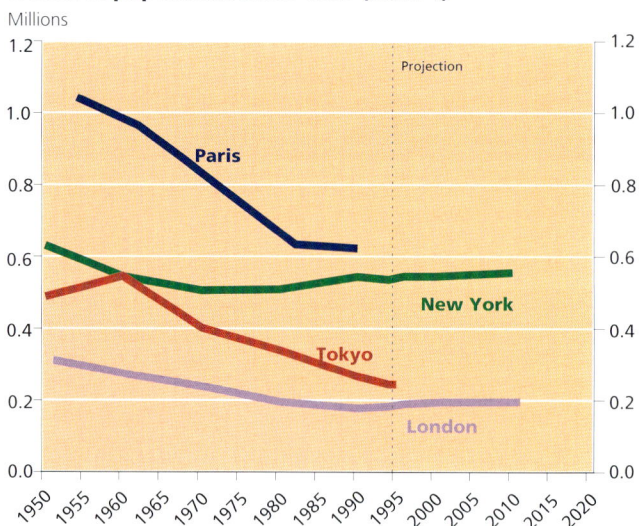

23 London   The figures for London are census data for 1951, 1961, 1971, and the London Research Centre's mid-year estimates for 1980, 1990, 1994 and 1996 and projections for 2001 and 2011. These projections are based on trend data but are constrained by forecasted housing availability.

New York   All data for New York state and New Jersey state are based on "Intercensal County Population Estimates: 1980 -1990" prepared by the United States Bureau of the Census, Population Estimates Branch. The source of the data is: the New York and New Jersey Federal - State Co-operative Program, the United States Bureau of the Census; with intercensal years adjusted by the census formula and Connecticut State Department of Health. The 1950 and 1960 data is estimated by the Regional Plan Association "The Region's Growth" (1967). The figure for 1994 is an estimate. The projection of future population is from the New York Metropolitan Transportation Council.

Paris   The figures for Paris are census data for 1954, 1962, 1968, 1982 and 1990.

Tokyo   The figures for Tokyo are census data. Data since 1995 are estimates from the Tokyo Metropolitan Government.

Figure 3b
Trends in population since 1950 (Zone 2)

Millions

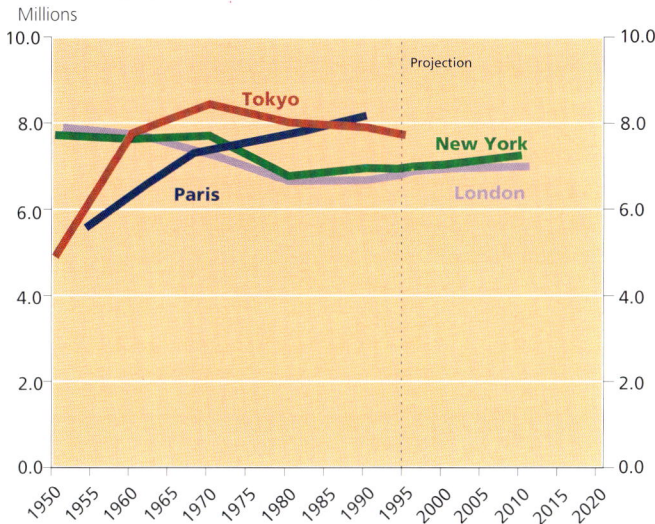

Figure 3c
Trends in population since 1950 (Zones 1 & 2)

Millions

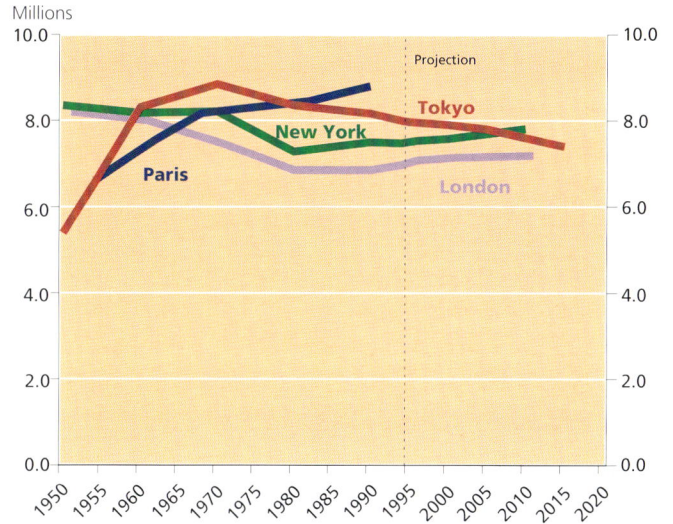

Although all four cities have some subsidised housing in their central area, the market rates for housing in the four city centres are generally much higher than elsewhere in their respective regions and countries. In New York, in addition to several large public-financed middle-income housing complexes, there remains a large population of low income residents, including many Hispanics and a growing Chinese population, who have low rents for sub-standard housing. Homelessness and people sleeping outdoors is also a feature of all the four cities' central cores.

London's central area (Zone 1) has been losing population for most of the 20th century. In 1901 London had a population of just under half a million, which fell to less than half of that by 1970, and to a low of 177,000 in 1990. The reasons for this are that the nature of the city and its transport structure have been changing. The 20th century led to suburbanisation with much greater living space per person and with efficient urban railways to enable people to work within the core of London. In very recent years there seems to have been some stabilisation of the resident population (with a small growth) but it is too early to be certain whether this is a long-term feature or a temporary halt to a continuing trend. Current population projections show

no further fall - and a slight rise by 2010. This is largely due to inward migration, including refugees and asylum seekers.

Population in Manhattan south of 60th street (Zone 1) has stabilised at about 530,000 residents in recent years, a reduction from a high of about 630,000 in the 1950s. The fall of population has halted due to new immigration (especially Chinese and Hispanic) and the conversion of former commercial and industrial areas in lower Manhattan. In the financial district, an experiment is underway to transform obsolete office skyscrapers into expensive housing and the entire area into a partially residential district among the banks and brokerages. However, only a modest growth of 25,000 new residents is projected by 2010.

Central Paris, with a population of over 600,000, continues to have more residents than the other three cities; but in 1950 it had well over a million inhabitants. Since then it has lost over 400,000 residents, most of the loss occurring between 1954 and 1975. Population grew in the inner suburbs (Zone 2) and since 1968 also in the outer ones (Zones 2 & 3). Since 1975 the depopulation of Paris' Zone 1 area has slowed down and the population has somewhat stabilised.

Population, employment and car ownership

Figure 3d [24]
Trends in population since 1950 (Zone 3)

Millions

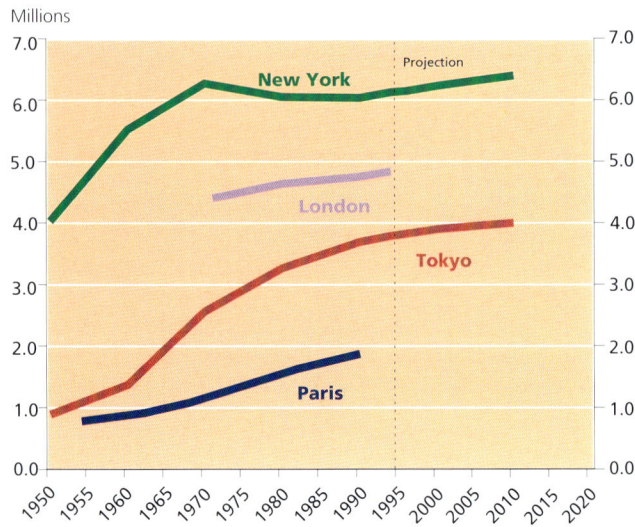

Figure 3e
Trends in population since 1950 (Zones 1, 2 & 3)

Millions

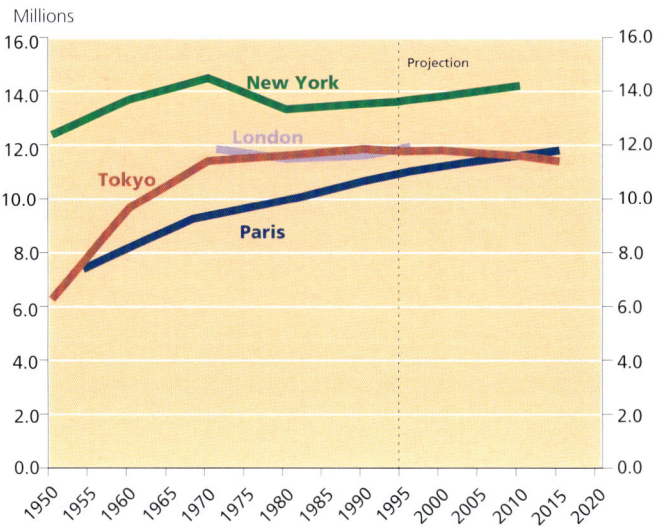

Like London, Tokyo had a large central area population which has been decreasing for most of the 20th century. The population of Tokyo's Zone 1 was 817,000 in 1920. Tokyo has experienced a pronounced "hollowing out" of its population as commercial development out-priced and displaced homes. This was accentuated in the 1980s with high demand for office space pushing land prices and rents to record highs. Although the Tokyo Metropolitan Government and the concerned ward authorities are trying to restore the night-time population, it is generally accepted that it is a very difficult task.

There is no common pattern of population growth in Zone 2, though in all four cities these areas are essentially residential. Greater London (Zones 1 & 2) has lost over a million inhabitants between 1960 and 1990. The trend of population loss has reversed recently. London's population would have continued to fall were it not for continuing migration by foreign nationals into the capital. For instance, the net international inflow for the five year period 1991 to 1996, was 295,000.

In New York, population in Zone 2 declined steadily from the 1950s until it stabilised at nearly 7 million people in about 1985, down from a high of 7.7 million

in the period 1950-1970. The loss in residents is explained by migration of former city residents to Zones 3 & 4 and other areas of the country, especially states in the "sunbelt". However, this shift has been offset by considerable immigration from foreign nationals, a pattern which is expected to grow. Both in London and New York, the population is expected to grow by 300,000 by 2010.

The population of Paris' Zone 2 is continuing to show a strong growth due to the continued development and expansion of the development areas. Its growth is based on the migration of people from Zone 1 in search of larger and more affordable homes, the attraction of new developments in Zone 2, and the fast connections to the centre by the expanding Réseau Express Régional regional rail line network.

In Tokyo, the overall population in the ward area (Zone 1 & 2) increased rapidly after the Second World War and reached its peak in 1970, after which it decreased. The rate of population decrease is not as marked as that of Zone 1. However, the population for Zones 1 & 2 in 1994 was still nearly 50% higher than it was in 1950.

24 **London**   Data before 1971 cannot be calculated because there have been wholesale boundary changes.

Figure 3f
Trends in population since 1950 (Zone 4)

Millions

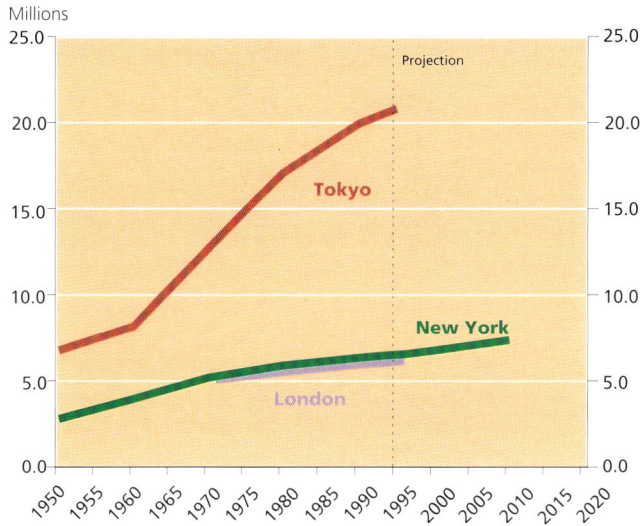

Figure 3g
Trends in population since 1950 (Zones 1, 2, 3 & 4)

Millions

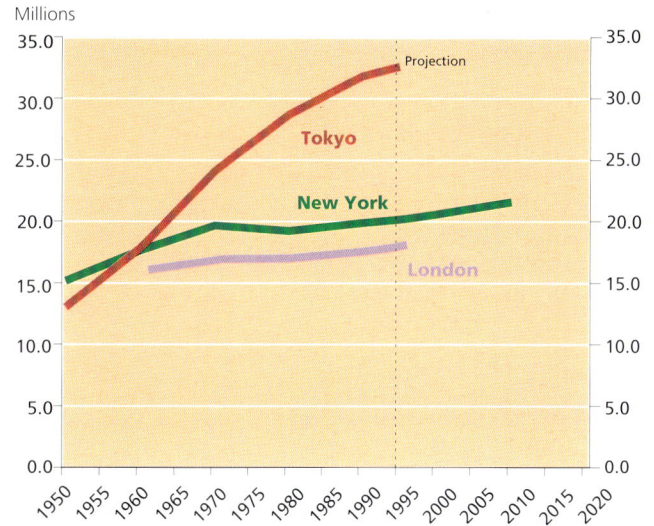

Zones 3 & 4 are major growth areas in all four cities, but the patterns of growth are different.

The south-east of England (Zones 1, 2, 3 & 4) has witnessed a large population growth of just under 2 million since 1960. Much of this has occurred in Zone 4. Within Zone 3 lies London's "green belt", an area which is generally designated as "open space" on which there are strict planning restrictions for new developments. The concept behind the creation of a green belt was that of keeping a demarcation between town and country. However, it has not contained London's spread, which has as a consequence leap-frogged the "green belt" and gone to the outer areas of Zone 3 and into Zone 4. Half of the total population growth of the entire south-east of England over the past three decades has been in Zone 4.

New York has also seen an expansion of population to the region's outer areas. The population in Zone 3 grew from about 4 million in 1950 to more than 6 million in the 1970s, one million of which was due to the shift of residents from Zones 1 & 2, lured by low-cost mortgages available to home buyers and the appeal of larger housing. The balance is partly a result of the

significant overall increase in black and Puerto Rican immigrants that occurred in the region between 1950 and 1970, partly due to a national shift of population from the interior to coastal states, and partly due to the post-Second World War "baby boom". Population in Zone 3 has since nearly stabilised at about 6 million and is projected to increase from 6 million to 6.4 million by 2010. Like London, Zone 4 is the New York region's major growth area. In Zone 4, the population has more than doubled between 1950 and 1990, reaching nearly 6.5 million in 1994. There are now more people living in Zone 4 than Zone 3 (although it is more than five times larger).

Roads and housing in London's Zone 3

Population, employment and car ownership

Zone 3 is the part of Paris that is experiencing the strongest growth in population, especially since 1968, but from a much lower original level. This is because the areas surrounding built-up Paris were low-density rural areas with small populations. The growth is underpinned by the availability of individual houses and low population densities. However, the population of Paris' Zone 3 is still relatively small and the area is still largely rural. The new schéma directeur (master plan) of the Ile-de-France, adopted in 1994, predicts and plans for the following evolution of population levels:

Large parts of Paris' Zone 3 are still rural

- **Zone 1** stabilisation

- **Zone 2** a very small growth

- **Zone 3** a moderate growth (of less than 1% per annum)

The schéma directeur of the Ile-de-France predicts that by 2015 the population of the region (Zones 1, 2 & 3) will have risen to 11.8 million from the 10.7 million figure of 1990. By contrast the Ville de Paris (within Zones 1 & 2) is predicted to have the same population in 2015 as it did in 1990, 2.1 million.

The fringes of Tokyo have seen the largest rates of population increase of the four cities. In the Tokyo Metropolis (Zones 1, 2 & 3), the population nearly doubled after 1950 (although it began to decrease in 1990). The Tama area (Zone 3) has shown a consistent increase since 1950, the largest rate of growth being in the 1960s due to the suburbanisation of Tokyo. Although the population is still increasing in Zone 3,

the rate of increase is declining due to the decrease in the population moving into Zone 3 seeking affordable housing.

Between 1980 and 1994 the population in the outer parts of the south-east region in England has grown by over one million inhabitants. It is expected that this trend will continue.

Zone 4 is the New York region's major growth area, where population has more than doubled between 1950 and 1990, reaching nearly 6.5 million in 1994. The same factors that led to the growth of Zone 3, plus the ease of creating new developments on former agricultural land, a major national highway building programme and the low cost of driving, attracted a growth of 3.5 million people in Zone 4 during this period. Population is projected to increase by nearly an extra million by 2010 to 7.4 million.

The population for the entire Tokyo region (Zones 1, 2, 3 & 4) has been increasing since 1950. This increase was particularly steep in the 1960s and 1970s. However, the rate of increase has been declining in recent years, and in 1994, the population moving out from the region exceeded that of the population moving in. Although, in Zone 4, the population has been increasing consistently since 1950, the rate of increase has been declining. By 1994 the population of Zone 4 was more than triple of what it was in 1950. It is projected that the population of the Tokyo region (Zones 1, 2, 3, & 4) will stabilise in the future.

3.5 Age distribution

The age distribution of a population reveals the numbers who are either too young or too old to drive, and, thus, are likely to have a dependence on public transport, as well as the number of people likely to enter or leave the work force. Women, as the predominant carers in families, whether or not they are employed outside the home, tend to make more non-work trips than men, and women's work trips are often linked with shopping or childcare arrangements. These responsibilities, frequently of a random spatial pattern, increase the need for flexible transport, an attribute better achieved by car than public transport. On the other hand, older women tend to drive less than do older men and be more dependent on public transport. Due to ease of access and travel patterns closer to residences, older citizens tend to use buses more than trains.

In London, New York and Paris, there is a common phenomenon of life-cycle demographic change. What can be noticed is that both men and women in their twenties come into the city centre or metropolitan area to find work and career, then have families and move out to probably better housing in the suburban or exurban areas. The migration by the young to the inner city is both national and international. For instance, in Greater London in 1995 there was a net inflow of 38,000 persons aged 16 to 24.

The distribution of Tokyo residents by age group reveals two distinct population bulges, one between the 40 to 44 bracket, the other of approximately age 20. These two groups consist of persons born during the post-Second World War baby boom and the second baby boom when the preceding baby boom generation became parents. This trend can be seen throughout Japan. The outward migration from Zone 1 formerly was explained by its residents seeking better housing conditions in the suburbs as the life cycle turned and the size of families grew. But during the "bubble economy" of the late 1980s, the outward migration was exacerbated by rising rents and taxes both due to increasing land prices.

There are relatively few children born in Zone 1 in all four cities, as those planning to set up a family move to the suburbs or the periphery. In London, New York and Paris, there is a further small dip in the age groups 5 - 15 as families that had children whilst living in Zone 1 move out as the children start to grow.

In Zones 1 & 2, in London, New York and Paris there are substantially more females than males. The pattern indicates that, in all cities except Tokyo, the inward migration of the young in search for jobs is greater for females than males. One peculiar phenomenon in London, is that at the 55 to 59 age group there are an equal number of men and women. The reason for this is the great wave of migration of young men from the Caribbean and especially the Indian sub-continent in the 1950s recruited to work in Britain. This is so for all Zones but is more pronounced for Greater London (Zones 1 & 2) where a large proportion of the foreign migrants set up home.

The travel implications of these age and gender patterns are larger numbers of people who need to make both work trips and many trips for shopping and other personal business on a flexible schedule and, often, in a random manner. Personal security is also very likely an important requirement of travel for the female population.

Population, employment and car ownership

Figure 4a
Age distribution of male and female residents - London (Zones 1 & 2)

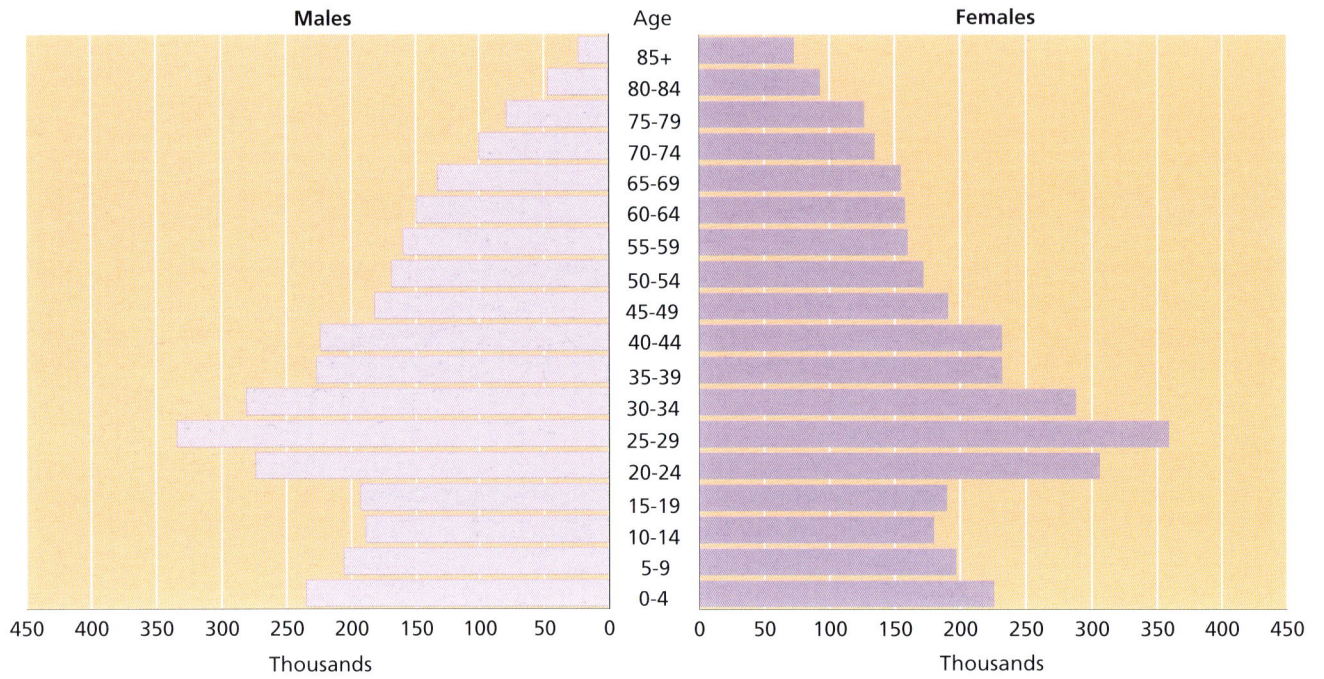

Figure 4b
Age distribution of male and female residents - New York (Zones 1 & 2)

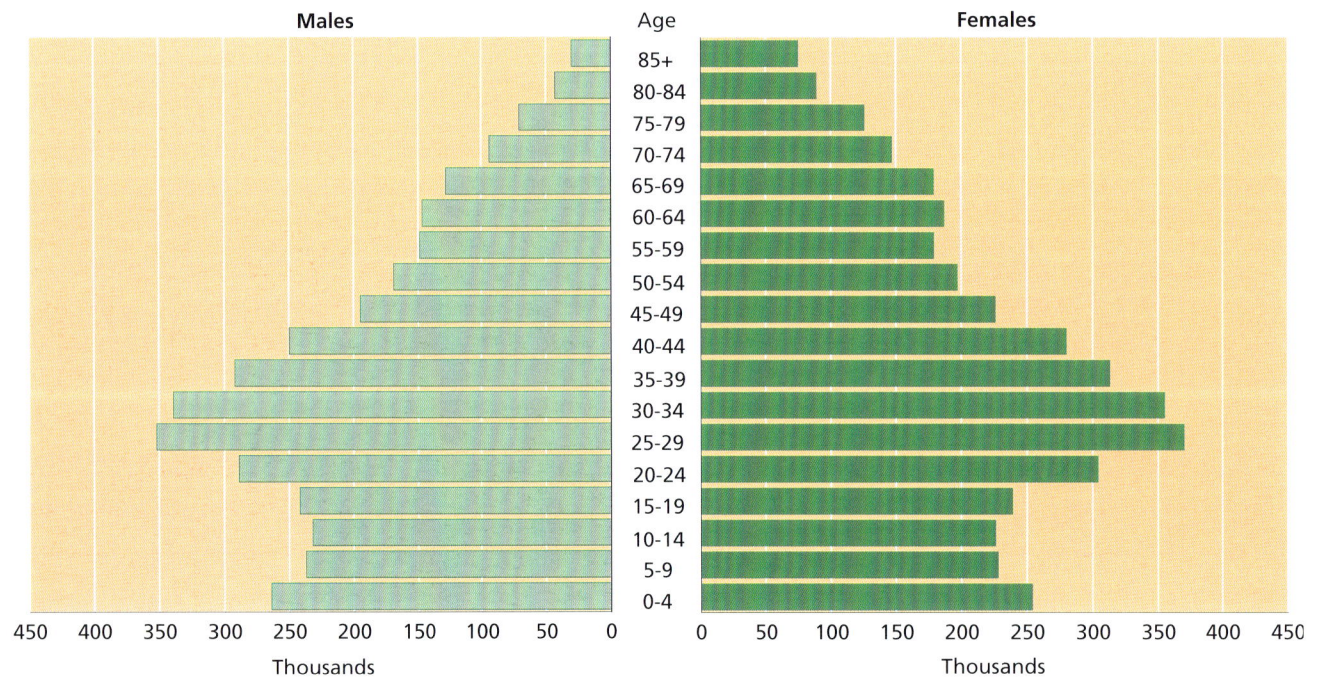

Figure 4c
Age distribution of male and female residents - Paris (Zones 1 & 2)

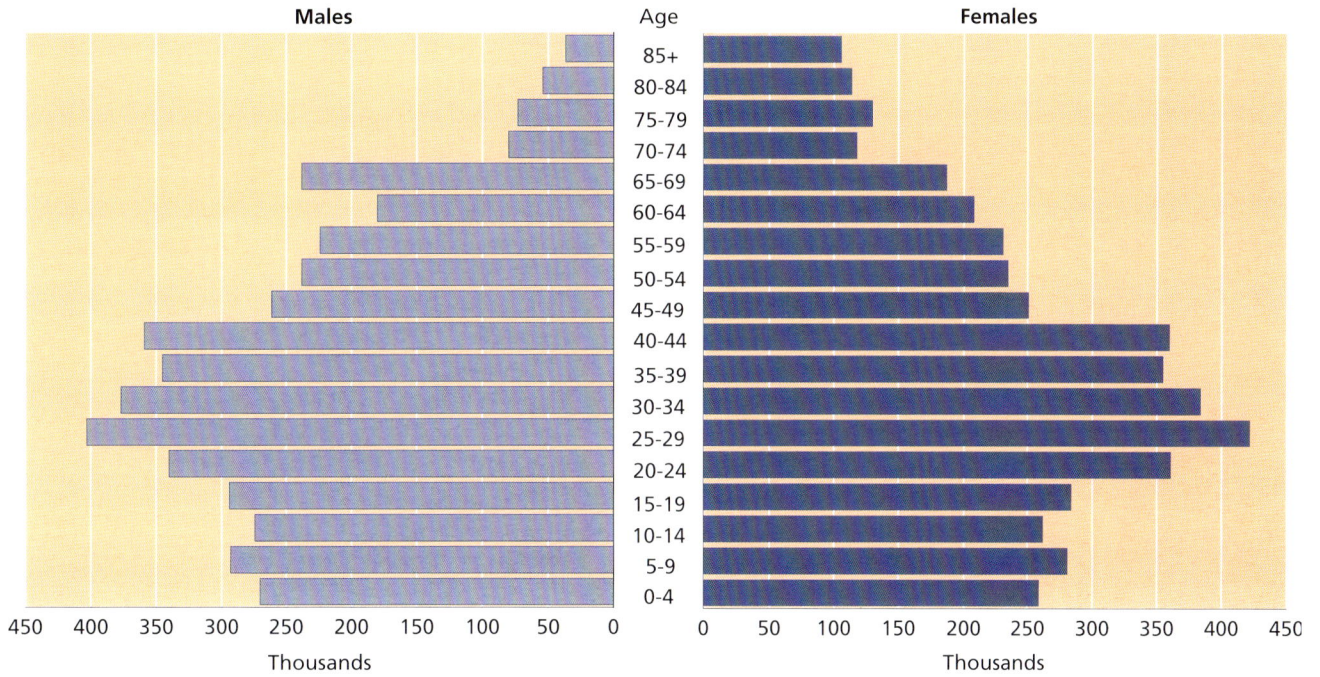

Figure 4d
Age distribution of male and female residents - Tokyo (Zones 1 & 2)

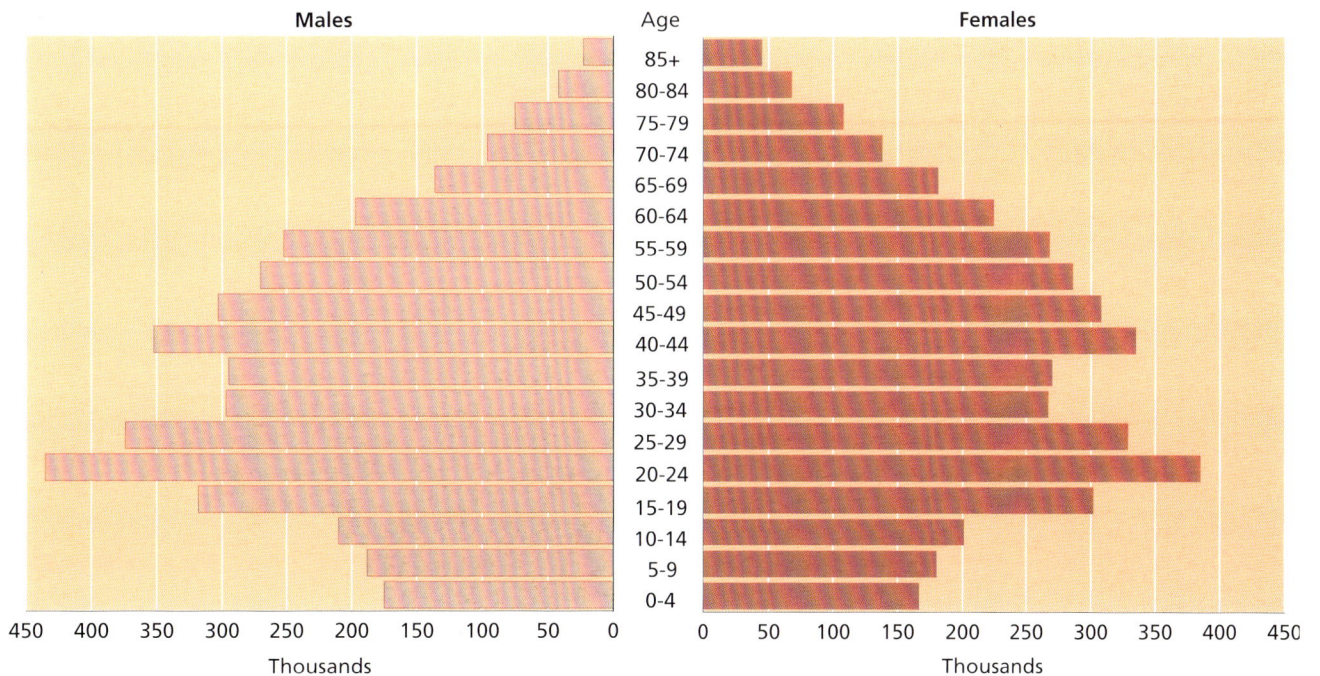

Figure 5a
Age distribution of male and female residents - London (Zones 3 & 4)

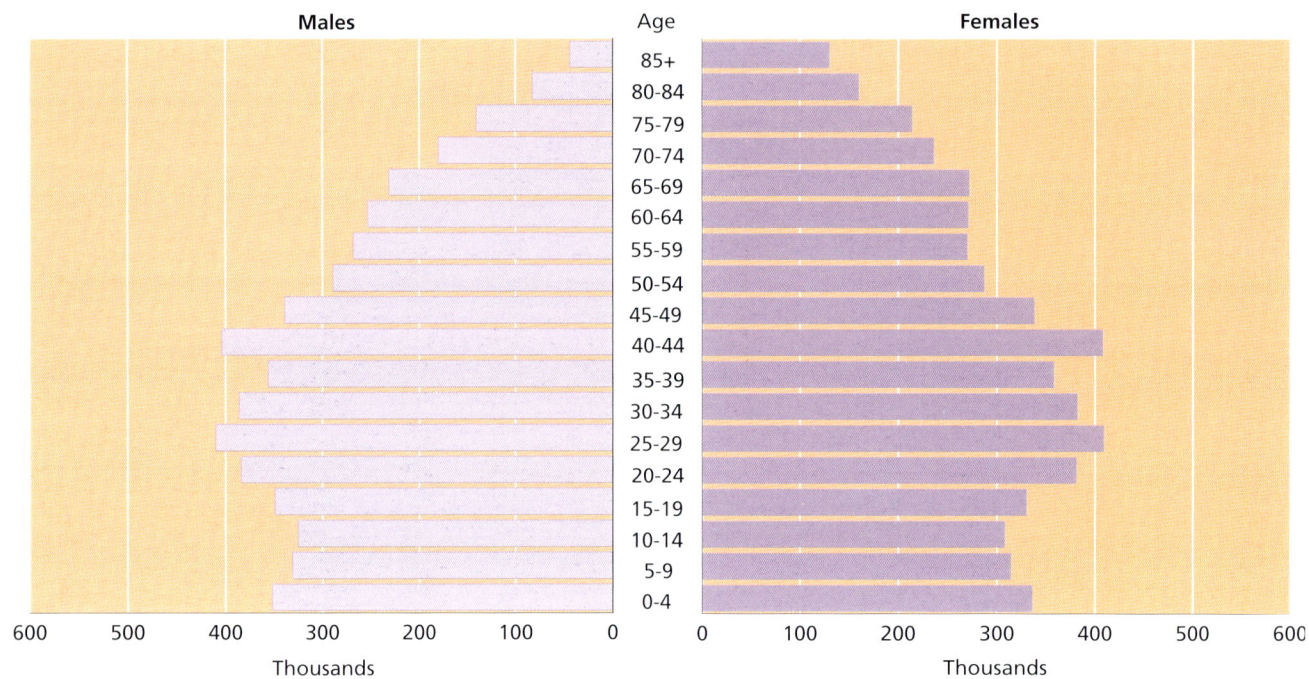

Figure 5b
Age distribution of male and female residents - New York (Zones 3 & 4)

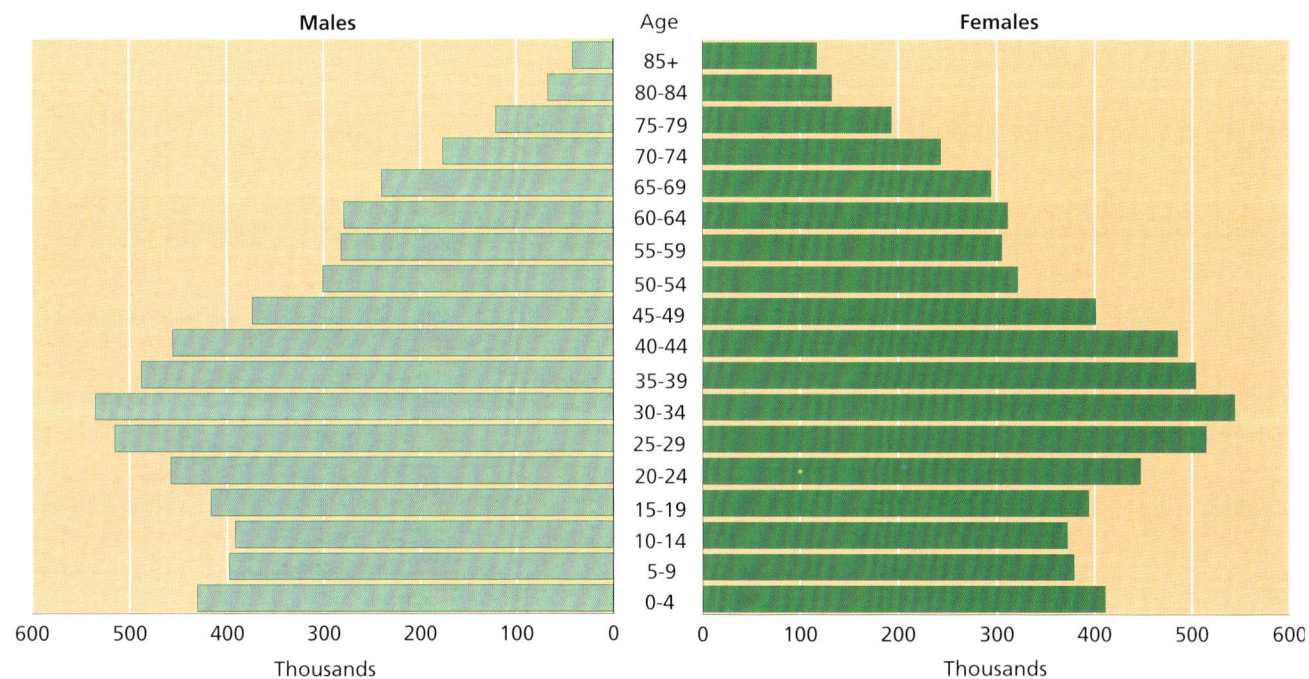

Figure 5c
Age distribution of male and female residents - Paris (Zone 3)

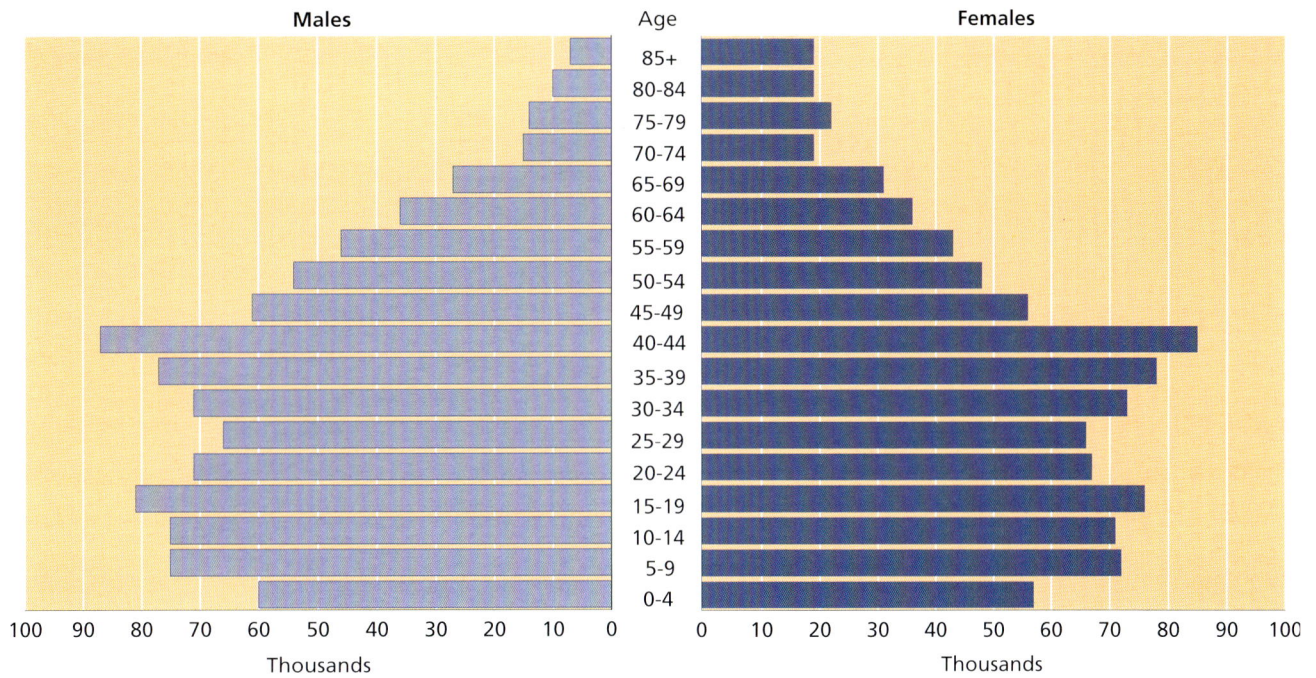

Figure 5d
Age distribution of male and female residents - Tokyo (Zones 3 & 4)

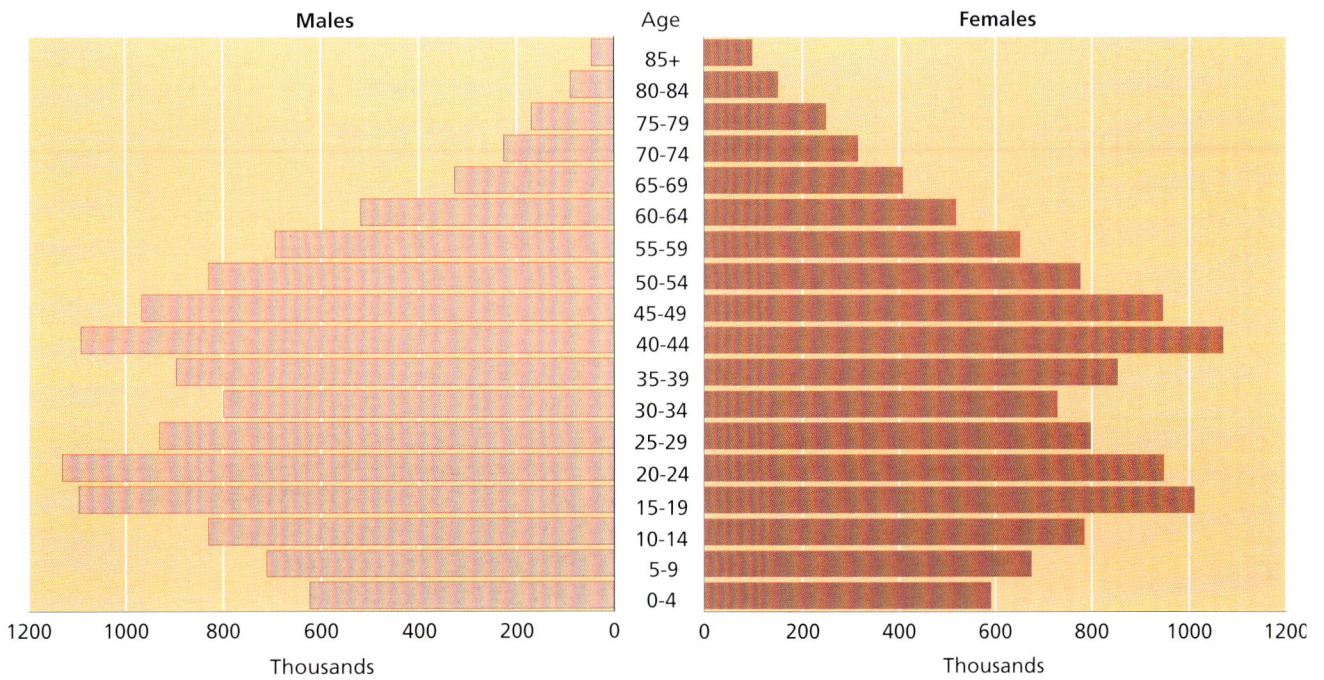

Map 5
Residential density of those aged 0 - 15 - the entire region (Zones 1,2,3 & 4)

London

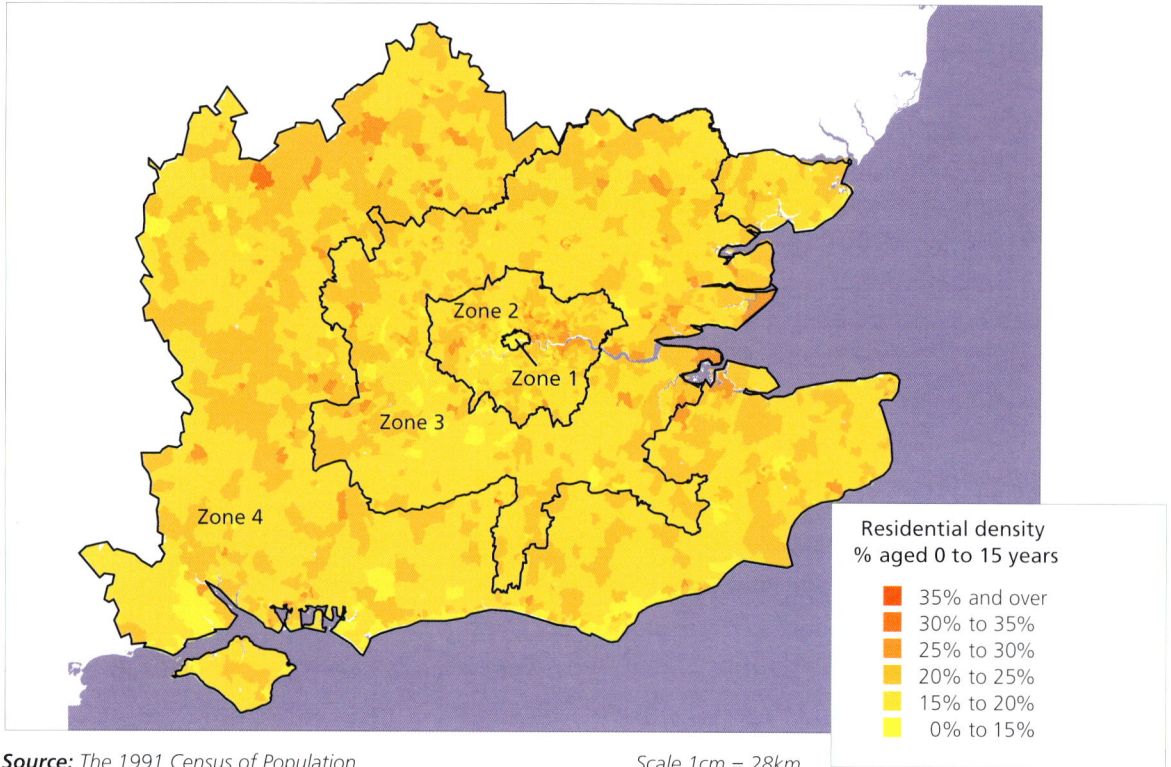

Zone 2
Zone 1
Zone 3
Zone 4

Residential density
% aged 0 to 15 years

- 35% and over
- 30% to 35%
- 25% to 30%
- 20% to 25%
- 15% to 20%
- 0% to 15%

Source: The 1991 Census of Population

Scale 1cm = 28km

New York

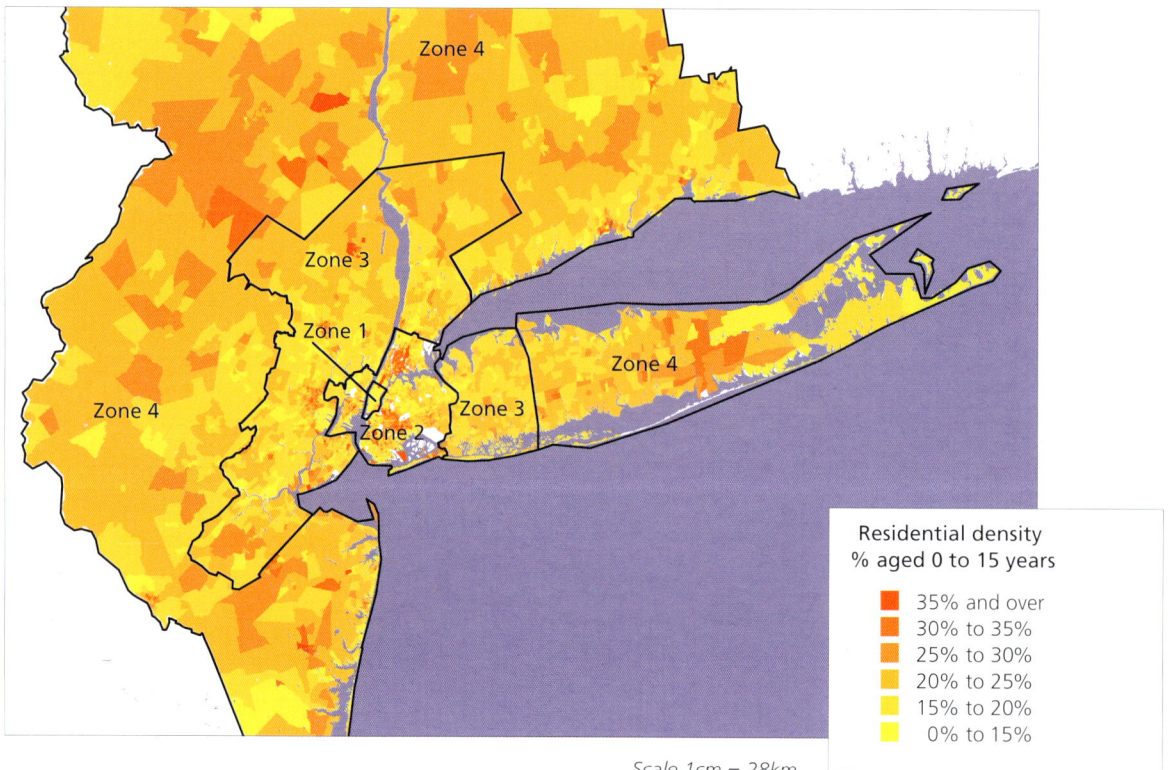

Zone 4
Zone 3
Zone 1
Zone 4
Zone 4
Zone 3
Zone 2

Residential density
% aged 0 to 15 years

- 35% and over
- 30% to 35%
- 25% to 30%
- 20% to 25%
- 15% to 20%
- 0% to 15%

Scale 1cm = 28km

Map 5
Residential density of those aged 0 - 15 - the entire region (Zones 1,2,3&4)

Paris

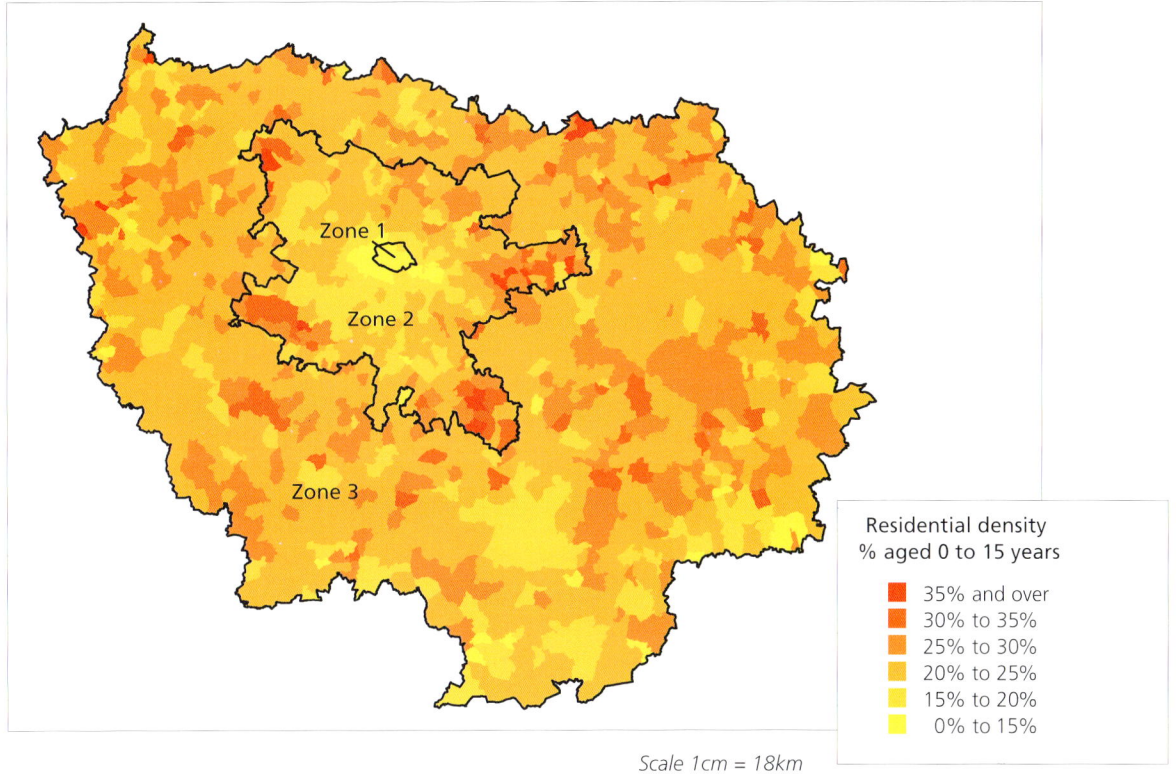

Residential density
% aged 0 to 15 years

- 35% and over
- 30% to 35%
- 25% to 30%
- 20% to 25%
- 15% to 20%
- 0% to 15%

Scale 1cm = 18km

Tokyo

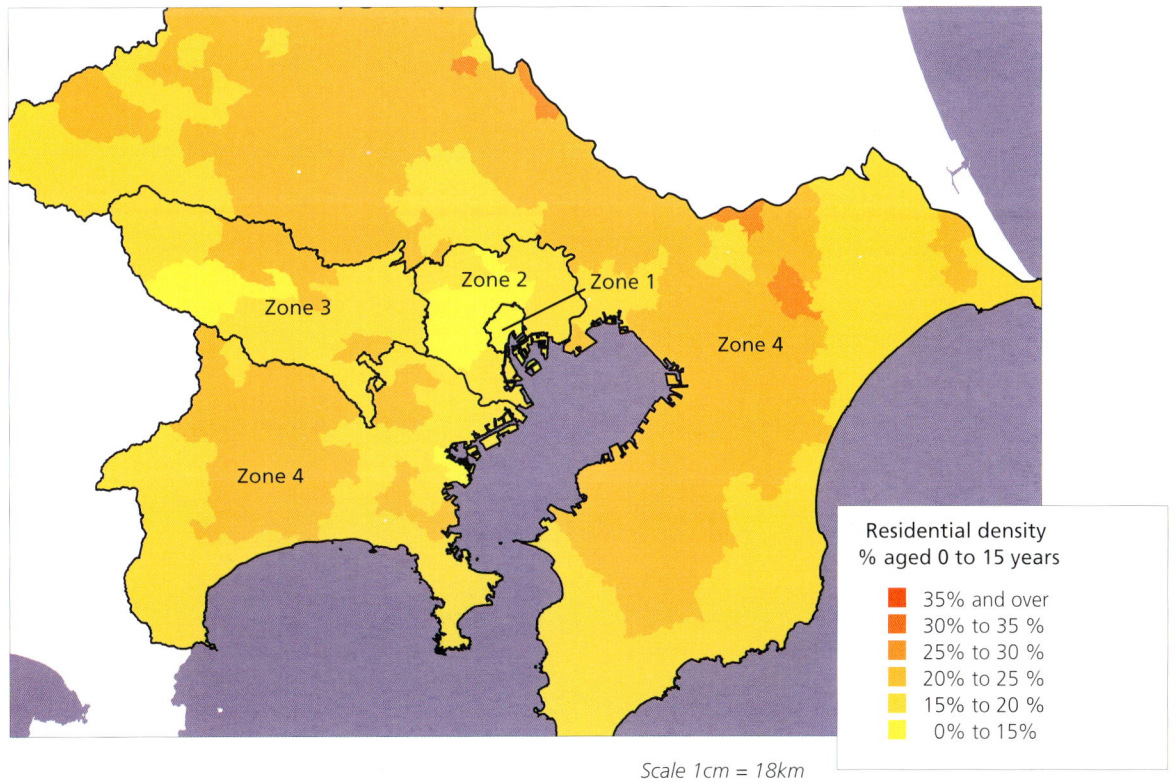

Residential density
% aged 0 to 15 years

- 35% and over
- 30% to 35 %
- 25% to 30 %
- 20% to 25 %
- 15% to 20 %
- 0% to 15%

Scale 1cm = 18km

Map 6
Residential density of those aged 65+ - the entire region (Zones 1,2,3 & 4)

London

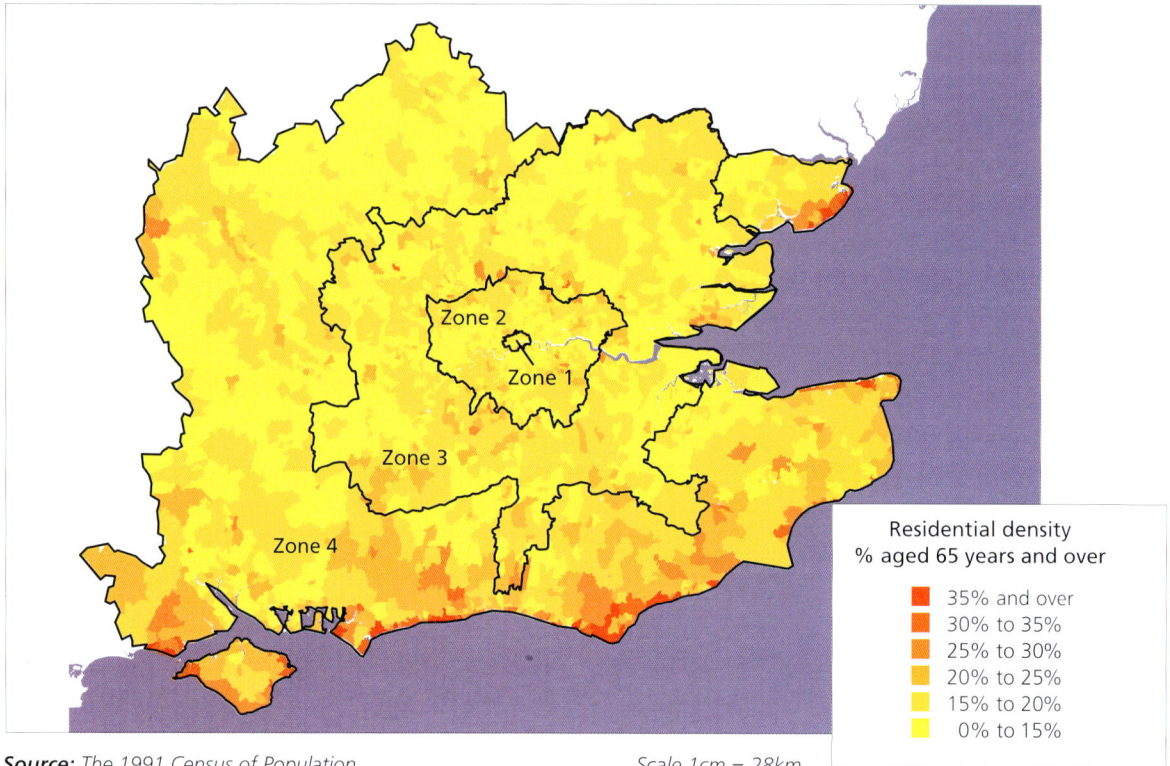

Residential density
% aged 65 years and over

- 35% and over
- 30% to 35%
- 25% to 30%
- 20% to 25%
- 15% to 20%
- 0% to 15%

Source: The 1991 Census of Population   *Scale 1cm = 28km*

New York

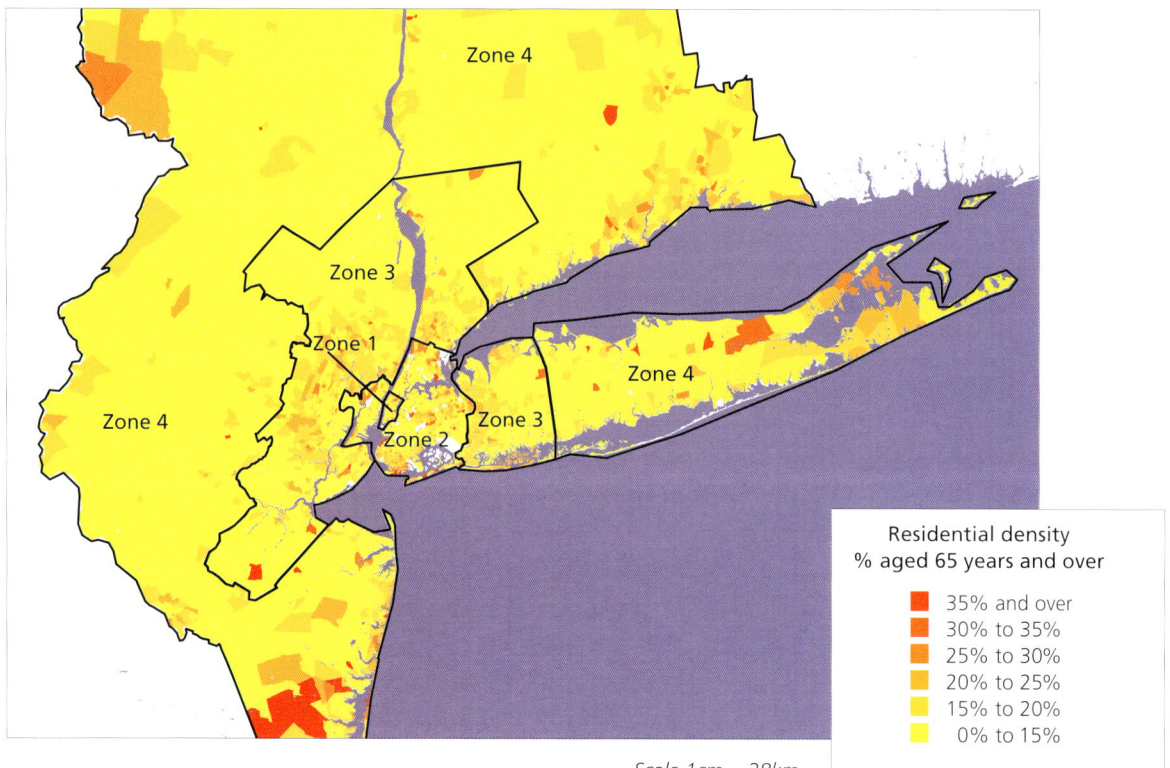

Residential density
% aged 65 years and over

- 35% and over
- 30% to 35%
- 25% to 30%
- 20% to 25%
- 15% to 20%
- 0% to 15%

Scale 1cm = 28km

Map 6
Residential density of those aged 65+ - the entire region (Zones 1,2,3 & 4)

Paris

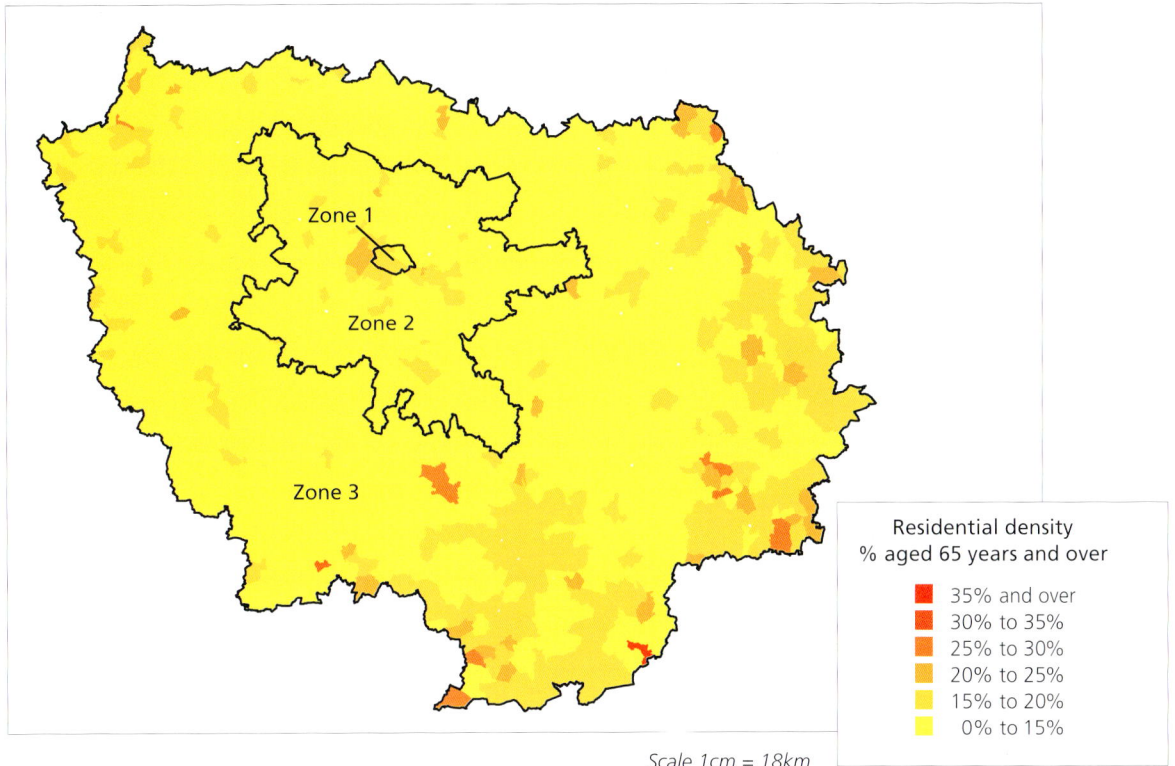

Residential density
% aged 65 years and over

- 35% and over
- 30% to 35%
- 25% to 30%
- 20% to 25%
- 15% to 20%
- 0% to 15%

Scale 1cm = 18km

Tokyo

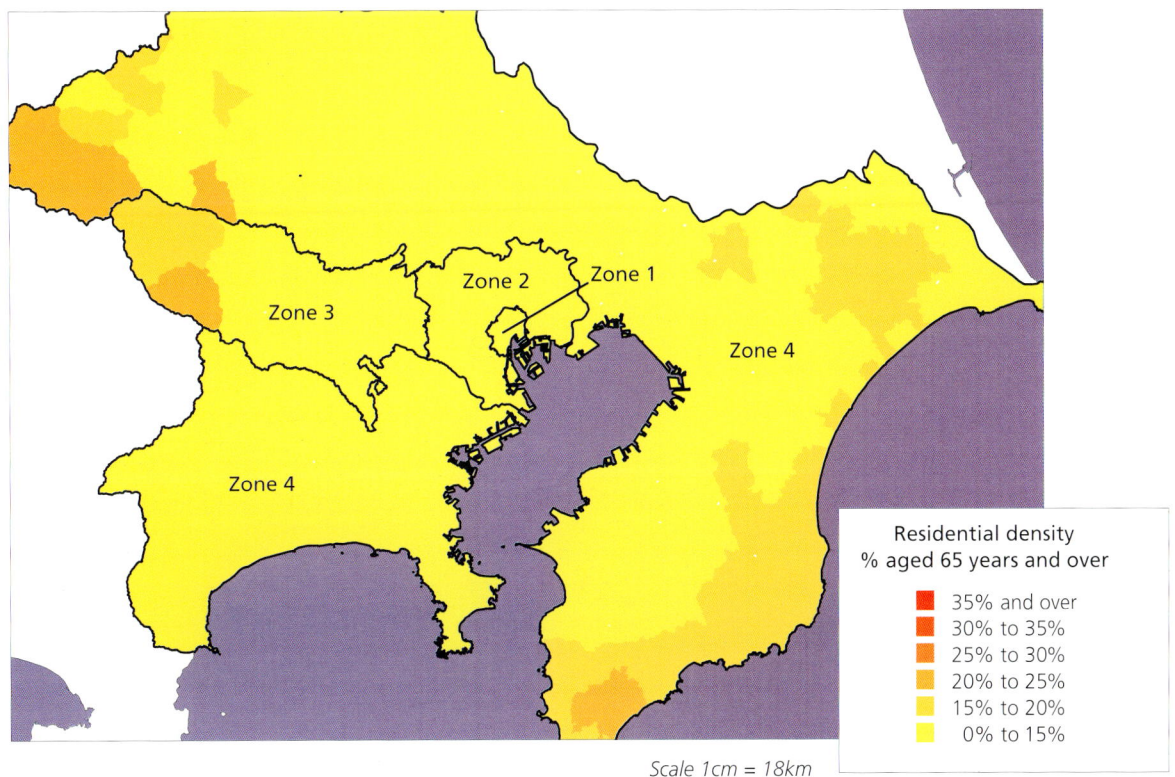

Residential density
% aged 65 years and over

- 35% and over
- 30% to 35%
- 25% to 30%
- 20% to 25%
- 15% to 20%
- 0% to 15%

Scale 1cm = 18km

In Zone 3 & 4, in all cities, the gender of virtually all age groups is balanced. Looking at the population age structure of the outer regions of the metropolises, it becomes apparent that there is no longer a bulge of young people and there is a relatively gradual population pyramid as young couples have moved out of the cities and have set up families. The situation for Tokyo is different in that the population of Zone 4 is the product of the relatively recent overall growth of the Tokyo region and is characterised by inward migration, hence the relatively small numbers of older people.

The establishment of retirement areas outside the metropolitan area is well illustrated in map 6, especially for London, where there is a high proportion of those aged over 65 settled all along the coast.

3.6   Employment

Since the journey to work is the greatest single purpose for many people's trips, the distribution and density of employment largely shapes the patterns of transport for all four cities.

Density of employment is very likely the most significant influence on travel patterns, determining peak travel demand, the viability of public transport and the propensity to walk for non-home based trips. The concentration of jobs in New York's Zone 1 makes it by far the most dense employment centre of the four cities. Yet Tokyo provides more jobs in Zone 1 than the other cities (about 400,000 more than the nearly 2 million in the Manhattan central area and more than twice as many as in the centres of Paris and London).

Tokyo's employment density in Zone 2 is comparatively high at 8,470 employed persons per square kilometre or about 15% of the density of its Zone 1. The other three cities' employment densities in Zone 2 are considerably less than half of Tokyo's and between 3% and 5% of the level in their respective central areas.

In all four cities, employment density in Zone 3 decreases dramatically, although the levels for New York and Tokyo remain much higher than for London and Paris. The low density of employment in Zones 3 & 4 coupled with the low density of habitation makes these areas very car dependent as it is difficult to link dispersed workplaces with dispersed dwellings.

Table 7a [25]

People in paid employment 1990 (totals and as a percentage of the total residential population in that Zone) (disaggregated Zones)

	London		New York		Paris		Tokyo	
Zone 1	917,000	518%	1,967,000	362%	1,025,000	165%	2,381,000	895%
Zone 2	2,432,000	36%	2,232,000	33%	3,469,000	42%	4,868,000	62%
Zone 3	1,930,000	39%	3,312,000	55%	581,000	12%	1,379,000	37%
Zone 4	2,496,000	33%	3,230,000	51%	-		7,813,000	39%
Total	7,775,000	44%	10,674,000	54%	5,075,000	48%	16,441,000	52%

25   London   The London data is from the 1991 census of population. It includes the self-employed.

New York   The data for New York excludes the self-employed.

Paris   The data for Paris includes the self-employed.

Tokyo   The data for Tokyo includes the self-employed.

Table 7b
People in paid employment 1990 (aggregated Zones)

	London	New York	Paris	Tokyo
Zone 1	917,000	1,967,000	1,025,000	2,381,000
Zones 1 & 2	3,349,000	4,132,000	4,494,000	7,249,000
Zones 1, 2 & 3	5,279,000	7,444,000	5,075,000	8,628,000
Zones 1, 2, 3 & 4	7,775,000	10,674,000	-	16,441,000

Table 8 [26]
Density of employment 1990 (employed persons per square kilometre per Zone) (disaggregated Zones)

	London	New York	Paris	Tokyo
Zone 1	33,960	85,550	35,340	56,690
Zone 2	1,570	3,040	1,710	8,470
Zone 3	210	660	60	1,190
Zone 4	120	120	-	690

It must be remembered that the data in the following tables refer to the place of employment not the residence of the employed.

All the cities have seen the number of jobs increase in all their Zones over the past 30 years. For instance, whilst Tokyo's Zone 1 had 1.3 million persons in employment in 1960, this figure had reached 2.4 million in 1990 [27].

3.7 Car ownership

New York has the lowest level of car ownership in Zone 1. Approximately one in five households own or lease a car in the Manhattan central business district. This low rate is due largely to the high cost of off-street parking and insurance in Manhattan's core, the scarcity and inconvenience of on-street parking (vacating curb space for street cleaning, car break-ins), and the easy access to most destinations by walking, taxi or public transport. Levels of car ownership in Zone 1 in both Paris and London are also relatively low. This is partially explained by the availability of frequent and comprehensive public transport and partly because of difficulties residents face with parking. Both Paris and London, but more so London, have severe parking restrictions - based on expensive parking metres and car parks. However, London's and Paris' Zone 1 car ownership is more than twice that of New York's, and London's is growing faster.

All four cities have fewer than one car per household in Zone 2 (from 0.47 in Tokyo to 0.91 in Paris).

In New York, while storage of private passenger cars in Zone 2 is not as costly as it is in the central business district, off-street space is still limited and bears a significant charge, unless in one's own driveway. Although on-street parking is scarce, parked cars have to be moved twice a week to permit street-cleaning. Thus, in New York, the level of car ownership is well below that of London and Paris. Nonetheless, there is no system of residential parking permits in New York, as there is in much of London and Paris.

In all four cities, most areas of Zone 2 have easy access to neighbourhood shops, services and schools by walking and bus, and good metro access to the central areas. This allows many households to live comfortably

---

26   This table has been constructed by dividing the figures of table 7a with the figures of table 4a

27   Tokyo has seen a rise in jobs in all four Zones.

Trends in persons in paid employment 1960-1995 in Tokyo (disaggregated Zones)

	Zone 1	Zone 2	Zone 3	Zone 4
1960	1,290,000	3,261,000	455,000	3,385,000
1970	1,721,000	4,170,000	860,000	5,183,000
1980	1,959,000	4,275,000	1,083,000	6,198,000
1990	2,381,000	4,868,000	1,379,000	7,813,000
1995	2,242,000	5,026,000	1,501,000	8,435,000

Population, employment and car ownership

Map 7
Employment density - the entire region (Zones 1,2,3&4)

London

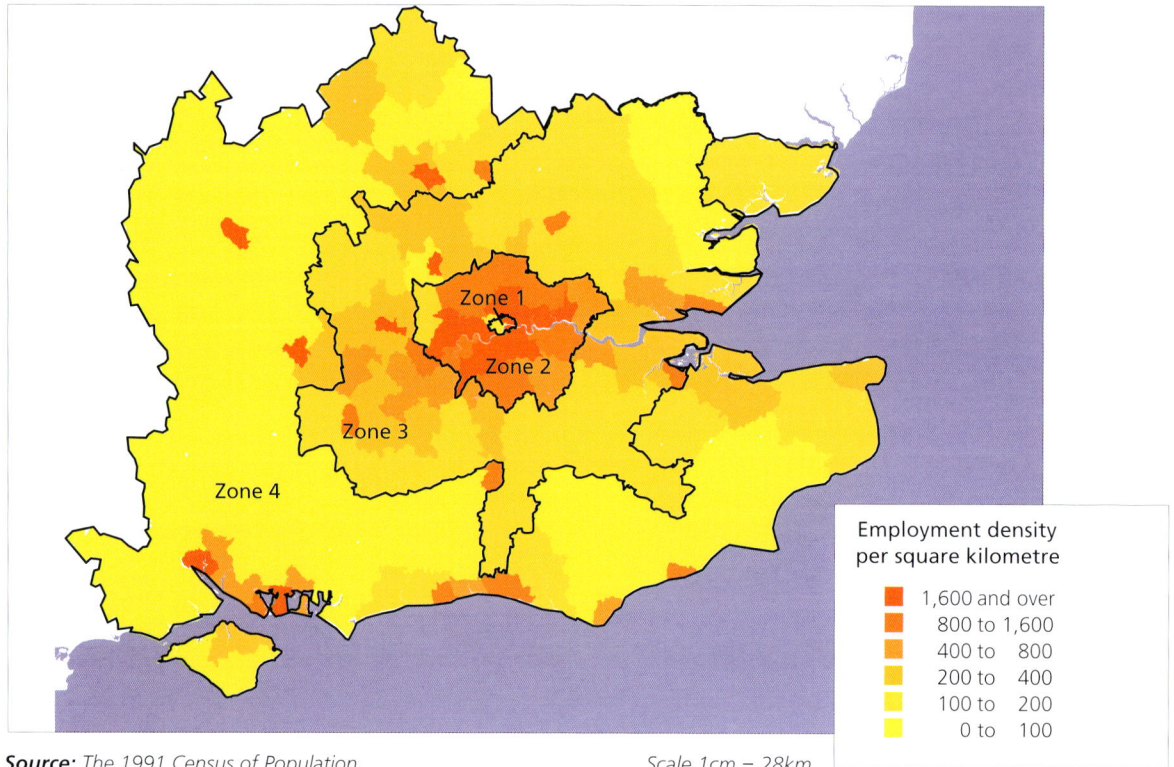

Source: *The 1991 Census of Population*

Scale 1cm = 28km

Employment density
per square kilometre

- 1,600 and over
- 800 to 1,600
- 400 to 800
- 200 to 400
- 100 to 200
- 0 to 100

New York

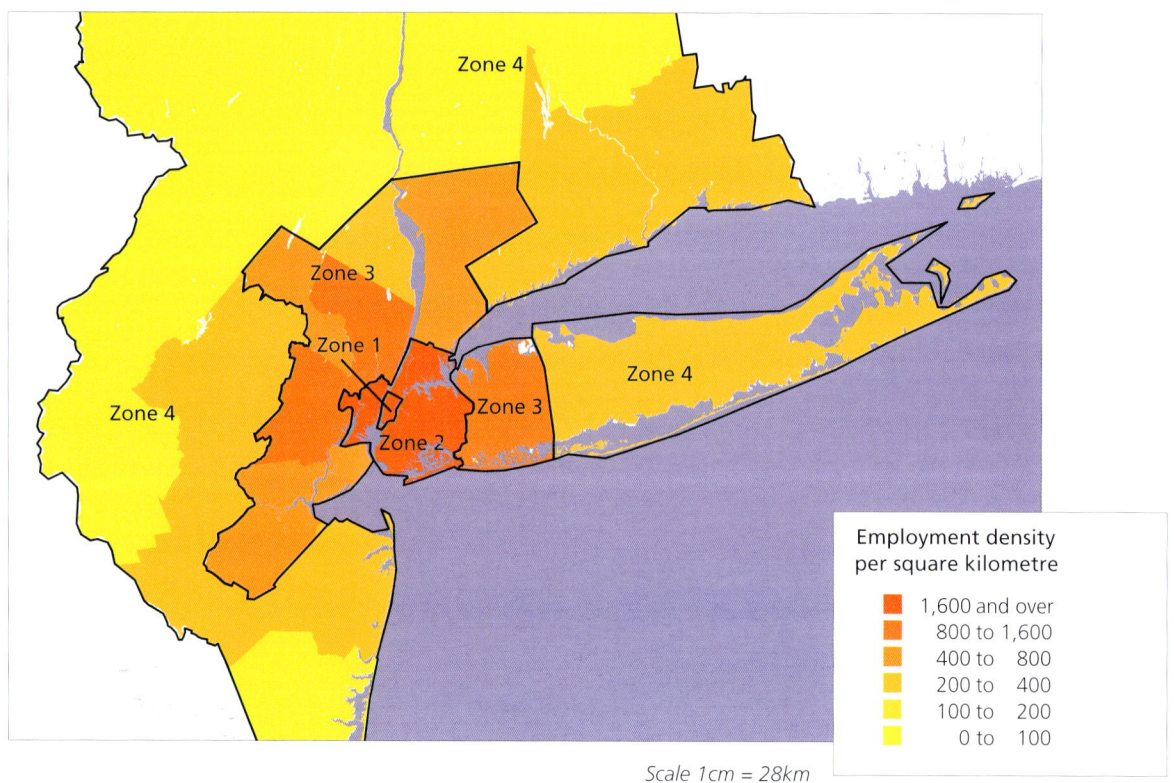

Scale 1cm = 28km

Employment density
per square kilometre

- 1,600 and over
- 800 to 1,600
- 400 to 800
- 200 to 400
- 100 to 200
- 0 to 100

Map 7
Employment density - the entire region (Zones 1,2,3&4)

Paris

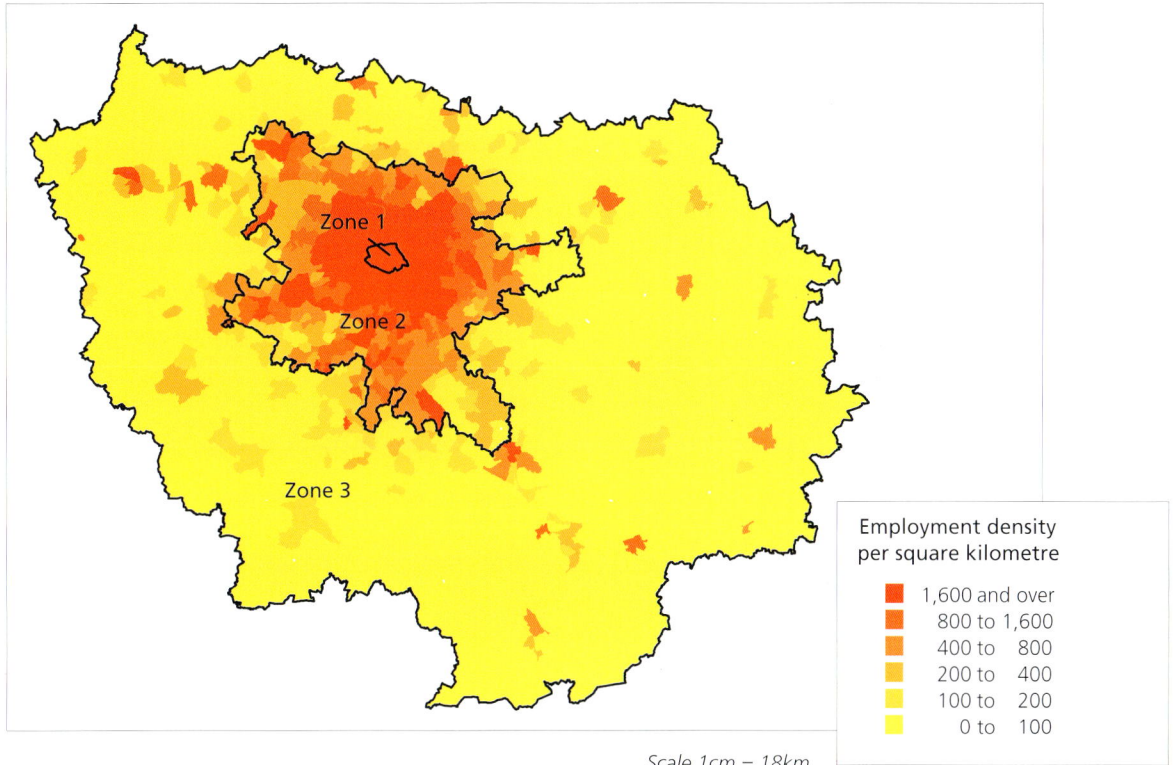

Employment density
per square kilometre

- 1,600 and over
- 800 to 1,600
- 400 to 800
- 200 to 400
- 100 to 200
- 0 to 100

Scale 1cm = 18km

Tokyo

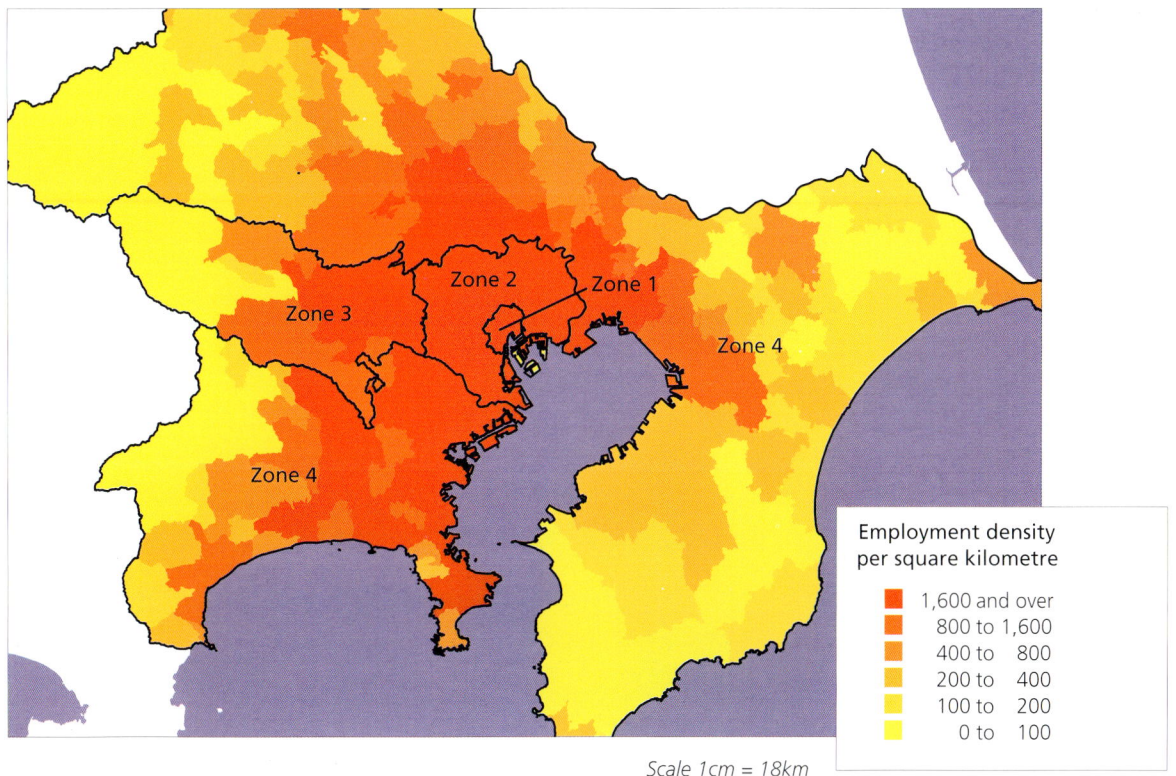

Employment density
per square kilometre

- 1,600 and over
- 800 to 1,600
- 400 to 800
- 200 to 400
- 100 to 200
- 0 to 100

Scale 1cm = 18km

London Research Centre **99**

Population, employment and car ownership

Map 8
Employment density - metropolitan area (Zones 1 & 2)

London

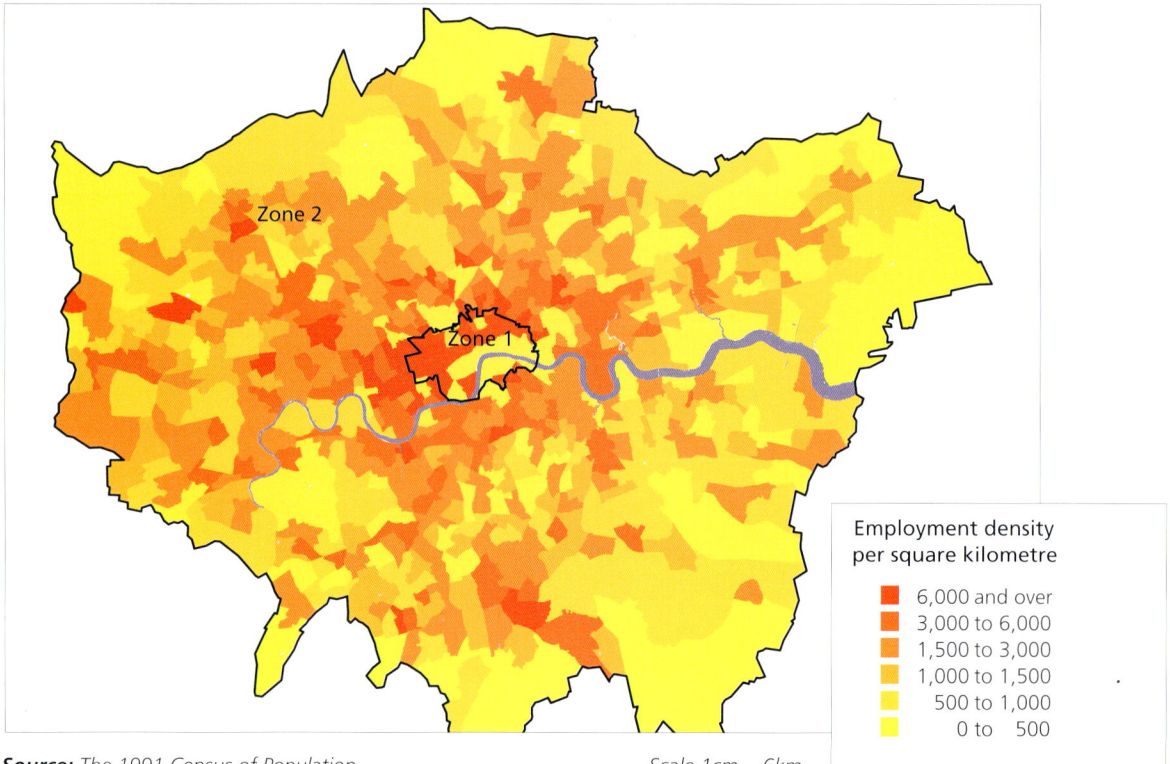

Source: *The 1991 Census of Population*

Scale 1cm = 6km

Employment density
per square kilometre

- 6,000 and over
- 3,000 to 6,000
- 1,500 to 3,000
- 1,000 to 1,500
- 500 to 1,000
- 0 to 500

New York

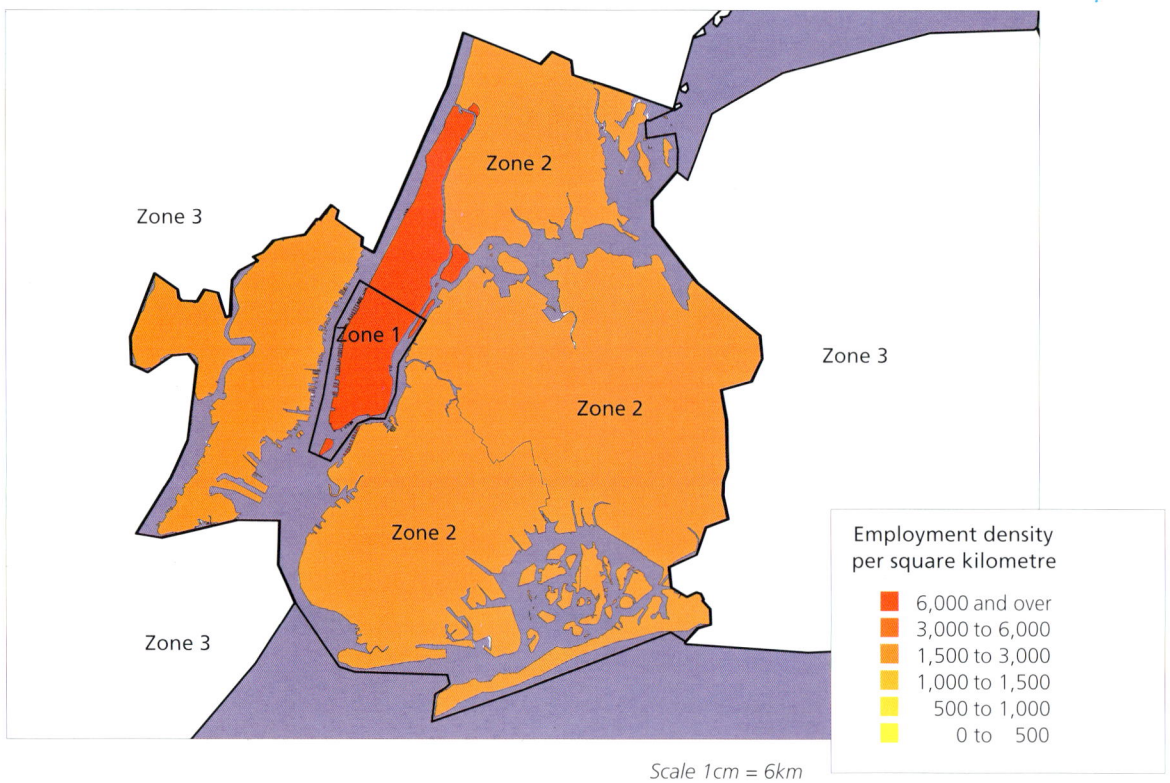

Scale 1cm = 6km

Employment density
per square kilometre

- 6,000 and over
- 3,000 to 6,000
- 1,500 to 3,000
- 1,000 to 1,500
- 500 to 1,000
- 0 to 500

Map 8
Employment density - metropolitan area (Zones 1 & 2)

Paris

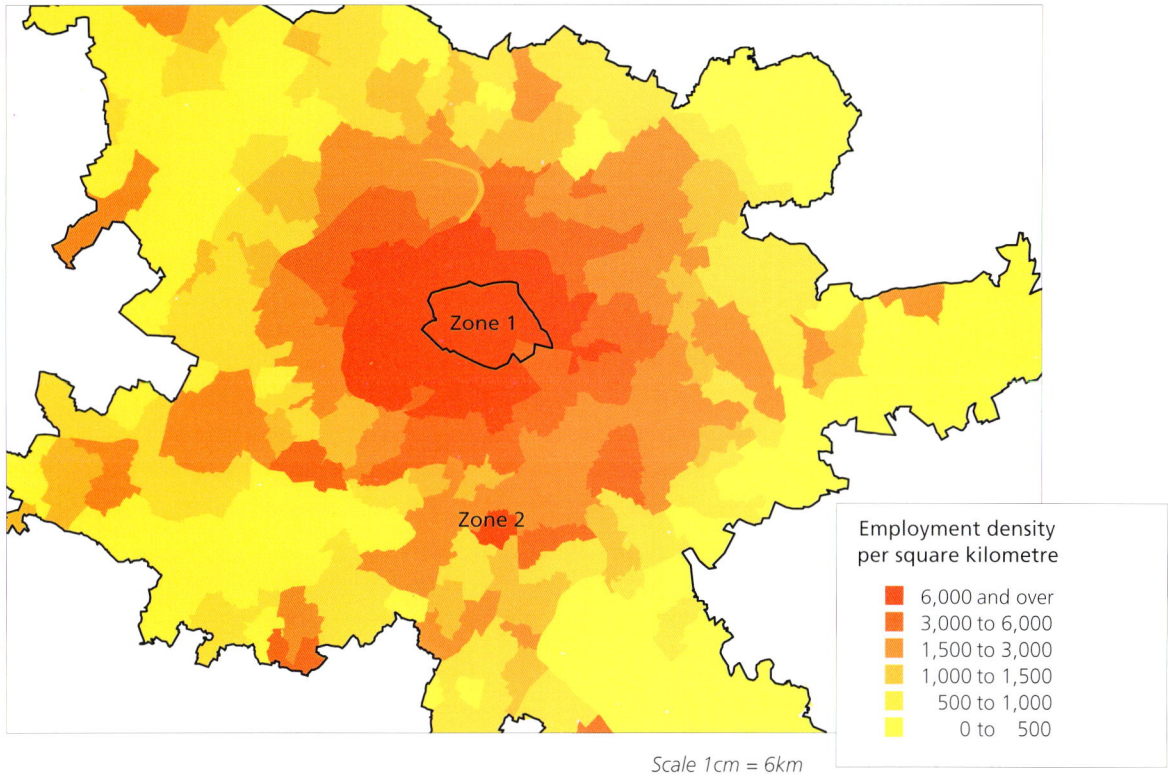

Employment density
per square kilometre

- 6,000 and over
- 3,000 to 6,000
- 1,500 to 3,000
- 1,000 to 1,500
- 500 to 1,000
- 0 to 500

Scale 1cm = 6km

Tokyo

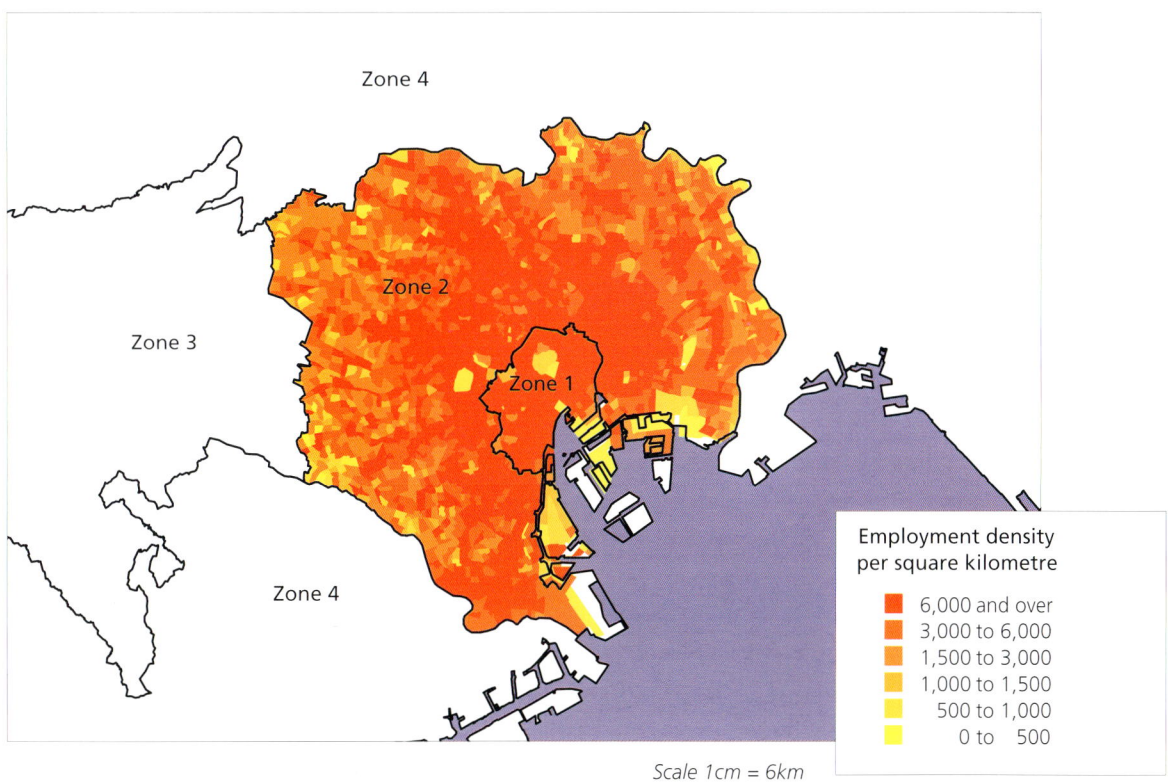

Employment density
per square kilometre

- 6,000 and over
- 3,000 to 6,000
- 1,500 to 3,000
- 1,000 to 1,500
- 500 to 1,000
- 0 to 500

Scale 1cm = 6km

Population, employment and car ownership

Table 9a [28]
Household car-ownership in vehicles/household and vehicles/person 1950-94 (Zone 1)

	London		New York		Paris		Tokyo	
	vehicles per household	vehicles per person	vehicles per household	vehicles per person	vehicles per household	vehicles per person	vehicles per household	vehicles per person
1950	n/a	n/a	n/a	n/a	n/a	n/a	n/a	n/a
1960	n/a	n/a	n/a	n/a	n/a	n/a	n/a	n/a
1970	n/a	n/a	n/a	n/a	0.32 [29]	0.13 [30]	n/a	n/a
1980	0.41	0.15	0.19	0.10	0.47 [31]	0.25 [32]	n/a	n/a
1990	0.54	0.27	0.22	0.12	0.49	0.26	n/a	n/a
1994	n/a	n/a	0.23	0.12	n/a	n/a	n/a	n/a

28 **London**   The London data originates from the Greater London Transportation Survey for 1971 and from the census of population for 1981 and 1991.

For 1971, the data comes in three categories: no car, 1 car, 2 cars and 2+ cars. The vehicle per household figure has been calculated using an arithmetic mean and by assigning the value of 2.5 for the category "2+ cars". For 1981 & 1991 the car-ownership data comes in four categories: no car, 1 car, 2 cars and 3+ cars. The vehicle per household figure has been calculated using an arithmetic mean and by assigning the value of 3 for the category "3+ cars".

New York   Data for Zones 1 & 2 is available only in aggregate format for the years 1950, 1960 and 1970.

The category "car ownership" includes light duty trucks and vans (which is a significant segment of passenger vehicles in the New York region).

Historical data for the New York region has been compiled from the census, the New York Metropolitan Transportation Council and the Regional Plan Association.

Paris   The Paris data originates from the census of population; thus the Paris data is for 1968, 1982 and 1990.

All the Paris data come in three categories: no car, 1 car, 2 cars and 2+ cars. The vehicle per household figure has been calculated using an arithmetic mean and by assigning the value of 2.5 for the category "2+ cars".

Tokyo   The Tokyo figures (provided by the Metropolitan Police Department) are a division of the number of registered cars as measured by the number of households. There will be an overestimate due to the fact that some car owning households include public service vehicles or company cars. The household car-ownership figures for Tokyo's Zone 1 are misleading because many company cars are registered at their company's headquarters in central Tokyo and have thus been omitted from table 9a; these figures are:

Year	Vehicles per household	Vehicles per person
1980	0.70	0.28
1990	1.07	0.32
1995	1.09	0.49

29 The figure is for 1968.

30 The figure is for 1968.

31 The figure is for 1982.

32 The figure is for 1982.

without owning a car. Yet, car ownership is still rising in Zone 2. In London, in the 1980s, nearly the entire growth in car use can be attributed to a growth in driving by women. Research in London has shown and continues to show that women are increasingly finding it unsafe to use public transport and are resorting to private car use [33]. Furthermore, in London there has been an increasing participation by women in the labour force: whilst women were 38% of Greater London's labour force in 1971, by 1996 they were 44% (1,577,000 economically active women).

The rate of car ownership in Tokyo is low compared to that of other cities. To purchase a car in Japan, the prospective owner must prove that he or she has an off-street parking space. But condominia do not always have attached parking spaces, and costs to rent spaces are exorbitant owing to high land prices, especially in Zones 1 & 2. On the other hand, the public transport systems are dense and efficient in the metropolitan area, making owning a car with all its accompanying high expenses for parking, fuel and safety inspection less attractive or necessary.

When car ownership data, arrayed geographically, as in Map 9, are compared to metro lines, shown in Map 10, it can be seen there is a high correlation between distance from metro lines and car ownership.

Table 9b [34]
Household car-ownership in vehicles/household and vehicles/person 1950-94 (Zone 2)

	London		New York		Paris		Tokyo	
	vehicles per household	vehicles per person	vehicles per household	vehicles per person	vehicles per household	vehicles per person	vehicles per household	vehicles per person
1950	n/a	n/a	0.50	0.15	n/a	n/a	n/a	n/a
1960	n/a	n/a	0.52	0.18	n/a	n/a	n/a	n/a
1970	0.55	0.19	0.56	0.20	0.48 [35]	0.16 [36]	n/a	n/a
1980	0.73	0.28	0.52	0.22	0.81 [37]	0.32 [38]	0.39	0.15
1990	0.83	0.34	0.63	0.24	0.91	0.36	0.47	0.19
1994	n/a	n/a	0.63	0.24	n/a	n/a	0.47	0.21

33 Research carried out by the Greater London Council in 1983 showed that only 17% of women in Zones 1 & 2 felt safe in taking the metro ("Underground") at night and only 15% felt safe whilst walking at night. (Greater London Council: Women's Committee, 1985 C, pp. 3 & 4). Recent research carried out by the London Research Centre has found that the issue of fear still predominates amongst women (London Research Centre, 1998).

34 For definitions, see table 9a.

London   The London data for 1971 comes from the Greater London Transportation Survey of 1971 and is an aggregation of Zones 1 & 2.

New York   The New York data for 1971 is an aggregation of Zones 1 & 2.

Tokyo   The figures for 1995, are: 0.50 vehicles per household and 0.22 vehicles per person.

35 The figure is for 1968.

36 The figure is for 1968.

37 The figure is for 1982.

38 The figure is for 1982.

Population, employment and car ownership

Map 9
Levels of car ownership - the entire region (Zones 1,2,3&4)

London

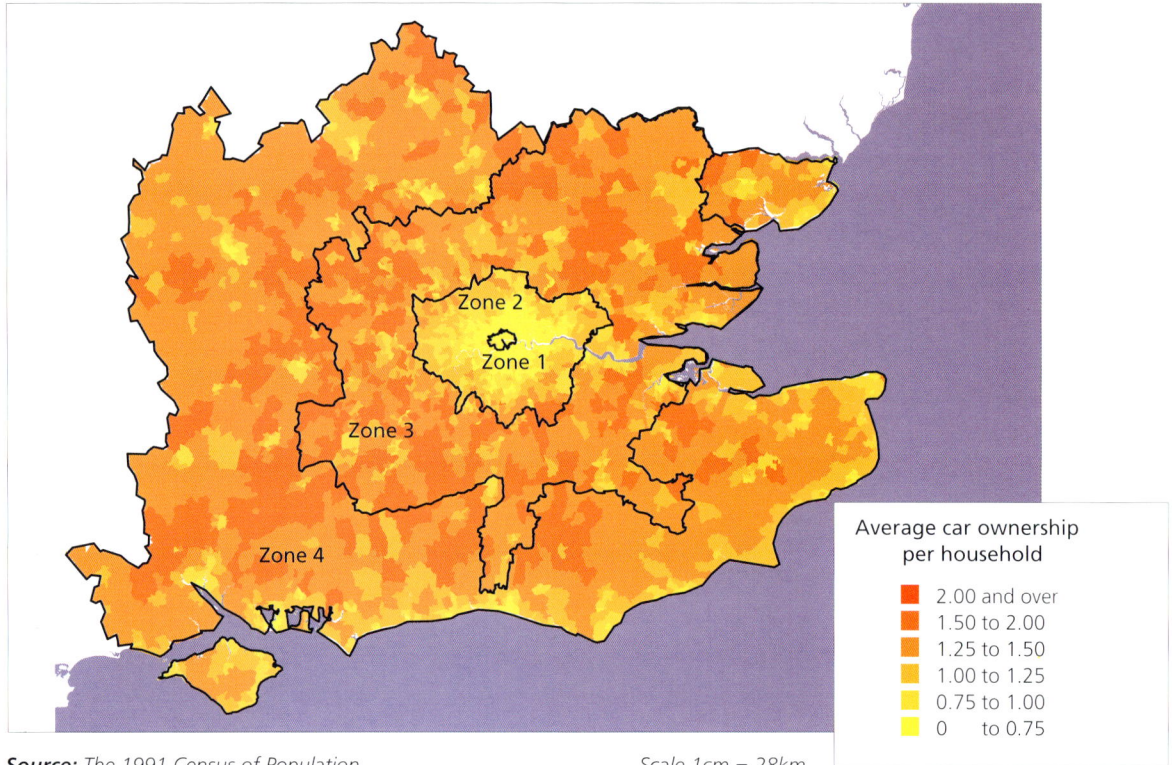

Source: *The 1991 Census of Population*   *Scale 1cm = 28km*

Average car ownership
per household

- 2.00 and over
- 1.50 to 2.00
- 1.25 to 1.50
- 1.00 to 1.25
- 0.75 to 1.00
- 0   to 0.75

New York

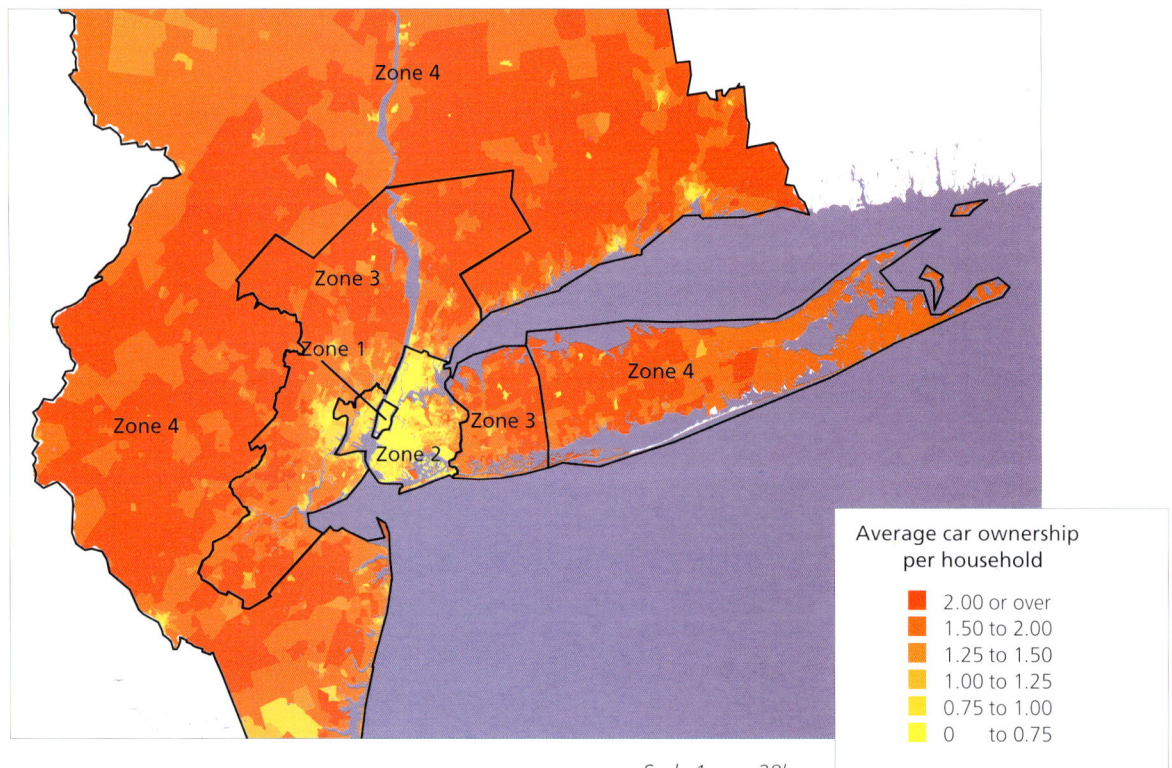

Scale 1cm = 28km

Average car ownership
per household

- 2.00 or over
- 1.50 to 2.00
- 1.25 to 1.50
- 1.00 to 1.25
- 0.75 to 1.00
- 0   to 0.75

Map 9
Levels of car ownership - the entire region (Zones 1,2,3&4)

Paris

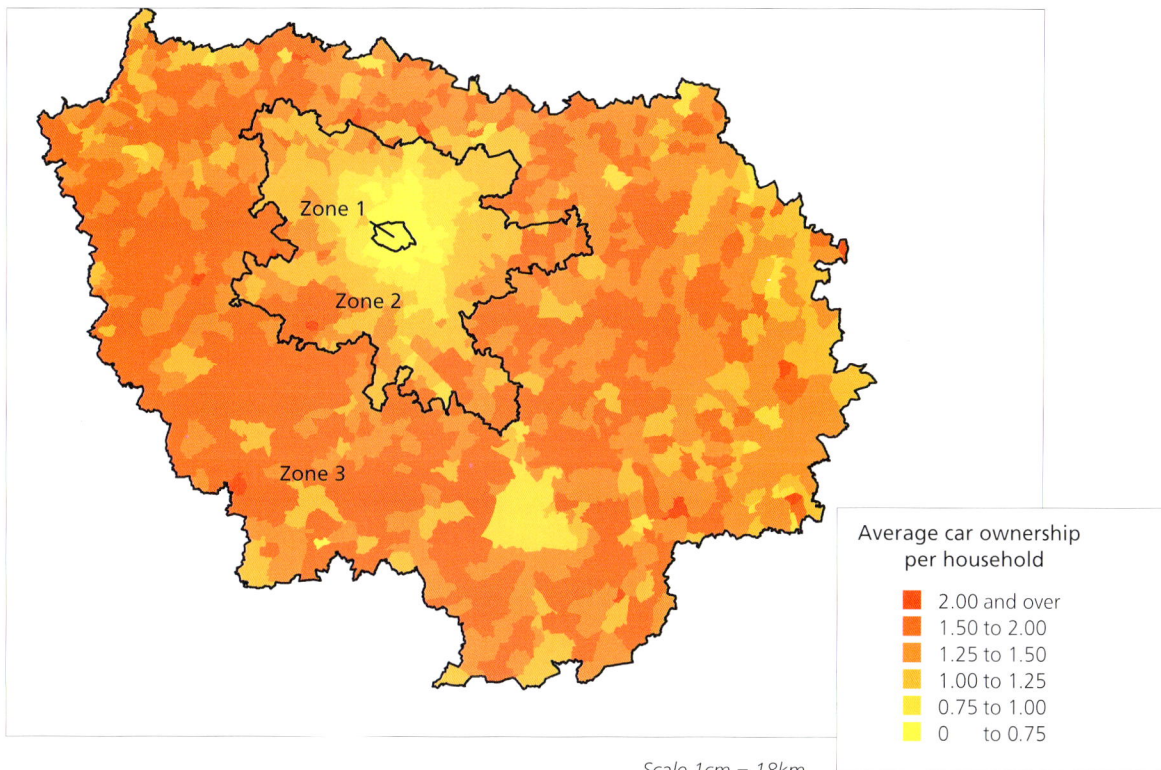

Average car ownership
per household

- 2.00 and over
- 1.50 to 2.00
- 1.25 to 1.50
- 1.00 to 1.25
- 0.75 to 1.00
- 0 to 0.75

Scale 1cm = 18km

Tokyo

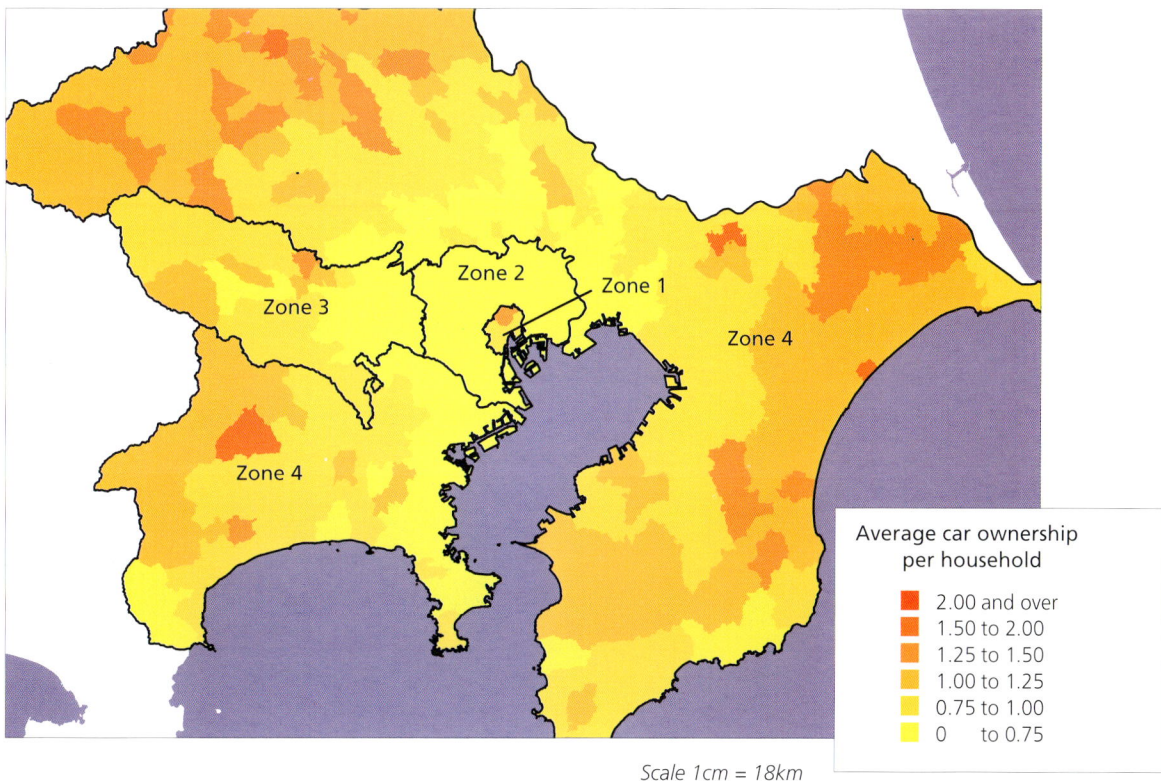

Average car ownership
per household

- 2.00 and over
- 1.50 to 2.00
- 1.25 to 1.50
- 1.00 to 1.25
- 0.75 to 1.00
- 0 to 0.75

Scale 1cm = 18km

Table 9c [39]

Household car-ownership in vehicles/household and vehicles/person 1950-94 (Zone 3)

	London		New York		Paris		Tokyo	
	vehicles per household	vehicles per person	vehicles per household	vehicles per person	vehicles per household	vehicles per person	vehicles per household	vehicles per person
1950	n/a	n/a	1.07	0.30	n/a	n/a	n/a	n/a
1960	n/a	n/a	1.24	0.36	n/a	n/a	n/a	n/a
1970	n/a	n/a	1.49	0.45	0.45 [40]	0.17 [41]	n/a	n/a
1980	1.04	0.37	1.62	0.55	1.13 [42]	0.37 [43]	0.43	0.14
1990	1.22	0.48	1.65	0.58	1.33	0.45	0.74	0.25
1994	n/a	n/a	1.65	0.57	n/a	n/a	0.72	0.28

Table 9d [44]

Household car-ownership in vehicles/household and vehicles/person 1950-94 (Zone 4)

	London		New York		Paris		Tokyo	
	vehicles per household	vehicles per person	vehicles per household	vehicles per person	vehicles per household	vehicles per person	vehicles per household	vehicles per person
1950	n/a	n/a	1.12	0.31	-	-	0.01	0.00
1960	n/a	n/a	1.30	0.37	-	-	0.04	0.01
1970	0.88 [45]	n/a	1.54	0.46	-	-	0.27	0.07
1980	0.89	0.33	1.62	0.54	-	-	0.68	0.16
1990	1.08	0.44	1.83	0.65	-	-	0.96	0.39
1994	n/a	n/a	1.86	0.68	-	-	1.05	0.37

39   For definitions, see Table 9a.

   Tokyo   The figures for 1995 are: 0.77 vehicles per household and 0.30 vehicles per person.

40   The figure is for 1968.

41   The figure is for 1968.

42   The figure is for 1982.

43   The figure is for 1982.

44   For definitions, see table 9a.

   Tokyo   The figures for 1995, are: 1.02 vehicles per household and 0.34 vehicles per person.

45   The figure is for 1972 and relates to Zones 3 & 4 combined.

Car ownership grew significantly in Zones 3 & 4 over the period from 1950 to the mid-1990s in all four cities, particularly for Tokyo where it started from nearly zero. In New York's Zone 3, car ownership increased from 1 car per household in 1950 to nearly 1.7 per household in 1994 (or 6 cars for every 10 people) and is the highest of the four cities. However, whilst New York's car ownership levels seem to have stabilised, there is still strong growth in the other cities, especially in Tokyo. In Tokyo's Zone 3, there was a 67% increase in household car-ownership between 1980 and 1994.

New York has the highest level of car ownership at 1.86 cars per household in Zone 4 and also the lowest residential density. In New York, of the households that are car owning, the majority own two or more vehicles. The reason for such high car ownership levels in New York is that most trips made within the counties making up Zones 3 & 4 remain within the county. Because few destinations in these areas can be reached on foot, and public transport services are infrequent in most areas (due to low densities and low passenger volumes), most people, especially two-income households, purchase a second car as soon as they can afford to, and frequently have more than two cars. Although the cost of maintaining a car in Zone 3 in New York is considerably less than in Zone 2, the investment required for each car, and the levelling off of the increase in women in the work-force, appears to have slowed the rate of growth in car ownership in recent years in Zone 3.

The further one moves from the centre in all cities the more car ownership grows (with the exception of London's Zone 4). Public transport serves badly suburb to suburb movements in both Paris and London (and in Zone 3 such services are virtually non existent). The pattern of increasing car ownership is not matched in London's Zone 4 which has a significantly lower car ownership level than Zone 3. This is due to the fact that Zone 4 has a more aged population (see map 6) and contains a number of historic self-contained villages and towns with high population densities and dense bus networks.

Because of low development densities and very dispersed destinations over a large area in New York's Zone 4, car use is essential for mobility. In the south-east of England car ownership is also rising but is far from reaching the levels of New York. Tokyo has the highest rate of increase in car ownership, but has started from a very low base, since there were very few cars in the 1950s. The level of car ownership in Tokyo's Zone 4 is still low compared with the other cities. Although public transport availability in Tokyo is much higher than in the other cities' Zone 4, car ownership is still growing. It must be remembered that, also in Tokyo, public transport services in Zones 3 & 4 are relatively less dense and convenient compared to the central area and it is easier to obtain a required parking space.

A car-dependent shopping centre in the New York region

Transport structure

Content

4   Transport Structure

The four world cities have well developed transport systems including metro, regional railways, buses and motorways. Tokyo is the city that most heavily uses its public transport system. New York (outside New York City) is, by contrast, car dominated.

With an understanding of the socio-demographic structure of the four cities, analysed in the previous chapter, it is possible to move to a description of the physical characteristics and performance of the transport system. This chapter also looks at the quality of service that can be expected in each city on the public transport system (metro and regional railways), concentrating on reliability, punctuality, and overcrowding. For roads a comparison is made of traffic accidents, looking at trends over the past fifteen years.

All four cities have very high levels of commuting to the city centre. The volumes of public transport passengers and car users are analysed as well as the mobility within the metropolitan area. Furthermore, origin-destination matrices are created to analyse movements between the study's four Zones.

The four metropolises need also to be well connected internationally to maintain their world city role and act as foci for international tourism and business. An investigation is made of how well the individual metropolises are connected to the rest of the world by looking both at airport accessibility (getting to and from the airport) and the number of international destinations served.

4.1   The overall structure of public transport and roads

All four cities have the following common public transport modes:

metro	("Underground" in London and "Subway" in New York) which is an urban rail system, with a frequent schedule, most often running underground
regional rail	a mostly over-ground heavy rail system serving suburban areas to/from the centre with frequencies much lower than the metro
bus	an urban bus system that covers the entire city

Aside from metro, regional rail and bus, each city has other forms of transport which contribute in differing amounts to the cities' overall transport infrastructure. These other forms of public transport are:

London	• an automated light railway, the Docklands Light Railway in inner east London (Zone 2)
	• express commuter coaches
New York	• express commuter coaches (known in New York as "express buses")
	• six ferry services

Paris   The most distinctive feature of Paris' transport system is the 4 lines of express regional rail trains, the Réseau Express Régional, which cross the city centre offering rapid through movement and connections to the metro system. Furthermore, Paris has:

- an automated metro: the OrlyVAL, connecting Orly airport with Antony station on the Réseau Express Régional B line (Zone 2)

- a tram line: from St. Denis to Bobigny and a line south-west of La Défense (both in Zone 2)

- a rack railway: at Montmartre (Zone 1)

- a segregated bus route: a 13 kilometre route from Créteil to Rungis (Zone 2)

Tokyo   Has recently invested in monorails and automated metro lines which complement an existing tram line (in Zone 2). These are:

- Five "new transit" rail lines. The "new transit systems" are automated electrically-powered light-rail trains. They run on elevated guide-ways with pneumatic tyres

  - the Tokyo Waterfront New Transit, an elevated automated metro line from Shinbashi (Zone 1) to Ariake (Zone 2)

  - the Ina line in Saitama prefecture (Zone 4)

  - the Seibu - Yamaguchi line in Saitama prefecture (Zone 4)

  - the Yukarigaoka line in Chiba prefecture (Zone 4)

  - the Kanagawa seaside line in Kanagawa prefecture (Zone 4). This is an automated rail line

- Three monorail lines:

  - the Tokyo monorail from Hamamatsucho (Zone 1) to Haneda airport (Zone 2)

  - the Chiba Urban Monorail from Chiba Minato to Senjodai (Zone 4)

  - the Shonan monorail from Ofuna to Shonan-Enoshima in Kanagawa prefecture (Zone 4)

- Tram:
  - 1 line in Zone 2

All of the above are excluded from the rail, metro and bus statistics presented further on, with the exception of London's Docklands Light Railway and Paris' Réseau Express Régional and Montmartre rack railway, which are incorporated within each cities' metro statistics.

Also, all the four cities have distinct liveried taxis which can be hailed on street, and hire cars which can be booked by phone.

4.1.1   London

London's public transport system is composed of an extensive, largely radial, regional rail network; the "Underground" (metro); and buses which operate at high frequency and density in Zones 1 & 2 and within towns and cities in Zones 3 & 4. London has also a motorway system of a radial nature and an orbital motorway (the M25) which coincides closely with the outer boundary of Zone 2.

4.1.1.1 London - metro

London's metro system (the "Underground") is operated by London Transport and is composed of deep bore

tunnels and cut and cover lines. London has 11 metro lines with a total of 356 route kilometres. All, except two metro lines, operate entirely within Zones 1 & 2. Most of the network was built before the Second World War, and some lines in the late 19th century. The system now requires heavy maintenance and much of the signalling and rolling stock needs renovation.

London's metro network was initially built in response to the impact of the developing regional rail network. By the middle of the 19th century there was a constant increase in road traffic in central London, much of it generated by the new surface railways. One of the features of this problem was the lack of direct rail services to the City (Britain's financial capital), with most of the regional rail terminals located around the edge of central London. The idea of linking the main line stations and the City with an underground railway was identified as one solution to the problem.

Over-ground extensions of the metro lines into the suburbs were subsequently seen as being more profitable than expensive construction work in the city so the metro lines were gradually extended over-ground and outwards from central London, initially to emerging commuter suburbs within inner London and then to outer London. Also, the new Central line showed the traffic potential of serving the theatre and shopping areas of the west end and contributed to a broadening of the initial prime concern of providing access to the city centre. The development of deep-level tunnelling was a further

Crowds entering the metro at Victoria Station in central London

Map 10
Rail and metro lines - London - the entire region (Zones 1,2,3&4)

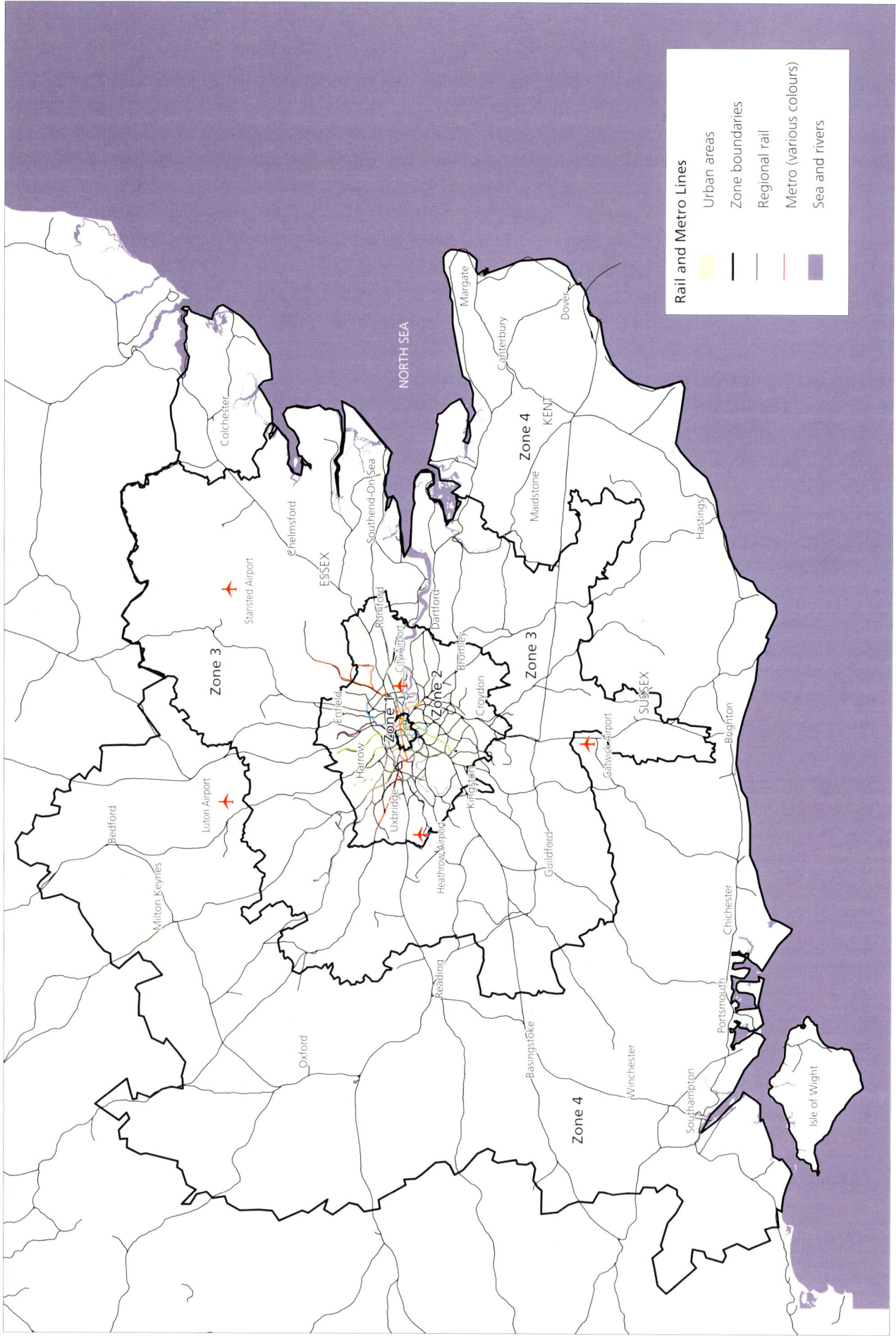

Rail and Metro Lines

	Urban areas
	Zone boundaries
	Regional rail
	Metro (various colours)
	Sea and rivers

Scale 1cm = 14km

NORTH SEA

Margate
Canterbury
Dover
KENT
Zone 4
Maidstone
Hastings

Colchester
Chelmsford
ESSEX
Southend-On-Sea
Stansted Airport
Zone 3
Romford
Dartford
City Airport
Bromley
Croydon
Zone 2
Zone 1
Enfield
Harrow
Uxbridge
Kingston
Heathrow Airport
Zone 3
Gatwick Airport
SUSSEX
Brighton

Bedford
Luton Airport
Milton Keynes
Oxford
Reading
Guildford
Basingstoke
Winchester
Zone 4
Southampton
Portsmouth
Chichester
Isle of Wight

© Bartholomew's 1997; generated from Bartholomew's digital database: MM-1197-72

Map 10
Rail and metro lines - New York - the entire region (Zones 1,2,3 & 4)

Scale 1cm = 14km

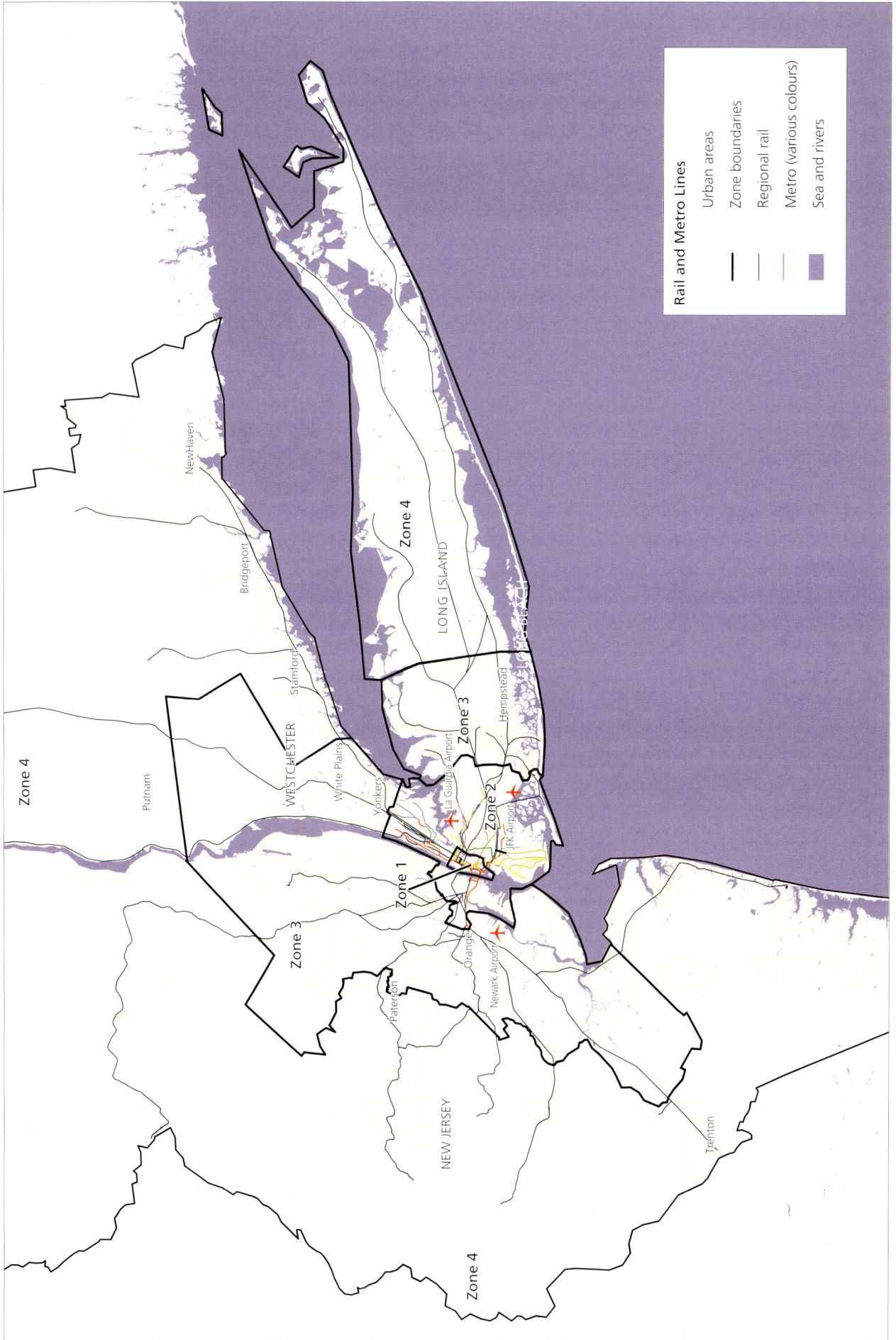

Rail and Metro Lines

Urban areas

Zone boundaries

Regional rail

Metro (various colours)

Sea and rivers

New Haven

Bridgeport

Stamford

Zone 4

LONG ISLAND

Zone 4

Putnam

WESTCHESTER

White Plains

Yonkers

La Guardia Airport

Zone 3

Hempstead

Zone 3

Zone 2

JFK Airport

Zone 1

Paterson

Orange

Newark Airport

NEW JERSEY

Zone 4

Trenton

Map 10
Rail and metro lines - Paris - the entire region (Zones 1,2,3 & 4)

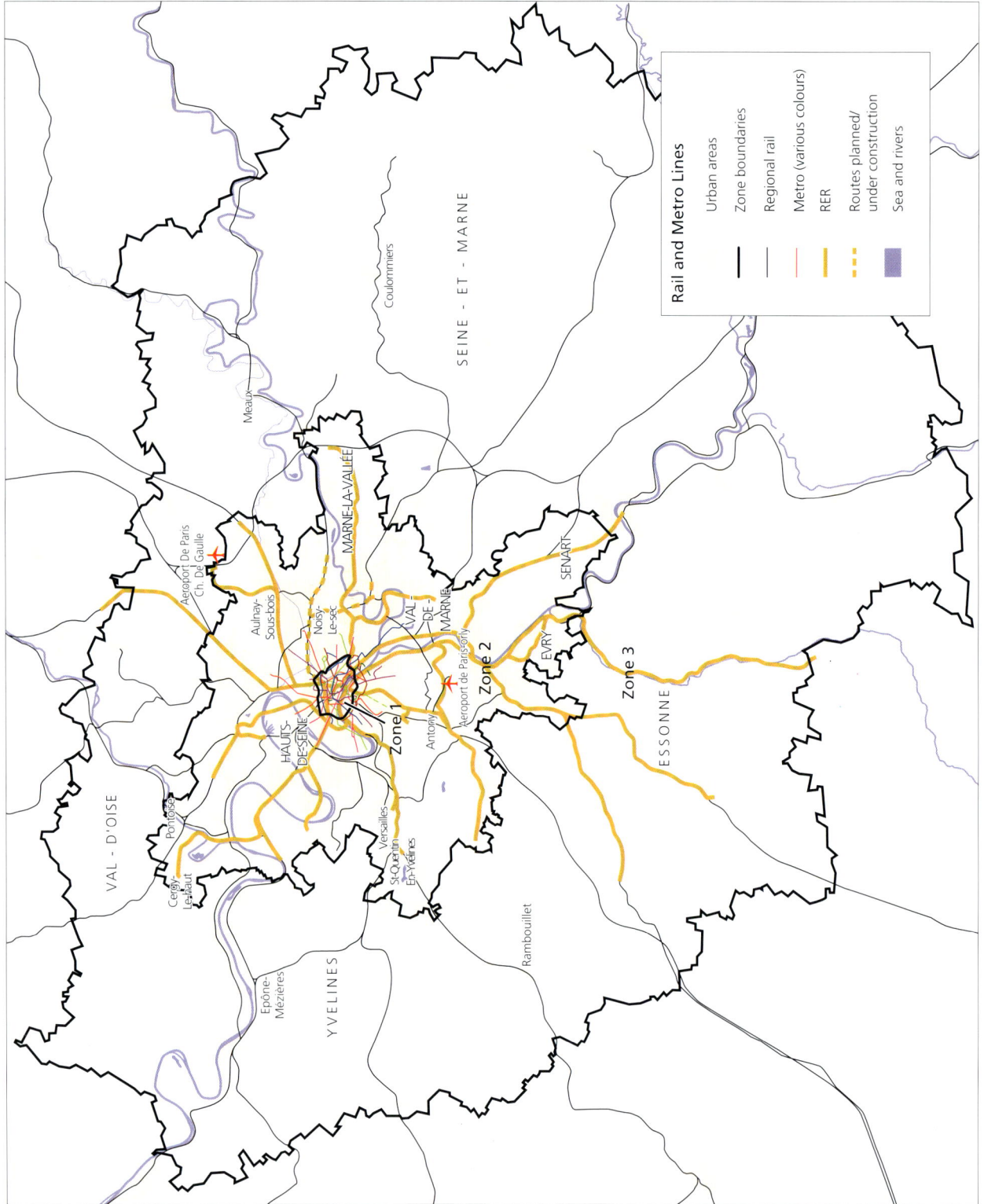

Rail and Metro Lines

Urban areas

Zone boundaries

Regional rail

Metro (various colours)

RER

Routes planned/
under construction

Sea and rivers

Scale 1cm = 8km

VAL - D'OISE

Pontoise

Cergy-
Le-Haut

Aéroport De Paris
Ch. De Gaulle

Aulnay-
Sous-bois

Noisy-
Le-sec

MARNE-LA-VALLÉE

SEINE - ET - MARNE

Coulommiers

Meaux

HAUTS-
DE-SEINE

Zone 1

VAL - DE -
MARNE

Antony

Aéroport de Paris Orly

Zone 2

EVRY

SENART

Zone 3

ESSONNE

Versailles

St-Quentin
En-Yvelines

YVELINES

Epône-
Mézières

Rambouillet

Map 10
Rail and metro lines - Tokyo - the entire region (Zones 1, 2, 3 & 4)

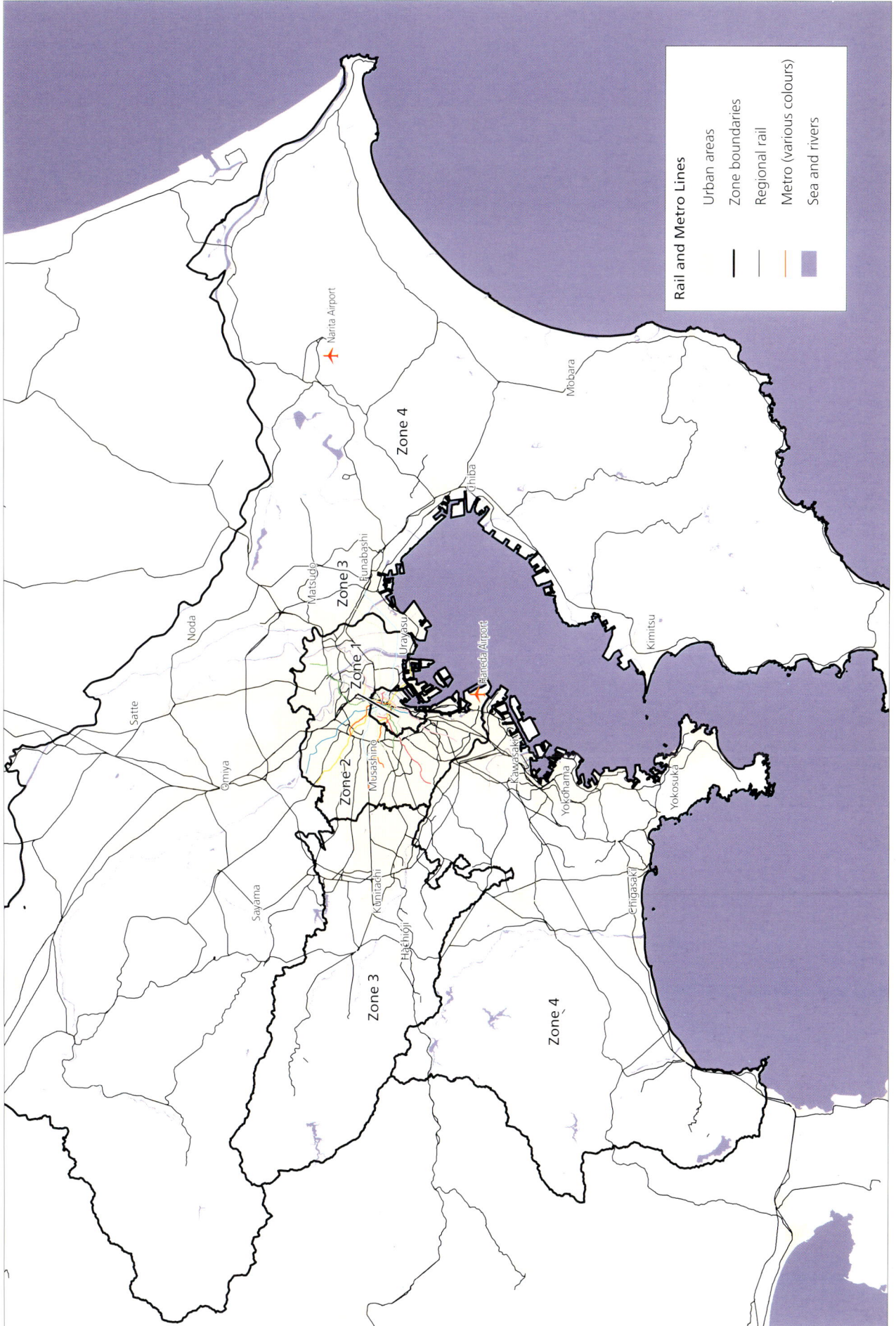

Rail and Metro Lines

Urban areas
Zone boundaries
Regional rail
Metro (various colours)
Sea and rivers

Scale 1cm = 9.5km

Narita Airport

Haneda Airport

Zone 1
Zone 2
Zone 3
Zone 4

Matsugo
Funabashi
Urayasu
Noda
Satte
Ōmiya
Musashino
Sayama
Kunitachi
Hachiōji
Chiba
Mobara
Kimitsu
Kawasaki
Yokohama
Yokosuka
Chigasaki

Map 11
Rail and Metro lines - London - the metropolitan area (Zones 1&2)

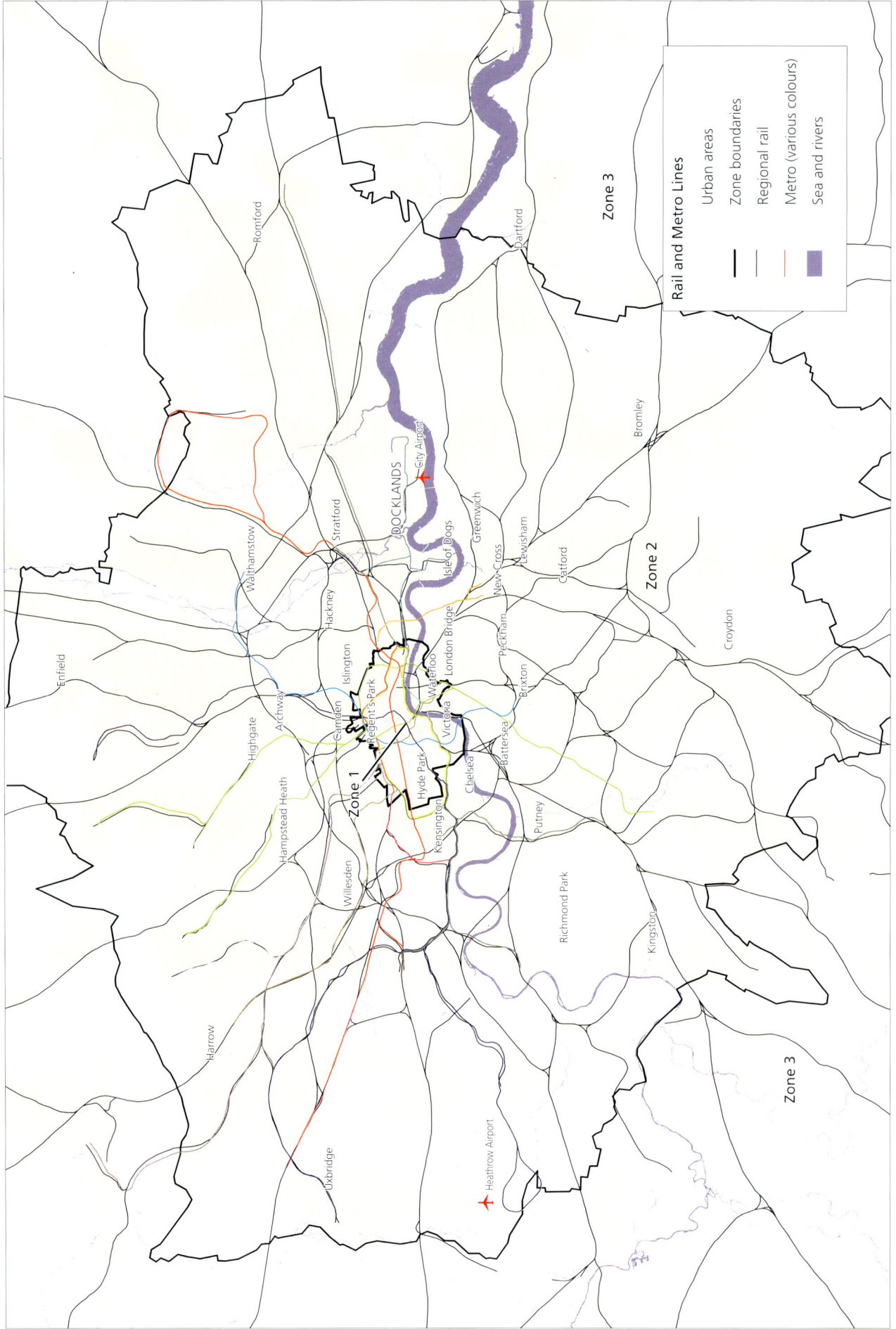

Scale 1cm = 3km

Rail and Metro Lines

	Urban areas
	Zone boundaries
	Regional rail
	Metro (various colours)
	Sea and rivers

Zone 3

Zone 2

Zone 3

Zone 1

Romford
Dartford
Walthamstow
Stratford
DOCKLANDS
City Airport
Isle of Dogs
Greenwich
New Cross
Lewisham
Catford
Bromley
Croydon
Enfield
Hackney
Archway
Islington
Camden
Regent's Park
Waterloo
London Bridge
Peckham
Brixton
Highgate
Hyde Park
Victoria
Battersea
Chelsea
Putney
Hampstead Heath
Kensington
Richmond Park
Kingston
Willesden
Harrow
Uxbridge
Heathrow Airport

© Bartholomew's 1997, generated from Bartholomew's digital database: MM-1197-72

Map 11
Rail and Metro lines - New York - the metropolitan area (Zones 1 & 2)

Scale 1cm = 3km

Rail and Metro Lines

Urban areas
Zone boundaries
Regional rail
Metro (various colours)
Sea and rivers

Zone 3

NASSAU

Zone 2

New Rochelle

Mount Vernon

Pelham Bay

Flushing

La Guardia Airport

JFK Airport

Jamaica

Bronx Zoo

BRONX

Harlem River

Astoria

QUEENS

Riverdale

MANHATTAN

Harlem

Central Park

EAST RIVER

Williamsburg

Brooklyn Downtown

BROOKLYN

Hudson River

Midtown

Greenwich Village

Wall Street

Brooklyn Heights

Cobble Hill

Verrazano Bridge

Hoboken

Jersey City

Zone 1

Ferry Terminal

STATEN ISLAND

Zone 3

Paterson

Zone 3

Newark

Newark Airport

Map 11
Rail and Metro lines - Paris - the metropolitan area (Zones 1&2)

Scale 1cm = 1.3km

Rail and Metro Lines

Urban areas	
Zone boundaries	
Regional rail	
Metro (various colours)	
RER	
Routes planned/ under construction	
Sea and rivers	

Aulnay-sous-Bois

ROSNY-SOUS-BOIS

CHAMPIGNY

LE BOURGET

BOBIGNY

BAGNOLET

Bois de Vincennes

ST.DENIS

Gare de l'Est

Gare du Nord

St-Michel Notre-Dame

Gare de Lyon

IVRY-SUR-SEINE

Gare St-Lazare

Gare Montparnasse

ASNIERES

LA DEFENSE

Bois de Boulogne

ARGENTEUIL

NANTERRE

VELIZY-VILLACOUBLAY

Map 11
Rail and Metro lines - Tokyo - the metropolitan area (Zones 1&2)

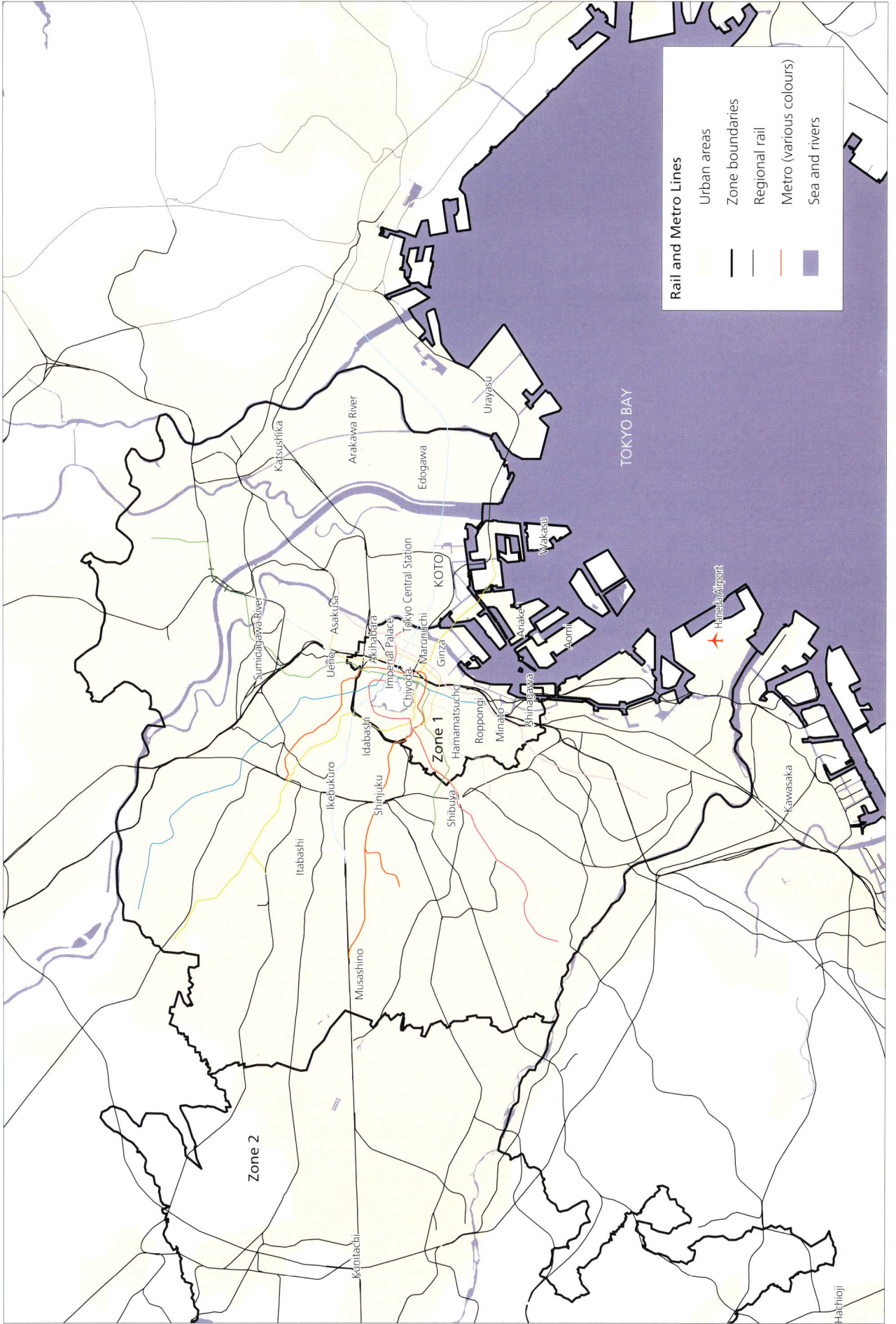

Scale 1cm = 3km

Rail and Metro Lines

Urban areas
Zone boundaries
Regional rail
Metro (various colours)
Sea and rivers

TOKYO BAY

Urayasu

Arakawa River

Katsushika

Edogawa

Wakasu

KOTO

Haneda Airport

Sumidagawa River

Ueno
Asakusa
Akihabara
Imperial Palace
Tokyo Central Station
Marunuchi
Chiyoda
Ginza
Ariake
Aomi

Idabashi
Hamamatsucho
Minato
Roppongi
Shinagawa

Zone 1

Ikebukuro

Shinjuku

Shibuya

Kawasaka

Itabashi

Musashino

Zone 2

Kunitachi

Hachioji

impetus for development of the network at the end of the 19th century.

When plans were put forward for the reconstruction of London, after the damage of heavy bombardment in the Second World War, they included a number of proposals for new "Underground" railways and two of the current metro lines had their origins in the recommendations of the London Plan Working Party Report of 1949. One became the Victoria line for which London Transport sought approval on the basis of social benefits that would accrue from relieving traffic congestion on the roads and overcrowding on the existing lines. The Victoria line opened in stages between 1968 and 1971. The other new metro line was the Jubilee which was opened in 1979. Its main benefit was the relief of the most heavily used section of the Underground network in central London, and there was the possibility of further extension east to the London Docklands area. The Jubilee line's extension to Docklands, which is currently being constructed and planned for completion in 1999, arose out of a need for public transport improvement to support major redevelopment in the Docklands.

Given the age of London's metro system, considerable investment is needed in renewals and modernisation even to maintain current levels of service. As well as tackling this problem London Transport has been gradually increasing the capacity and safety of the system through rolling stock renewal, signalling improvements, frequency enhancements and the refurbishment of stations.

The metro system carries about 2.5 million journeys on an average weekday and about 80% of these journeys involve travel within, or to and from, the central area of London.

4.1.1.2 London - regional rail

The first railways into London were built around 1840. The initial emphasis of the rail companies was to connect the major towns and cities. The shape and size of the rail network in the 19th century was largely determined by the forces of enterprise and profit rather than social benefit. However in the 1860s the rail companies started to develop lines and services in response to what was a clearly growing demand for suburban rail travel by commuters. The desire to put distance between the home and the workplace was a characteristic feature of Victorian society, and the rail network became a vital element in the development of London with its dense concentration of economic activity in the centre surrounded by a resident population which gradually spread outwards.

One problem to be overcome by the rail companies wanting to serve London was how to gain access to the central area. Among the earliest rail termini were those located at London Bridge and Fenchurch Street. Their proximity to the City led to their being adopted by a number of rail companies. However from 1846 restrictions were imposed and most of the lines terminated at the edge of what is now the central area. This aggravated the problem of traffic congestion on the streets leading to the terminals and this became worse as commuter and off-peak traffic grew. The first metro lines were constructed to overcome this problem.

Today the regional rail network within London is mainly radial in layout and extends throughout the metropolitan region. Generally, services provide for radial journeys to and from central London and there are relatively few opportunities for making cross-region or orbital journeys without passing through the central London termini and then on to the "Underground".

The trunk sections of the network carry a mixture of stopping and express services. The regional rail trains are run by private companies who hold franchises on clusters of routes. Regional rail trains have a higher passenger capacity than the metro system but service frequencies are lower.

London is the main hub of the national inter-city rail system and is also linked directly to the European continent by services operating through the Channel Tunnel.

The 20th century has seen improvements, such as electrification and refinements in signalling and rolling stock, rather than major changes to the basic rail network. To some extent in London the inability of the road network to cope with large volumes of people wanting access to the central area provided some protection to the rail companies from increasing competition from motor cars and buses. In the past decade, there has been growth in use of the London rail network which has led to overcrowding and resulted in a programme of train and platform lengthening, signalling improvements and new rolling stock designs.

The regional rail system brings about 340,000 commuters into central London in the morning peak on an average weekday and there are an additional 260,000 arrivals at the central London terminals through the remainder of the day (1991 figures [46]).

4.1.1.3 London - buses

London Transport bus services currently carry about 3.7 million journeys on an average weekday (far more than the "Underground") with a third of these journeys in Zone 2 and about 20% to and from the central area.

In the early 20th century, buses and tramways provided an increasingly competitive alternative to the metro for moving people within London, although the regional railways continued to be the principal mode for bringing people into the heart of London. In the early part of the 20th century, the acquisition of bus and tram operators by the dominant metro operator meant that the street level systems began to be used as feeders to the underground rather than as competitors.

The number of people using buses, and the number of services provided, grew until ownership of private motor cars came within the financial reach of middle-income households in the early 1950s. By that time, rising incomes and the increasing availability of affordable private motor cars were leading to a decline in the number of people using buses. Also the rising popularity of private cars was creating severe congestion on many parts of the road network leading to delays to bus services.

London's bus network offers the vast majority of Greater London (Zones 1 & 2) residents a service within five minutes walk of their homes or workplaces. However, the heavy volumes of traffic on many sections of the road network result in delays to bus services and consequent unreliable time-keeping. A key strategy has been and continues to be the improvement of service reliability through carefully targeted service improvements - such as reductions in the length of some routes - and by the application of bus priority schemes. At bus stops on a number of routes a real time information system has been installed which informs passengers of the expected arrival times of buses.

Outside Greater London (Zones 3 & 4), bus services were deregulated and are now operated by numerous private bus companies. Only in the larger cities and

---

46   1996 figures indicate that there were 400,000 commuters into central London in the morning peak on an average weekday and an additional 230,000 arrivals through the remainder of the day. However, these figures are not comparable with those of 1991 which were obtained through the London Area Transport Survey.

towns is there a comprehensive bus service. Even then, the evening and Sunday services are infrequent or non-existent.

4.1.1.4 London - other public transport modes

An automated light rail system was built in the 1980s to serve the Docklands area and link it to the main metro system but this was not enough to provide adequate public transport access to the area. The Jubilee line will now serve the Docklands. Currently the Docklands Light Railway is being extended under the river Thames to Lewisham in south-east London. The financing and construction of the extension is being undertaken by the private sector. There are also plans to link the railway to the City airport in the Royal Docks area of Docklands in Zone 2.

Between 20,000 to 25,000 people enter central London by coach each weekday in the morning peak. These are either privately run commuter coaches or tourist coaches. Many of the coach services compete with the regional railways, offering a commuting service at lower fares.

4.1.1.5 London - roads

The south-east of England has a motorway network that emanates radially from London. Metropolitan London is bounded by the M25 motorway within its "green belt" which is roughly in the Zone 2/3 boundary. London's motorways do not penetrate to the city centre but end within Zone 2. London's city centre is completely free of motorways.

Although London's motorway system is not as extensive as the other cities it also has a large network of dual carriage way roads. In Zone 1, London has 11 kilometres of dual carriageway, in Zone 2, 247

kilometres and over 1,100 kilometres in Zones 3 & 4 (Focas & Navarre, 1994, p. 77). Many of the historic towns and villages in Zones 3 & 4 now have by-passes to alleviate through-traffic.

Few people use the car to commute to central London. Since 1980 there has been a slight decline in persons entering Zone 1 by car to about 150,000 persons per weekday (out of a total of 855,000). In Central London, the car is the slowest mode for door-to-door journey times and car speeds have been falling since the 1960s. In Zones 3 & 4 the car is the predominant mode of travel. But even in Zones 1 & 2, 64% of non-walk journeys are undertaken by car.

The main innovation in Greater London has been the designation of "priority" roads ("red routes") where parking restrictions are strictly policed. Locally nearly all the boroughs are adopting traffic calming measures to cut speeds on residential roads.

4.1.2 New York

The New York region has 420 kilometres of "Subway" metro lines and a 1,600 kilometre regional rail network, which is about two-thirds the length of the 3,000 kilometre motorway network. The rail network, which is mostly radial, was built towards the end of the 19th century and the early part of the 20th century mostly by private entrepreneurs.

4.1.2.1 New York - metro

New York has a total of 30 separate metro lines (some of which run on the same or parallel tracks for part of their routes).

Nearly all the New York metro service (underground and elevated lines) is contained within Zones 1 and 2, operated by New York City Transit, a division of the Metropolitan Transportation Authority, which was created in 1968 to co-ordinate public transit in the New York portion of the region. Some distinct features of New York metro are that it has a 24 hour operation and that it offers parallel express and local services, with the express travel times much shorter than metro in other cities (operating more like a regional rail). New York City Transit carried an average of 3,650,000 passengers per weekday in 1995. Ridership appears to be increasing due to a stronger economy and the introduction in 1997 of free bus-subway transfers, for use with an electronic fare card which charges a flat fare regardless of distance and time of day. The fare card also allows discounts for purchasers of 10 or more fares and even greater discounts for regional rail passengers who transfer to the metro.

Beyond Zone 2, the metro systems are far smaller than the New York City Transit. The Port Authority Trans Hudson line carries an average of 207,000 passengers per weekday, who pay a $1.00 flat fare, in two rail tunnels under the Hudson River to two points in Zone 2 in Hudson county; one of the routes extends to Essex county in Zone 3. Essex County also has a 7 kilometre light rail line in the City of Newark, which carries 14,000 passengers daily. The other Zone 3 service is another division of the Metropolitan Transportation Authority, the Staten Island Railway (23 kilometres entirely within Staten Island), which serves as a feeder line to free ferries that go to the southern tip of Zone 1, carrying about 17,000 passengers on weekdays.

4.1.2.2 New York - regional rail

New York's regional rail network is composed of three principal regional systems and one inter-city system, each with its own administrative structure, rolling stock, fares, operating policies, planning and marketing.

Two of the regional rail systems operate under the auspices of the Metropolitan Transportation Authority: Metro-North and the Long Island Rail Road. Metro-North operates two routes from Zone 1 to four counties north of Manhattan, east of the Hudson River, and one route from Zone 1 to the north-east to New Haven, Connecticut. Metro-North had an average of 211,000 passengers per weekday in 1995, a number that has been increasing for several years. Long Island Rail Road operates nine branch lines to four counties east of Manhattan, the furthest extending 193 kilometres to the eastern tip of Long Island. Long Island Rail Road served an average of 261,000 daily passengers in 1995. The third major rail system, and the largest, is New Jersey Transit, which operates 12 rail lines in the region to the west, south-west and north-west of Manhattan.

Amtrak operates inter-city lines between New York and major cities to the south, west, north and north-east. Its most heavily used route, the Northeast Corridor line, is between Washington and Boston and crosses through the New York region.

Shore Line East was created in 1990 by the Connecticut Department of Transportation to subsidise Amtrak to operate a local rail system on Amtrak lines 80 kilometres east of New Haven and 115 kilometres from mid-town Manhattan. It is a two-train, peak period-only service that serves just 2,400 passengers per day.

4.1.2.3 New York - buses

New York has approximately 830 separate bus routes serving the region. Bus use is by far the heaviest in Zones 1 and 2. Outside Zone 2, commuter coaches (called "express buses") are the dominant mode of transit from New Jersey to Zone 1.

Buses are operated primarily by public agencies, although there are a substantial number of private companies that receive federal and state subsidies. The principal bus systems are:

- New York City Transit and New York City Franchised Buses. New York City Transit operates 197 bus routes in Zones 1 & 2, with flat fares of $1.50 and free bus-to-bus and bus-to-metro transfers. In addition, New York City Transit has 30 express routes, used primarily for commuting from distant parts of Zone 2 to Zone 1, at fares of $4.00. Together, these services carried 1,817,000 passengers in 1995. Another 128 commuter routes from Zone 2, carrying about 278,000 passengers, are operated by private bus companies who receive federal subsidies administered by the City of New York.

- New Jersey Transit. This operates local buses at a $1.00 flat fare and express buses to Zone 1. Complementary commuter services are offered by private carriers. Together, they carried 689,000 passengers a day in 1995 on 222 routes from and within Zones 2, 3, and 4. The fact that express bus ridership is four times greater than rail use from New Jersey into Zone 1 indicates the significance of commuter coach services in the regional transport system.

- New York State and Connecticut Systems. In Zone 3, bus services are provided in Westchester County by Bee-Line, which carried 105,000 people a day in 1995 on 50 routes. In Nassau and Suffolk Counties there are 52 routes. The Metropolitan Transportation Authority's Long sland Bus carried 62,000 passengers in 1995 and other Long Island bus lines carried 18,000 passengers a day, considerably fewer than in Westchester though the number of jobs and population is far greater. This is because jobs

and population are somewhat more clustered in Westchester. In Zone 4 counties, private bus services on 174 routes move about 50,000 passengers a day in the remaining counties of New York State and about 40,000 people in Connecticut.

4.1.2.4 New York - other public transport modes

There are six ferry services to Zone 1.

In addition, there are three heliports in Zone 1.

There are approximately 50,000 taxis and radio dispatched vehicles operating in Zones 1 & 2. Except in bad weather, taxis are easy to hail almost anywhere in Manhattan but not in Harlem (north of 96th street), a neighbourhood of predominantly black residents.

4.1.2.5 New York - roads

New York's transport system is dominated by a network of 91,000 kilometres of all types of roads, mostly under county and municipal jurisdiction. Of these roads, approximately 3,000 kilometres are motorways (also called "expressways", "freeways" or "parkways"). However, the 3% of the total roads that are motorways carry 40% of the region's traffic and provide the principal infrastructure for goods' movement, 90% of which is transported in lorries. Motorways are under the jurisdiction of the three state Departments of Transportation and three toll-collecting authorities: the New York State Thruway Authority, the New Jersey Turnpike Authority and the New Jersey Highway Authority. Sixteen major bridges and tunnels are operated by the Port Authority of New York and New Jersey or the Metropolitan Transportation Authority Bridges and Tunnels. Since 1996, nearly all motorways have been designated as part of the National Highway System.

Motorways in New York's Zones 1 & 2 and some of Zone 3 were built largely as public works projects during the 1930s, following an overall plan for roads and transit developed by the Regional Plan Association in 1929. In the 1950s, the region was well-poised to take advantage of the petrol-tax supported Interstate Highway System to expand its motorways in Zones 3 & 4, which now constitute 88% of all motorways. When the region's roads are viewed as a whole, the network appears to have a basically radial pattern, oriented to Zones 1 & 2. There are also several partial orbital routes.

Development has followed motorways, clustering around its entrances and exits, generating a diffused travel pattern that results in nearly two-thirds of all motorways in New York being routinely congested during peak periods. Due to local opposition to new road building, there is little likelihood of significant road expansion. New York intends to use minor reconstruction of bottlenecks and surveillance and response technologies to improve traffic flow and permit modest increases in capacity.

4.1.3 Paris

Paris' public transport system dates well back to the 19th century. Yet much of it is quite new and parts of it incorporate the latest technological advances. This has come about

through three decades of continuous and consistent funding within the region's structure plan framework. The road system has also benefited from this structured approach and most of Paris' motorway network was built after 1965.

4.1.3.1 Paris - metro

A large number of Paris' 15 metro lines have in recent years been extended into Zone 2; otherwise the near entirety of the system lies within Zone 1.

The first metro line opened in 1898, fifteen years after the decision to go ahead, delayed by disagreements between the state, which wanted an underground extension of existing regional railway lines to the centre of Paris, and the Ville de Paris, which wanted an independent narrow gauge network. The state gave way to the Ville de Paris, and between 1900 and 1910, Paris

Paris metro

saw the construction of six lines including an orbital one within Zone 1. By 1939, every Parisian in Zone 1 was less than 400 metres from a metro station. Also by 1939 the decision was taken to extend the metro lines beyond the boundary of the Ville de Paris. The extension of the metro lines to the suburbs started during the Second World War and is still continuing.

4.1.3.2 Paris - regional rail

The first railway line in the region, inaugurated in 1837, linked central Paris to the suburbs. But it was not until 1850 to 1870 that the network of radial lines and a loop line were built.

The urban rail network was largely completed before the end of the 19th century with the construction of a second orbital railway at a radius of about 15 kilometres from the centre and a few suburban extensions to existing lines that followed the spread outwards of the population.

A number of interconnecting local railway and tram lines were built after 1900 but were closed down after the First World War. The network went into a period of decline until the Second World War, even though it was nationalised in 1938. Both the inner and outer orbital railway lines were closed to passenger traffic during this period.

The network saw heavy reconstruction work take place after the Second World War. By the 1970s the network formed part of the new Parisian structure plan, the Schéma Directeur d'Aménagement et d'Urbanisme of 1976. Many lines were taken over for the construction of the Réseau Express Régional which provides rapid transit through the central area. Most Réseau Express Régional lines were built by linking the city centre termini of existing regional rail lines. Some were created through new extensions to reach the new towns and the Charles de Gaulle airport.

From 1980, construction started on the high speed "TGV" (trains à grande vitesse) railway network. Paris became the hub of a network of high-speed trains linking most parts of France and beyond.

4.1.3.3 Paris - buses

The first buses were introduced in Paris before the First World War, but the bus network largely developed in the inter-war period. Bus routes progressively replaced tram routes (when the franchises on the tram routes ran out and were not renewed) as priority was given to cars and the metro system.

The present regional bus network is composed of three separate networks:

- The Paris buses run by the Régie Autonome des Transports Parisiens which operate on up to 60 routes mainly within the Ville de Paris (mostly in Zone 1). Some routes extend further out in the suburbs, mainly where there is an inadequate coverage by the metro, and especially to the suburban riverside communes.

  The average speed of the buses is 12 kilometres per hour despite numerous bus priority schemes including 134 kilometres of bus lanes and a 13 kilometre segregated bus lane.

  The average frequency is 4 to 5 minutes during the peak and 7 to 8 minutes in the off-peak.

- The suburban buses which are also run by the Régie Autonome des Transports Parisiens operate on about 220 routes. These serve inner suburbs, outside the Ville de Paris. The routes cover both the main radial roads to the centre and provide orbital connections from suburb to suburb. They also form a feeder service to railway stations.

- A network of privately owned buses operated by 90 companies grouped into two trade associations: the Association Professionelle des Transports Routiers and the Association pour le Développement et l'Amelioration des Transports Routiers en Région Ile-de-France. These run 837 routes in the region, but do not cover the city centre and the inner suburbs. Many of these routes are feeder services to railway stations. There are also a number of express bus services between départements.

4.1.3.4 Paris - other public transport modes

Paris has two tram lines, a funicular, an automated light-metro line and one entirely segregated bus line.

All of Paris' original tram lines have been dismantled but two new ones have been built. The first, opened in 1992, runs between Bobigny and Saint Denis in the northern part of Zone 2 and is 9 kilometres long with 21 stops. The second line, opened in 1997, links La Défense with the south western suburbs. It is 11 kilometres long and has 13 stops.

The automated light-metro line, the OrlyVAL, links the two airport terminals at Orly with Anthony station on line

B of the Réseau Express Régional. It is 7 kilometres long and has no intermediate stops.

The segregated bus line was opened in 1993. It links the southern suburb of Créteil with the Rungis employment area, north of Orly airport (Zone 2). It is 13 kilometres long and has 23 stops.

Furthermore, Paris has a small Rack railway operation in Montmartre (Zone 1) of a total 0.1 kilometres. It is run by the Régie Autonome des Transports Parisiens and serves mostly tourists.

4.1.3.5 Paris - roads

Motorways developed relatively late in France compared to other European countries. France, more rural than other countries, saw car ownership grow quite slowly, and progress towards constructing a national road network comprising good quality roads was also slow.

The idea of urban motorways came from what was happening in other European countries, notably Italy

Line B of the Réseau Express Régional crossing the A6 motorway in Paris

and Germany. A plan elaborated in 1935 developed a network of five radial motorways and an orbital one at about a radius of 20 kilometres from central Paris. But the execution of the plan was stopped by the Second World War and by 1945 only 20 kilometres of motorway had been built.

In the post-war years, congestion on the road network started to become an important issue, especially as car ownership started to rise as did the development of new urban areas. Many plans were designed but few of these left the drawing board. A few new roads were built, notably the Boulevard Périphérique, opened in 1957 (an orbital motorway encircling the Ville de Paris), the southern motorway, opened in 1960, and the northern motorway, opened in 1966.

Whilst economic growth was continuing, funding priorities changed and in 1960 the funds given to transport doubled. This allowed the start of construction of a regional motorway network, plans for which were further developed in the first regional structure plan (the "Schéma Directeur d'Aménagement et d'Urbanisme") of 1965. It was no longer merely a transport plan like its predecessors, but a structural plan for the whole region, where transport acted as a pivotal support to the region's future growth.

The plan provided for the construction of 14 radial motorways emanating outwards from the Boulevard Périphérique, to connect Paris to the rest of France, serve the distant suburbs and serve also the new towns. It also called for two new orbital motorways:

- The A 86 motorway (in Zones 2 & 3) aimed to serve the areas which are being redeveloped (at present being completed); and

- The A 87, the Francilienne, which links the new towns, and aims to redirect traffic that would have otherwise crossed through Paris (but has so far only been completed in the east).

The petrol crises of the 1970s led to priority being given to the improvement of public transport. The construction of road schemes slowed down. This slow-down was further reinforced by the downward revision of population estimates. The effect was to abandon the notion of new highways in central Paris (other than the one on the right bank of the river Seine) and use existing roads to build up the Francilienne, rather than create it entirely through new road construction. The 1980s saw an even greater slowdown in new road construction. Ambitious plans, developed in the early 1990s, for a privately built network of underground roads in central Paris have been progressively abandoned.

4.1.4   Tokyo

Tokyo's transport structure is characterised by heavy levels of commuting into the central area. And, although Tokyo has a developed system of urban motorways and public transport consisting of metro networks, automated metro lines, numerous regional railways, buses and monorail systems, it still strains during the week-day peak hours with heavy levels of overcrowding and congestion.

4.1.4.1 Tokyo - metro

The Tokyo region has 14 metro lines. Two of these are in Yokohama, to the south of the Tokyo Metropolis, and do not provide access to central Tokyo.

The first metro system in Tokyo was opened in 1927 by a private operator and in 1938 a second private metro company began operation. The two companies were merged to form the Teito Rapid Transit Authority and this gradually added new lines from 1954 to 1991, making up the present eight lines with a total length of 169 kilometres.

Owing to the rapid increase of population and cars in the 1950s, a more rapid development of the metro network became a political priority. The government-sponsored Urban Transportation Council suggested in 1956 that the Tokyo Metropolitan Government take responsibility for the construction of new metro lines. The Transport Bureau of Tokyo Metropolitan Government started metro operations in 1960, after which it opened new lines in 1968, 1978 and 1991. It has a current total of four lines with a total length of 68 kilometres.

In 1996 the Teito Rapid Transit Authority carried over 2,000 million passengers over its eight lines, and the Transport Bureau of Tokyo Metropolitan Government carried more than 500 million. The average number of passengers carried per kilometre per day by the Teito Rapid Transit Authority is 255 thousand, much higher than the 152 thousand carried by the Transport Bureau of Tokyo Metropolitan Government.

4.1.4.2 Tokyo - regional rail

Since the private railway companies (except Japan Railways) do not own lines in the central area of Tokyo Metropolis, within the circular Yamanote line, commuters are required to transfer to either metro or Japan Railways lines to go to their work places in this Zone 1. However, several private lines have arrangements to operate through-train services on metro line tracks. This measure has greatly eased the inconvenience for commuters. At present, three Japan Railways lines and eight owned by private operators run through-train services on metro tracks.

Of Teito Rapid Transit Authority's eight metro lines, five connect with Japan Railways and other private railways, and the Authority has agreements for the through-running of train services with six regional rail operators.

Through-train services are offered for rapid, express and local trains. Two of the Transport Bureau of Tokyo

Metropolitan Government's lines are used by four other operators and offer through-train services. Through-train frequency varies according to line. On most of the lines, through-trains operate all day, although some lines offer through-train services only during the morning and evening peak hours on weekdays.

In the through-running of regional rail trains on metro tracks, the trains with their passengers go through, but the crews change at connecting stations before proceeding to the next operator's track.

Railway stations in Tokyo, whether located in the central area or the suburbs, are staffed from about 05:00 to 01:00, but the last trains leave around midnight in the central area.

4.1.4.3 Tokyo - buses

In 1919 the first bus system in Tokyo was introduced by a private company. It was four years later that public bus operations commenced. The public bus system in Tokyo originally was intended to supplement the city's tram system, which was devastated in the 1923 earthquake. Later, several private bus firms, which form the basis of the present network, started services and all sectors of the public and private bus and tram networks continued to expand in competition with each other until the outbreak of the Second World War.

By the end of the war, passenger numbers had dropped substantially. It was not until 1950 that the volume of bus passengers returned to its 1938 pre-war peak. Bus operations continued to grow until around 1965. Worsening traffic congestion, a shrinking population in the central area, and the expansion of the metro network, caused bus ridership to decline from the late 1960s. There were 1,300 million bus passengers in Tokyo in 1970. By 1994 the figure had fallen to 900 million (or only 69% of the volume of 1970).

Inner-city elevated expressways in Tokyo

4.1.4.4 Tokyo - other public transport modes

Tokyo has 3 monorail lines and a tram line. The 3 monorail lines have a combined length of 37 kilometres.

There are no commuter coaches in Tokyo, but there are some "midnight express" buses for people who have missed the last train home. The "midnight express" buses run mainly from core areas in Zones 1 & 2 to residential areas in Zones 3 & 4, only on weekdays.

4.1.4.5 Tokyo - roads

Tokyo's motorways comprise "urban expressways" and "inter-city expressways". The urban expressways meander through the densely built-up area of the centre often at an elevated level and/or at multiple levels, up to four levels in height. The urban expressways consist of the inner loop route in Zone 1 and seven radial routes extending from it toward Zones 2, 3 & 4. Two of the radial routes connect directly with the inter-city expressways at the western border of Zone 2.

After the Second World War, the volume of traffic on Tokyo's inadequate road system grew dramatically, creating congestion at every intersection and traffic jams on every artery in the metropolitan area. To cope with this worsening situation and changes in the urban structure, construction of motorways was planned.

The Metropolitan Expressway Public Corporation was established in 1959, to construct Tokyo's inner city motorways. The original plan aimed to complete the entire expressway network by the end of 1965. A motorway network from Haneda Airport to competition sites was built for the Tokyo Olympics of 1964. An inner-city ring-road (the "Inner Loop") in Zone 1 and radial routes were built within loop Route 6 (not a motorway). At that time there was no plan for orbital motorways in the suburbs.

After 1965 Japan experienced rapid economic growth. In Tokyo population growth and motorisation accelerated, and the number of car owning households increased dramatically. Traffic congestion on motorways became a major problem. The extension of each route, and construction of orbital routes, was then seen as essential in order to alleviate congestion. The Outer Loop around Zone 2 was specifically built to eliminate the need to pass through the centre of Tokyo to travel between Kanagawa Prefecture and Saitama Prefecture, both in Zone 4. The construction of the Central Loop in Zone 2 is aimed at relieving congestion on the Inner Loop. Radial motorways have been and are continuing to be extended.

Road construction slowed down after 1975 owing to an economic slump and worries over deteriorating air quality. Nevertheless, the volume of traffic persistently grew and traffic congestion worsened. To ease the situation, the Bayshore Road and the Outer Loop were constructed, and the Metropolitan Expressway was extended to Zone 4. However, these measures have not been successful in reducing traffic congestion.

Currently, in the Tokyo Metropolitan Region there is an urban expressway and an inter-city expressways network with a total length of 911 kilometres. These motorways are either radial or part of three orbital rings:

- an Inner Loop in Zone 1

- a Central Loop in Zone 2 (parts of which are either under construction or still at the planning phase) and

- an Outer Loop (with a radius of 20 kilometres from the city centre) in Zones 3 & 4, parts of which are still in the planning phase

Traffic volume on the urban expressways exceeded its planned capacity as early as 1975, and a mounting number of vehicles has proved to be a continual cause of congestion ever since. Tokyo's motorways are still frequently heavily congested.

4.2 Metro and Regional Railways

Although the metro systems of the four cities share a similarity of purpose, that of catering for the movement of the inhabitants and visitors of the metropolitan area, the different density of lines and stations can mean that they play a somewhat different role. The regional rail systems in all four regions are primarily geared to commuters, and link the main towns and cities of the region.

4.2.1   Infrastructure

Within Zones 1 & 2, London and New York have just under 400 kilometres of metro lines which is nearly twice as much as Paris and Tokyo. However, as can be seen from table 11, the densities of the systems vary greatly.

As for regional rail routes, the south-east of England has the largest network with routes totalling 3,071 kilometres, slightly more than Tokyo's total and nearly double the totals for the Ile-de-France and the New York regions. However, route kilometres of rail and metro do not necessarily correlate with the number of passengers. For example, Tokyo, which has not quite double the route kilometres of New York, moves many more passengers.

Table 10a [47]
Route length of metro and regional rail lines in kilometres (disaggregate Zones)

	London	New York	Paris	Tokyo
METRO				
Zone 1	69	73	86	84
Zone 2	303	317	115	134
Zone 3	42	30	0	0
Zone 4	0	0	-	45
REGIONAL RAIL				
Zone 1	25	7	23	25
Zone 2	763	160	625	382
Zone 3	923	558	753	298
Zone 4	1,360	877	-	2,160
TOTAL				
Zone 1	94	80	109	109
Zone 2	1,066	477	740	516
Zone 3	965	588	753	298
Zone 4	1,360	877	-	2,205

Table 10b
Route length of metro and regional rail lines in kilometres (aggregate Zones)

	London	New York	Paris	Tokyo
METRO				
Zone 1	69	73	86	84
Zones 1 & 2	372	390	201	218
Zones 1, 2 & 3	414	420	201	218
Zones 1, 2, 3 & 4	414	420	-	263
REGIONAL RAIL				
Zone 1	25	7	23	25
Zones 1 & 2	788	167	648	407
Zones 1, 2 & 3	1,711	725	1,401	705
Zones 1, 2, 3 & 4	3,071	1,602	-	2,865
TOTAL				
Zone 1	94	80	109	109
Zones 1 & 2	1,160	557	849	625
Zones 1, 2 & 3	2,125	1,145	1,602	923
Zones 1, 2, 3 & 4	3,485	2,022	-	3,128

On the other hand, in the cities other than New York, regional rail systems complement the metro by providing travel throughout the region, while New York's regional rail system is used principally for commuter travel from Zones 3 and 4 to Zone 1. In London and Paris, both the regional rail systems and the land area are very similar in size in Zones 1, 2 and 3. Their regional rail lines are more than twice as extensive as the regional rail systems in New York and Tokyo (in

those three Zones, but the land area of New York is roughly half the size of London and Paris, and Tokyo's is less than one-fifth as large).

It is in Zone 4 where the four regional rail systems differ most significantly. Tokyo's rail network in its outermost Zone is by far the largest, London's is about two-thirds its size, while New York's is a little more than a third the size of Tokyo's.

47   Route length is measured by "route right of way", rather than the length of individual routes that may share portions of the same track, or have parallel tracks in the same "right of way".

Paris   In Zone 2 Paris also has one tramway of 9 kilometres in length, not included in the above statistics.

Tokyo   In Zone 2, Tokyo also has one tramway, not included in the above statistics.

Furthermore, Tokyo also has three monorail lines with a total length of 37 kilometres, and five "new transit" lines with a total length of 42.1 kilometres. These are also not included in the above statistics.

Table 11 [48]

Route length of metro and regional rail lines in kilometres per square kilometre

	London	New York	Paris	Tokyo
METRO				
Zone 1	2.56	3.17	2.97	2.00
Zone 2	0.20	0.43	0.06	0.23
Zone 3	>0.00	0.01	-	-
Zone 4	-	-	-	>0.00
REGIONAL RAIL				
Zone 1	0.93	0.30	0.79	0.60
Zone 2	0.49	0.22	0.31	0.66
Zone 3	0.10	0.11	0.08	0.26
Zone 4	0.08	0.03	-	0.19
TOTAL				
Zone 1	3.48	3.48	3.76	2.60
Zone 2	0.69	0.65	0.37	0.90
Zone 3	0.11	0.12	0.08	0.26
Zone 4	0.08	0.03	-	0.19

Figure 6a

Route length of metro lines in kilometres per square kilometre

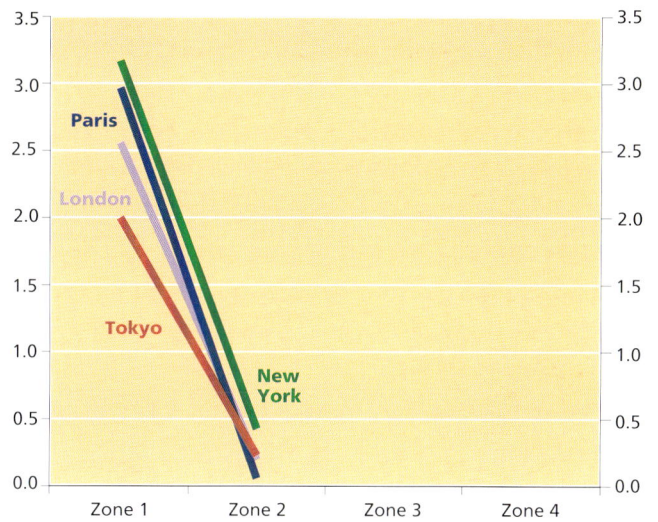

Figure 6b

Route length of regional rail lines in kilometres per square kilometre

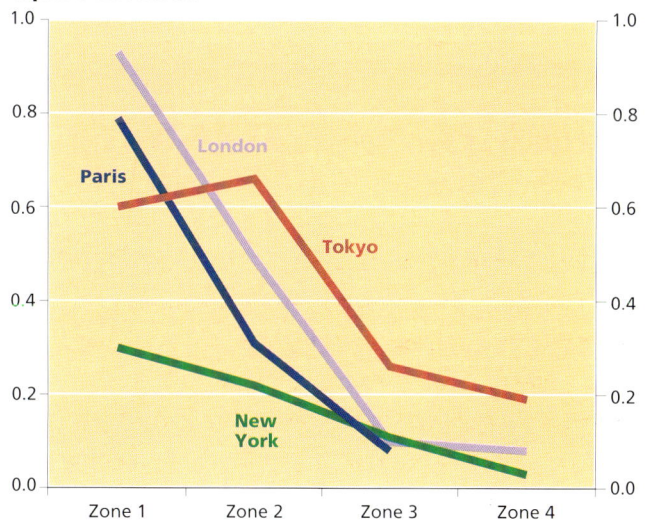

As can be seen from table 11, Tokyo, except in Zone 1, has an overall higher density of metro and rail lines than the other cities. In Zones 3 & 4 it is significantly more than the other cities. New York, with a very extensive outer area, has only 0.03 kilometres of rail track per square kilometre in Zone 4, less than a sixth of the density in Tokyo, but it also has a much lower population density than Tokyo in Zone 4.

Table 12a reveals that in Zone 1, Paris has more stations than the other three cities (twice the number in London and Tokyo and 35% more than New York). However, looking at the entire metro system, New York has many more stations than London and Paris and more than three times as many as Tokyo. Since the geographical area of Zones 1 & 2 in New York, shown in Table 4b, is much smaller than in any city but Tokyo, metropolitan New York has the greatest density of metro stations, resulting in the shortest walking distances to the metro.

48   For definitions see table 10a. The "total" figures of table 10a are divided by the figures of table 5a.

Yet in the central area (Zone 1), it is Paris that has the densest metro network. In Paris the average inter-station distance is approximately 500 metres and one in three stations is served by more than one metro line.

As shown in tables 10b, 12b and map 10, New York has the most extensive metro system with a total of 420 kilometres of lines and 513 stations, most located within New York City. Nearly all the metro stations are within Zones 1 & 2; the exceptions are the 14 serving the Staten Island Railway, the 11 on the Newark metro, and the Port Authority Trans Hudson line which extends to Essex county in Zone 3.

In Tokyo, most of the stations in Zone 1 belong to Japan Railways or the metro companies. Among them, three serve only Japan Railways trains, while 11 function in tandem with metro lines and two with other private railways, producing a total of 16 stations for Japan Railways in Zone 1, although 13 of them are jointly maintained with other operators. In spite of its relatively small area, Zone 1 is served by 62 metro stations, among which 50 are used exclusively for metro traffic, while 11 connect with Japan Railways and one with the Keihin Electric Express Railway. Since none of the other six private railway companies has stations in Zone 1, their passengers who commute from other Zones to Zone 1 must transfer to either metro or Japan Railways.

The picture of regional rail stations is very different from that of the metro. Paris, over the past two decades has developed a system of through regional trains

crossing the central area, the Réseau Express Régional [49]. As can be seen in maps 10 and 11, these lines link the outer suburbs with central Paris but also allow quick through travel in the capital, as well as linking the main rail termini.

In London, the only such scheme is the Thameslink line with 15 minute intervals in the central area - but which also necessitates a change of traction.

In New York plans for Réseau Express Régional style schemes have been put forward recently by the Regional Plan Association in its third regional plan [50], but do not have any statutory authority.

Tokyo is slightly different in that it has the Yamanote circular railway and has some through-running of regional rail trains on metro tracks (and some metro trains running on regional rail tracks).

In Zone 1, New York has just two regional rail stations (both terminals), while London, Tokyo and Paris have at least seven times as many stations (in Paris, two of these are only termini, whilst the others are also served by the Réseau Express Régional).

The greatest contrast is in Zone 2, where London, Paris and Tokyo have eight or more times as many regional rail stations as does New York.

In Tokyo's Zone 2 all private regional railway lines have interchange stations on the Yamanote circular line and/ or other metro lines. Their lines radiate in all directions

---

49   There are four Réseau Express Régional lines with multiple branches and one is currently under construction, the line E (EOLE). The lines currently in operation are:

   Line A   operates in an east-west direction; it is jointly run by the Régie Autonome des Transports Parisiens and the national railway company, the Société Nationale des Chemins de fer Français;

   Line B   operates in an north-south direction and links Paris' northern airport at Roissy with its southern one, Orly via the OrlyVAL automated railway at Antony station; it is jointly run by Régie Autonome des Transports Parisiens and the Société Nationale des Chemins de fer Français;

   Line C   operates in an east-west direction; it is run by the Société Nationale des Chemins de fer Français;

   Line D   operates in an north-south direction; it is also run by the Société Nationale des Chemins de fer Français.

50   See, (Yaro & Hiss, 1996).

Table 12a [51]
**Number of metro and regional rail stations
(disaggregated Zones)**

	London	New York	Paris	Tokyo
METRO				
Zone 1	52	88	119	50
Zone 2	203	392	177	90
Zone 3	15	33	0	0
Zone 4	0	0	-	23
REGIONAL RAIL				
Zone 1	16	2	14	17
Zone 2	305	39	265	235
Zone 3	254	188	158	140
Zone 4	173	146	-	751
TOTAL				
Zone 1	68	90	133	67
Zone 2	508	431	442	325
Zone 3	269	221	158	140
Zone 4	173	146	-	774

Table 12b
**Number of metro and regional rail stations
(aggregated Zones)**

	London	New York	Paris	Tokyo
METRO				
Zone 1	52	88	119	50
Zones 1 & 2	255	480	296	140
Zones 1, 2 & 3	270	513	295	140
Zones 1, 2, 3 & 4	270	513	-	163
REGIONAL RAIL				
Zone 1	16	2	14	17
Zones 1 & 2	321	41	279	252
Zones 1, 2 & 3	575	229	437	392
Zones 1, 2, 3 & 4	748	375	-	1,143
TOTAL				
Zone 1	68	90	133	67
Zones 1 & 2	576	521	575	392
Zones 1, 2 & 3	845	742	732	532
Zones 1, 2, 3 & 4	1,018	888	-	1,306

51   Interchange stations are counted only once.

Tokyo   Interchange stations of metro and rail are only counted in the "rail" category and excluded from "metro". The number of stations in the "rail" category includes those shared between different operators (including metro).

These are:
- 14, in Zone 1
- 44, in Zones 1 & 2
- 50, in Zones 1, 2 & 3
- 97, in Zones 1, 2, 3 & 4

The number of metro stations in Zone 4 includes those in the metro system operated by Yokohama City which runs within the Kanagawa Prefecture.

In Zone 2, Tokyo also has one tramway with 29 stops, not included in the above statistics.

Furthermore, Tokyo also has three monorail lines and five "new transit" lines not included in the above statistics. They have stations in the following Zones:

- 7, in Zone 1
- 13, in Zone 2
- 0, in Zone 3
- 59, in Zone 4

Some of these stations may be included in the statistics as they may interchange with other metro or regional rail lines.

Table 13 [52]

Number of metro and regional rail stations per square kilometre (disaggregated Zones)

	London	New York	Paris	Tokyo
METRO				
Zone 1	1.93	3.83	4.10	1.19
Zone 2	0.13	0.53	0.09	0.15
Zone 3	>0.01	0.01	-	-
Zone 4	-	-	-	>0.00
REGIONAL RAIL				
Zone 1	0.59	0.09	0.48	0.40
Zone 2	0.20	0.05	0.13	0.41
Zone 3	0.03	0.04	0.02	0.12
Zone 4	0.01	0.01	-	0.07
TOTAL				
Zone 1	2.52	3.91	4.59	1.60
Zone 2	0.33	0.59	0.22	0.57
Zone 3	0.03	0.04	0.02	0.12
Zone 4	0.01	0.01	-	0.07

Figure 7a

Number of metro stations per square kilometre

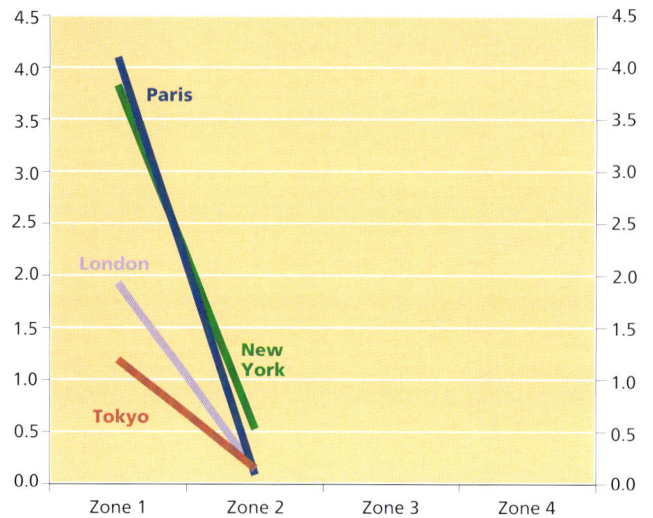

through Zone 2 and beyond. These railways have an aggregate of 189 stations, among which 20 are interchange stations with Japan Railways and/or the metro network. Metro lines and private railways (including Japan Railways' Chuo line) have some through-running on the same track of each others' trains outside Yamanote loop line.

In Zone 3, when adjusted for the geographical size, the four cities are more similar. Overall, Tokyo is better served by rail in Zones 3 & 4, having the highest number of stations and comparatively also the greatest density of stations. The Parisian regional rail stations in Zone 3 are about three kilometres apart and most are equipped with park-and-ride facilities.

The most significant attribute of regional rail stations in New York is the very limited availability of car parking, the general scarcity of which acts as the principal constraint on expanding ridership. Most regional rail stations (in all Zones) are located in fully developed commercial areas with little space to devote to storing cars of commuters who provide little local benefit. Even stations on the edge of suburban areas have little space for car parking. Stations are, generally, under the jurisdiction of the local communities, nearly all of which resist expansion of parking and restrict most of the use to resident permit holders. Feeder public transport services have limited practicality due to the very dispersed pattern of residences. The station facilities themselves range from quaint, historic structures to utilitarian. Few offer more than a waiting room, and a staffed ticket window and a coffee vendor during peak hours.

The regional rail system in the south-east of England was largely developed in the last century and has a mostly radial pattern emanating from central London. Nonetheless, there are a few non-radial lines, such as the one on the south coast linking Southampton with Portsmouth, Brighton, Eastbourne and Hastings. Many

52   For definitions see table 12a. The "total" figures of table 12a are divided by the figures of table 4a.

Figure 7b
Number of metro and regional rail stations per square kilometre

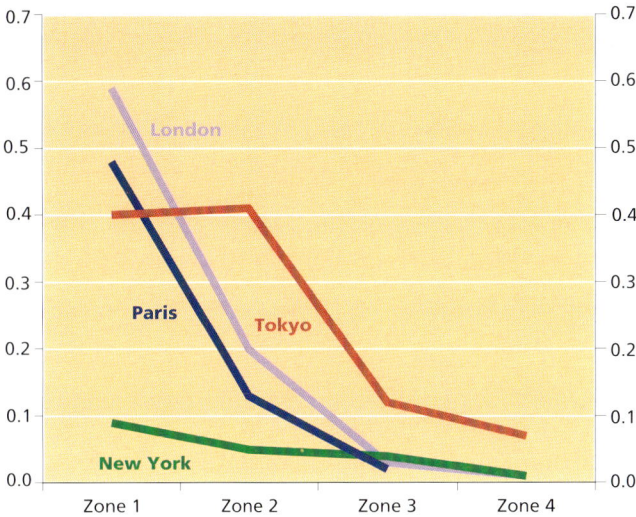

Figure 8a
Number of metro stations per million inhabitants

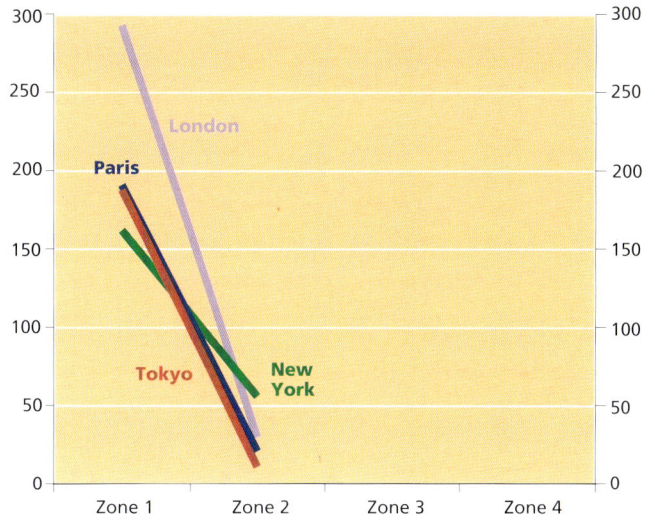

Table 14 [53]
Number of metro and regional rail stations per million inhabitants (disaggregated Zones)

	London	New York	Paris	Tokyo
METRO				
Zone 1	293	162	191	188
Zone 2	30	56	21	11
Zone 3	3	5	-	-
Zone 4	-	-	-	1
REGIONAL RAIL				
Zone 1	90	4	23	64
Zone 2	46	6	29	30
Zone 3	53	31	84	38
Zone 4	29	23	-	38
TOTAL				
Zone 1	384	166	214	252
Zone 2	76	62	54	42
Zone 3	57	37	84	38
Zone 4	29	23	-	39

Figure 8b
Number of regional rail stations per million inhabitants

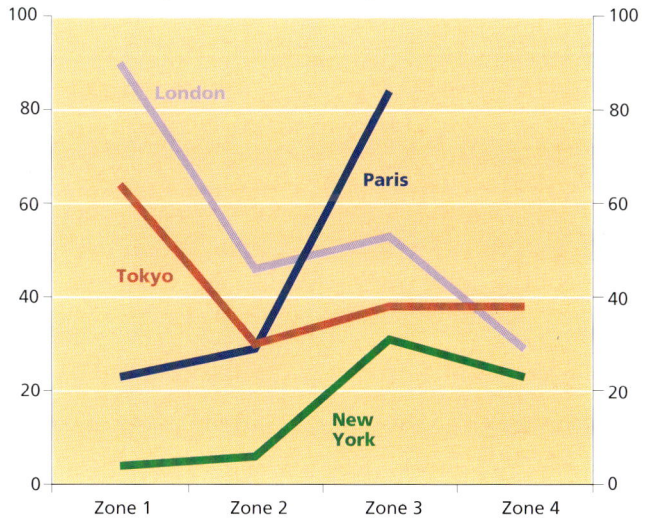

stations on these lines are small but a large proportion of them are equipped with car parks.

4.2.2 Frequency of service

All cities except Tokyo have a high frequency metro service, both peak and off-peak, in their central area (Zone 1) - Tokyo's falls in the off-peak. High frequencies

53 For definitions *see* table 12a. The "total" figures of table 12a are divided by the figures of table 5a.

Table 15 [54]

Scheduled average wait times of metro services in the Monday to Friday peak (07:00 - 09:59) and the off-peak (12:00 - 12:59)

Average wait		London		New York		Paris		Tokyo	
		peak	off-peak	peak	off-peak	peak	off-peak	peak	off-peak
Zone 1	less than 5 mins	100%	100%	93%	85%	100%	84%	100%	68%
	5 to 10 mins	0%	0%	7%	15%	0%	16%	0%	32%
	over 10 mins	0%	0%	0%	0%	0%	0%	0%	0%
Zone 2	less than 5 mins	95%	80%	83%	40%	100%	73.5%	87%	36%
	5 to 10 mins	5%	20%	17%	54%	0%	26.5%	11%	62%
	over 10 mins	0%	0%	0%	6%	0%	0%	2%	2%
Zone 3	less than 5 mins	37%	32%	0%	0%	-	-	-	-
	5 to 10 mins	44%	25%	100%	0%	-	-	-	-
	over 10 mins	19%	43%	0%	100%	-	-	-	-
Zone 4	less than 5 mins	-	-	-	-	-	-	18%	6%
	5 to 10 mins	-	-	-	-	-	-	82%	94%
	over 10 mins	-	-	-	-	-	-	0%	0%

Figure 9a
Metro services with less than a scheduled 5 minute wait in the Monday to Friday peak (07:00 - 09:59)
Percentages

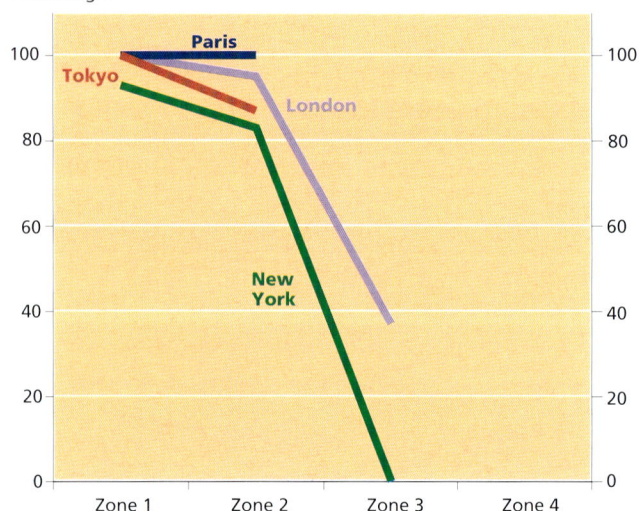

Figure 9b
Metro services with less than a scheduled 5 minute wait in the Monday to Friday off-peak (12:00 - 12:59)
Percentages

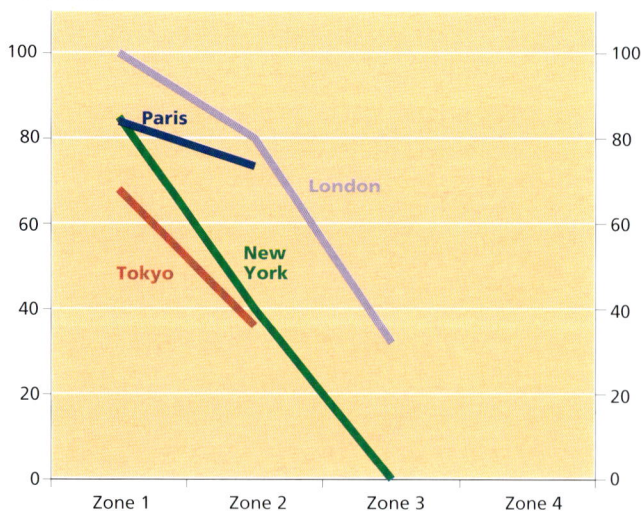

54   The scheduled average wait time is half the scheduled interval between trains.

Table 16 [55]

Scheduled average wait times of regional rail services in the Monday to Friday morning peak (07:00 - 09:59) and the off-peak (12:00 - 12:59)

	Average wait	London		New York		Paris		Tokyo	
		peak	off-peak	peak	off-peak	peak	off-peak	peak	off-peak
Zone 1	less than 5 mins	50%	50%	43%	9%	100%	12%	95%	65%
	5 to 10 mins	40%	30%	34%	9%	0%	88%	5%	35%
	over 10 mins	10%	20%	23%	82%	0%	0%	0%	0%
Zone 2	less than 5 mins	35%	25%	51%	12%	12%	2%	98%	89%
	5 to 10 mins	45%	45%	30%	8%	48%	21%	2%	11%
	over 10 mins	20%	30%	29%	80%	40%	77%	0%	0%
Zone 3	less than 5 mins	40%	10%	32%	0%	1%	0%	76%	45%
	5 to 10 mins	20%	45%	36%	0%	10%	1%	21%	51%
	over 10 mins	40%	45%	32%	100%	88%	99%	3%	4%
Zone 4	less than 5 mins	15%	15%	25%	6%	-	-	70%	34%
	5 to 10 mins	30%	20%	27%	12%	-	-	25%	53%
	over 10 mins	55%	65%	48%	82%	-	-	5%	13%

Figure 10a

Regional rail services with less than a scheduled 5 minute wait in the Monday to Friday peak (07:00 - 09:59)

Percentages

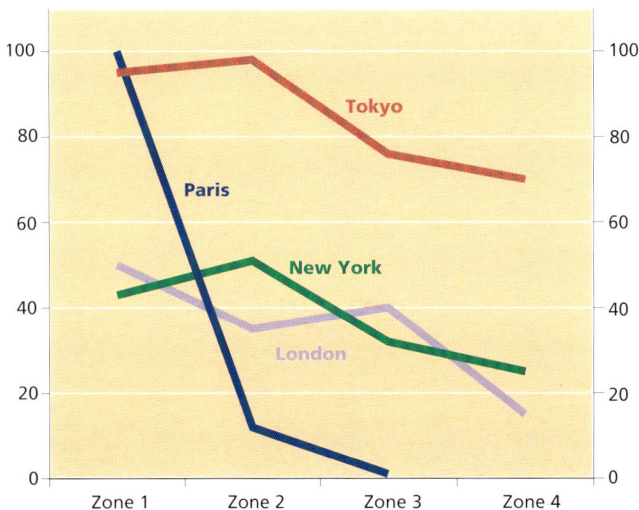

Figure 10b

Regional rail services with less than a scheduled 5 minute wait in the Monday to Friday off-peak (12:00 - 12:59)

Percentages

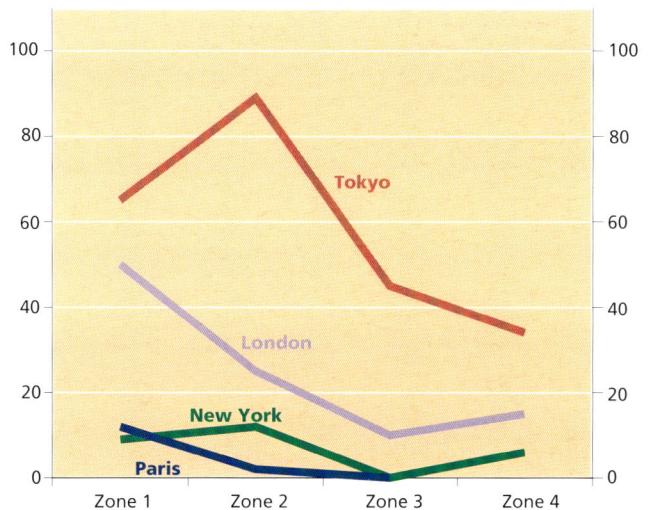

55   London   The figures have been obtained by taking a representative sample of stations and have been rounded to the nearest 5%.

are maintained in London and Paris in the off-peak in Zone 2.

In Paris, 60% of all metro stations have less than a 2 minute interval between trains.

Tokyo is the only city to offer a consistently high frequency regional rail service in all Zones in both the peak and off-peak. Since the regional rail and the metro operate punctually and conveniently, they attract an enormous number of passengers, who prefer them to other transport modes. In other words, high frequency of service brings a high rate of use of rail and metro systems.

London maintains a reasonable peak and off-peak service in Zone 1, but in Zones further out there is a poor service with the exception of railway stations in the larger towns and cities which have frequent services both in the peak and off-peak.

Paris in the off-peak, in all Zones except Zone 1, has a very infrequent service at all times.

In New York, in the off-peak period, rail services, depending on the line, run either one or two trains an hour; branch lines are even less frequent, in some cases not operating at all during off-peak hours.

4.2.3   Overcrowding

There are many aspects of quality of service that matter to passengers. These can range from cleanliness to perceived security while travelling. It has not been possible to gauge many aspects of quality of service in the four cities that are comparable. However, it has been possible to gain some measure of the level of crowding on the metro and regional rail.

The methods of measuring overcrowding are different in each city and within each city different operators measure congestion in different ways. The images of railway staff pushing commuters into extremely congested trains in Tokyo are well known world-wide. Although congestion levels may often be extreme in Tokyo, they can also be severe at peak hours in the other cities too.

In Tokyo, the "congestion ratio" of trains is calculated by dividing the total number of passengers during rush hours by the overall capacity of railway cars in service at the time. Train car capacity is regarded as the total number of seats and strap-hangers plus standing passengers holding columns near doors (viable standing capacity) in normal conditions. Viable standing capacity differs depending on train car types. For instance, most "Bullet" train cars feature forward-facing seats accommodating two or three passengers abreast with a narrow aisle in-between. By contrast, all metro and the vast majority of regular commuter trains have longitudinal seats facing inward and an abundance of straps and columns so as to accommodate anticipated heavy loads of standing passengers.

Congestion during peak hours, in Tokyo, averages 194% for rail and metro [56]. This means that about half the passengers do not have a seat, or even a rail or strap to hold on to; rail cars are so jammed that passengers are pressed against one another and jostled virtually in unison as the train starts and stops.

As for the metro, the Chiyoda (Machiya to Nishi-Nippori), the Tozai (Monzen Nakacho to Kayabacho) and Hibiya (Minowa to Iriya) lines report congestion ratios of more than 200%. As measures to augment passenger capacity, such as the construction of new lines, lengthening trains, revising schedules and increasing service frequency, continue to progress, congestion tends to ease. In spite of this, however, attaining a long-range congestion ratio goal of even 150% appears difficult. Meanwhile, plans have been made to achieve a more immediate congestion ratio of 180% through the construction of new lines.

56   The following are some typical examples. They are lines of most congestion. The figures show the percentage of overcrowding.

Rail line	From:	To:	Time period:	1955	1965	1975	1985	1995
Metro								
Chiyoda	Machiya	Nishinippori	7:45 - 8:45			216	230	223
Tozai	Monzennakacho	Kayabacho	7:50 - 8:50			219	221	204
Hibiya	Minowa	Iriya	7:50 - 8:50	224	224	231	203	199
Marunouchi	Shinotsuka	Myogadani	8:00 - 9:00	254	222	216	206	197
Regional rail								
Keihin-Touhoku	Oimachi	Shinagawa	7:30 - 8:30	298	274	224	254	268
Yamanote	Ueno	Okachimachi	8:00 - 9:00	297	283	223	243	255
Soubu	Kinshicho	Ryougoku	7:30 - 8:30	286	288	231	270	248
Joban	Kameari	Ayase	7:30 - 8:30	275	284	206	259	248
Yamanote	Yoyogi	Harajuku	7:30 - 8:30	298	268	246	263	246
Chuo	Nakano	Shinjuku	8:00 - 9:00	280	289	260	259	236
Yokosuka	Shinkawasaki	Shinagawa	7:30 - 8:30	255	307	292	243	231
Saikyo	Ikebukuro	Shinjuku	7:30 - 8:30					207
Seibu-Ikebukuro	Shiinamachi	Ikebukuro	7:42 - 8:42	210	244	225	203	206
Odakyu	Setagayadaita	Shimokitazawa	7:43 - 8:43	235	231	229	206	200
Tokyu-Toyoko	Yutenji	Nakameguro	7:50 - 8:50	209	230	237	204	197
Tobu-Isezaki	Kosuge	Kitasenju	7:30 - 8:30	227	220	201	184	195
Seibu-Shinjuku	Shimoochiai	Takatanobaba	7:43 - 8:43	264	264	217	199	193

Source: Annual report of urban transport 1995 (Japan Transport Economics Research Centre)

Definition of overcrowding is as follows:

Percentage: Number of passengers/capacity of trains x 100
Capacity of trains: Frequency x number x capacity
Frequency: frequency of a line in each period
Number: number of cars in a train
Capacity: capacity of a car
Capacity of a car: is calculated by three different methods:

- method 1:   car which has long seats (commuter train), the train's floor-space/0.35
- method 2:   car which has cross seats ("Bullet" train), number of persons fully seated
- method 3:   car which has both long seats and cross seats, the train's floor-space/0.40

Criteria for measuring congestion Levels

100%   Filled to capacity. Passengers can ride comfortably being seated, hanging on a strap, or holding a column by the door.

150%   Crowded to the extent that passengers contact one another, but they still can read newspapers easily.

180%   Crowded to the extent that passengers bodily touch one another, but they still can read newspapers.

200%   Jammed to the extent that passengers jostle one another and are subjected to considerable pressure, but passengers still can manage to read magazines.

250%   Whenever the train jolts, passengers are forced to assume a slanting position, unable to move their bodies or even their hands.

In New York, the Metropolitan Transportation Authority guidelines for metro and buses specifies a minimum standing space of three square feet per passenger, equivalent to 0.28 square metres per person, or 1.12 square metres for four passengers, which is slightly more generous than the Paris metro standard of 1.0 square metre for four passengers. During the weekday peak period, in New York, metro cars are reported to operate at about 66% of the "crush" criterion, although that varies along a route, worsening as trains approach Manhattan in the morning peak period. The metro route that connects the Bronx to Manhattan is 40% to 80% over capacity at peak times.

In Paris, the percentage of trains on which more than four people were standing per square metre, was:

Zone 1: 7.8 kilometres (6.5% of route length);

Zone 2: 16.3 kilometres (5.5% of route length).

The new railways that have been and are being built in Paris have, as a major objective, the relief of congestion. Particular attention is being paid to the diminution of congestion on line A of the Réseau Express Régional. Other measures are also being taken on that line, such as the introduction of on-board signalling to reduce train headways.

In London congestion on the metro is not evenly distributed along the network, but is in the form of "bottle-necks". No major measures have been undertaken in London to reduce congestion on the metro. However, some relief has been offered to passengers of the Central line through new and more spacious rolling stock and modernised signalling.

Congestion on the metro and trains in London and New York is related to the economic cycle - when the economy is booming and the number of commuters increases, the congestion is at its worst.

The guidelines in New York for regional rail, are a seat for all passengers, which is achieved statistically on Metro-North and New Jersey Transit. On the Long Island Railroad there are about 870 more passengers than seats, among just under 39,000 peak period passengers as trains enter Zone 2. Yet on all commuter lines, passengers often stand due to the uneven distribution of passengers along the train.

In Tokyo, among private rail operators, passenger capacity has all but doubled from that of 1965 by lengthening trains and increasing the frequency of service. As a result the congestion ratio dropped from 240% to 174%, improving matters to where passengers could read not only magazines but also newspapers. Still, certain sections of private railways, specifically the Seibu Ikebukuro line (from Shiinamachi to Ikebukuro), the Odakyu line (from Setagaya Daita to Shimo-Kitazawa), and the Tobu Isezaki line (from Kosuge to Kita-Senju), remain highly crowded, with a congestion ratio exceeding 200%.

Japan Railways has expanded its passenger capacity 1.8 times since 1965, thus reducing the congestion ratio from 268% to 206%. Nevertheless, all major Japan Railways commuter lines continue to show an average congestion ratio of over 200%. In particular, the Yamanote Loop line (from Ueno to Okachimachi), the

Tokyo's "New Transit System"

Keihin Tohoku line (from Oimachi to Shinagawa), and the Joban line (from Mikawajima to Nippori) have amazing congestion ratios of about 250%. Under these conditions, eight or nine persons are wedged into one square metre of floor space, which means that when trains start or stop, passengers cannot help but lean with everyone else, and some are unable to move even their hands. Such degrees of congestion in Japan are commonly termed "commuter hell".

4.2.4   Punctuality and reliability

The measure for reliability in this study is the proportion of train journeys commenced as a proportion of those scheduled. The measure for punctuality is the proportion of journeys that have been undertaken that arrive at their destination within a certain time period after the time they were scheduled to arrive. Passengers perceive reliability in terms of cancellations of trains and punctuality in terms of trains arriving late.

Tokyo has exemplary reliable and punctual rail and metro systems and passengers take this kind of service for granted. Tokyo's punctuality and reliability record (both close to 100%) is even more remarkable when one takes into account the level of overcrowding that the systems experience in the peak hours. To cope with the very large number of persons boarding and alighting, on several routes in Tokyo, the number of doors per car have been increased or wider doors provided. On some routes, the number of cars has been increased to make the trains longer and platforms have been extended. Overall, Tokyo's figures are far better than those achieved by the other cities.

The figures for Paris have been distorted by strikes taking place in 1995. Although performance is better when there are no strikes, the system is not infrequently strike bound, and the Parisian figures for 1995 cannot be considered completely atypical.

London's and New York's punctuality figures for metro and regional rail are poor, especially in view of the more stringent thresholds in Paris and Tokyo. In 1995, in London, 15% of scheduled metro services arrived more than 5 minutes late compared to 2% of Tokyo's metro services arriving more than 60 seconds late. Targets are set by the government in London for punctuality and reliability for all train and metro operators. However even the targets are well below what is achieved in Tokyo and often they are not met. London's regional rail system has the poorest performance of the four cities.

Table 17
Reliability of metro and regional rail services in 1995

	London	New York	Paris	Tokyo
METRO (% of journeys undertaken as a proportion of schedule)	97%	97%	91% (7% was due to strike action)	99.9%
REGIONAL RAIL (% of journeys undertaken as a proportion of schedule)	99% (Monday to Friday)	99.6%	99% [57]	n/a

57   The data refers to number of trains run as a percentage of roster.

Table 18
Punctuality of metro and regional rail services in 1995

	London	**New York**	**Paris**	**Tokyo**
Metro	85% (no more than 5 minutes late)	80% (no more than 5 minutes late during the day and 10 minutes during the late night/early morning)	87.5% [58] (no more than 3 minutes late in the peak and 6 minutes late in the off-peak)	98% (no more than 60 seconds late) data for metro system of the Transport Bureau of Tokyo Metropolitan Government
Regional rail (% of trains arriving no more than 5 minutes late)	88% (in the peak)	95% Metro-North 91% Long Island Railroad 96% New Jersey Transit	91% [59] (in the peak) 94.5% [60] (whole day)	n/a

Table 19a [61]
Compound index of service quality for metro services

City	Services with a scheduled wait of 5 minutes or less in the peak	Services with a scheduled wait of 10 minutes or less in the off-peak	Proportion of scheduled services run	Services no more than 5 minutes late	Compound service quality measure
London	98	100	97	85	380
New York	88	97	97	80	362
Paris	100	100	91	88	379
Tokyo	94	99	100	100	393

58   Figures are for the first ten months of 1995. November and December were deemed to be "unrepresentative".

59   Figures are for the Société Nationale des Chemins de fer Français lines, and only for the first eleven months of 1995 (December was deemed to be "unrepresentative").

    The figures for the Réseau Express Régional lines, run by the Régie Autonome des Transports Parisiens, were 93%.

60   Figures are for the Société Nationale des Chemins de fer Français lines, and only for the first eleven months of 1995 (December was deemed to be "unrepresentative").

    The figures for the Réseau Express Régional lines, run by the Régie Autonome des Transports Parisiens, were 95%.

61   The indices on frequency are the mean of the figures for Zone 1 and Zone 2. The indices for punctuality and reliability are for the entire metro network.

    Tokyo   The index for Tokyo's punctuality is put at 100 since 98% of trains arrive no later than 60 seconds from their schedule.

Table 19b [62]
Compound index of service quality for regional rail services

City	Services with a scheduled wait of 5 minutes or less in the peak	Services with a scheduled wait of 10 minutes of less in the off-peak	Proportion of scheduled services run	Services no more than 5 minutes late	Compound service quality measure
London	30	53	99	88	270
New York	36	13	100	94	243
Paris	7	8	99	93	207
Tokyo	81	94	100	95	370

Tables 19a and 19b amalgamate the data of tables 15 to 18, which measure the frequency, reliability and punctuality of the metro and regional rail in the four cities, as compound indices. These compound indices provide an overall measure of performance of the rail systems of all the four cities.

In tables 19a and 19b each individual index has a maximum score of 100 for frequency (all trains running with a scheduled wait of 5 minutes or less in the peak and 10 minutes or less in the off-peak), for reliability (no cancellations), and punctuality (no trains delayed).

The compound indices show how the performance of metro and regional rail services in Tokyo is well above that in the other cities, especially for regional rail. New York and Paris score below London for both metro and regional rail, held down by very low frequency of service.

4.3 Buses

Travel by bus is significant in all four cities. London and Tokyo have the largest networks (see table 19) but it is London and New York that have the largest number of passengers (see tables 28 and 29f). In addition to the buses, London has a small number of commuter coaches, many of which are based in Kent; whilst New York has a significant number of commuter coaches.

62   The indices on frequency are the mean of the figures for Zone 2, Zone 3 and Zone 4. The indices for punctuality and reliability are for the entire regional rail network.

      London   The index for London's regional rail punctuality has been calculated based on services during the peak.

      New York   The index for New York's regional rail punctuality has been calculated as the average of Metro North, Long Island Railroad and New Jersey Transit services.

      Paris   Indices on frequency have been calculated for only Zones 2 & 3.

              The index for Paris' regional rail punctuality has been calculated as the average between peak and off-peak services.

      Tokyo   The index for Tokyo's regional rail reliability has been put at 100, based on 100% of metro trains arriving no later than 60 seconds from their schedule. There are no reliability data for regional rail services.

              The index for Tokyo's regional rail punctuality has been put at 95, based on 98% of metro trains arriving no later than 60 seconds from their schedule. There are no punctuality data for regional rail services.

4.3.1   Network and operating characteristics

In London's Zones 1 & 2, a large proportion of public transport passengers are carried by bus. The buses are in the hands of private companies but are co-ordinated and regulated by the government-owned London Transport. In Zones 3 & 4 the bus system is completely private and run on free market principles, except where local authorities want to subsidise particular "socially necessary" routes. Outside Zone 2, in most areas, off-peak services are either non-existent or infrequent. Buses play a significant role only in the major towns and cities of south-east England. There are no accurate statistics for buses outside London.

There are approximately 430 separate bus routes serving the New York metropolitan area (Zones 1 & 2). Bus use is by far the heaviest in these Zones. However, commuter coaches (called "express buses" in New York) carry almost as many commuters from Zones 3 & 4 to Zone 1 as does regional rail.

In central Paris, the bus plays a lesser role than it does in the other cities; in central Paris this can be explained by the fact that the metro system has more stations per square kilometre than do the other cities. In Paris' Zones 1 & 2, the Régie Autonome des Transports Parisiens has 274 bus routes and there are also a smaller number of routes run by private operators. In Zone 3, buses are a significant mode of transport. Suburban routes are mostly linked to serving railway stations, although there are some longer distance routes in the mainly rural parts of Zone 3.

There is a large and complex network of bus routes in Tokyo because bus services are provided for every 0.5 to

Table 20 [63]
Number of bus routes (aggregate Zones)

	London	New York	Paris	Tokyo
Zone 1	111	38	53	n/a
Zones 1 & 2	649	430	≈300	n/a
Zones 1, 2 & 3	n/a	670	1,074	1,989
Zones 1, 2, 3 & 4	n/a	830	-	6,574

1 square kilometre in Zone 1, and every 1 to 2 square kilometres in Zones 2 & 3. Moreover, there are other reasons for the bus route network being so large and complex. In the Tokyo region, there are numerous bus services that have the same origin and destination but take different routes, with some even turning back part way. There are also numerous circular routes. For Tokyo's figure in table 20, each of these route variations is counted as a separate route.

Another reason for Tokyo region's many bus routes is that to abolish a bus route requires approval by the Ministry of Transport, which takes into account the profitability of the company's entire bus network, not just the route the firm wishes to abandon; the theory is that maintaining bus routes protects people living in areas where no other means of public transport are available. Furthermore, many bus services are run by firms affiliated to train companies, and are provided for the convenience of the railways' passengers.

Apart from some rare exceptions, most bus companies in Tokyo generally do not share the same routes since the Ministry of Transport assigns specific service areas to each operator to preclude competition. However, at major railway stations and along important arteries

---

63   The table is produced to give a rough guide to the extensiveness of the service. A bus route is defined as one with a separate number. Routes for special purposes of a very limited variety such as school journeys are not included.

   Paris   Reliable data available only for Zones 1 and Zones 1, 2 & 3 combined. The figure for Zones 1 & 2 is a rough estimate. There are 274 bus routes operated by the Régie Autonome des Transports Parisiens and a small number of routes operated by private companies.

   Tokyo   Data is only available for the Zones 1, 2 & 3 combined (the Tokyo Metropolis) and for the entire region. The figures are of 1995.

               Each bus route variation is counted as a separate route.

Table 21 [64]
Route length of bus services in kilometres (aggregate Zones)

	London	New York	Paris	Tokyo
Zone 1	490	370	280	n/a
Zones 1 & 2	3,410	5,240	≈3,000	n/a
Zones 1, 2 & 3	n/a	10,710	16,470	15,000
Zones 1, 2, 3 & 4	n/a	15,485	-	n/a

Table 22 [65]
Average route length of bus services in kilometres (aggregate Zones)

	London	New York	Paris	Tokyo
Zone 1	4	10	5	n/a
Zones 1 & 2	5	12	9.5	n/a
Zones 1, 2 & 3	n/a	16	15	8
Zones 1, 2, 3 & 4	n/a	19	-	n/a

leading to them, buses of different companies converge and therefore share part of their routes for limited distances.

There are more bus routes in both Zones 1 and 2 in London than there are in those zones in New York and Paris.

Route lengths increase with distance from the centre in all four cities, reaching a maximum average of just under 20 kilometres in New York's Zone 4.

The function of buses is somewhat different in the four cities. In London, in Zones 1 & 2, buses carry more passengers than the metro, on a dense network of routes. In Zones 3 & 4 they are less frequent, especially at off-peak times, due to the regime of complete deregulation that exists in Great Britain, except in Greater London. Only in major towns and cities, such as Oxford, do they play a significant role in the population's mobility.

In New York's Zones 3 & 4, except for the cities and parts of Westchester County, local bus services are very infrequent and are used for less than 1% of total trips.

The longer route lengths in New York are due to the widely dispersed origins and destinations on local routes in Zones 3 & 4.

4.3.1 Quality of service

Crowding, punctuality and reliability are the main indicators of quality of service by bus.

In New York, local buses within Zones 1 & 2 are scheduled to meet the maximum loading standard at the maximum loading points. Since bus delays increase passenger loadings along a route, schedule adherence is used as an indicator of crowding. In 1995, over a 24 hour period, a little more than half the routes ran within 50% of their scheduled intervals.

In London efforts are made to improve bus reliability by creating shorter bus routes and through installing more bus lanes. However since buses remain often quite unreliable, London Transport is introducing "countdown", a real time information system at bus stops to let passengers know approximately how long they are likely to wait.

---

64   For definitions, see table 20.

    New York   Data for Zones 3 & 4 are based on estimates from New York Metropolitan Transportation Council, New Jersey Transit and Connecticut Transit.

    Tokyo   The Tokyo figure for Zones 1, 2 & 3 is a rough estimate.

65   For definitions see tables 20 and 21.

Table 23 [66]

Reliability and punctuality of bus services in 1995

	London	New York	Paris	Tokyo
Reliability	99%	n/a	97% (in central Paris)	n/a
(% of bus kilometres run as a proportion of schedule)			98% (in the suburbs)	
Punctuality	70% (no more than 2 minutes early or 5 minutes late)	68% New York City Transit (no more than 5 minutes late)	n/a	n/a
		93% New Jersey Transit (no more than 5 minutes late)		

All the cities suffer from road congestion which makes punctuality of bus services hard to achieve, and overcrowding is common.

4.4 Roads

4.4.1 Motorways

Whilst all cities have a developed motorway network in their region, New York is the city with the largest and densest network. London has no motorways in the city centre, while Tokyo has numerous, many of which are elevated on multiple tiers. Paris and Tokyo are still continuing to build new motorways in their regions.

Motorways are defined as limited access roads without cross-roads.

New York has by far the most motorway kilometres of the four cities. Well over half are in Zone 4 and a third in Zone 3. Tokyo also has a substantial urban motorway

Table 24a

Length of motorways in kilometres (disaggregate Zones)

	London	New York	Paris	Tokyo
Zone 1	0	8	5	43
Zone 2	62	337	431	142
Zone 3	n/a	998	346	39
Zone 4	658*[67]	1,653	-	687

Table 24b

Length of motorways in kilometres (aggregate Zones)

	London	New York	Paris	Tokyo
Zone 1	0	8	5	43
Zones 1 & 2	62	345	436	185
Zones 1, 2 & 3	n/a	1,343	782	224
Zones 1, 2, 3 & 4	720	2,996	-	911

66 London The London figures are for London Transport buses only, which operate almost entirely in Zones 1 & 2.

67 The figure for London is a combination of Zones 3 & 4.

Table 25 [68]
Density of motorways (motorway kilometres per square kilometre of land area)

	London	New York	Paris	Tokyo
Zone 1	0	0.78	0.17	1.02
Zone 2	0.04	0.46	0.21	0.25
Zone 3	n/a	0.20	0.03	0.03
Zone 4	0.05	0.06	-	0.06

Figure 11
Density of motorways (motorway kilometres per square kilometre of land area)

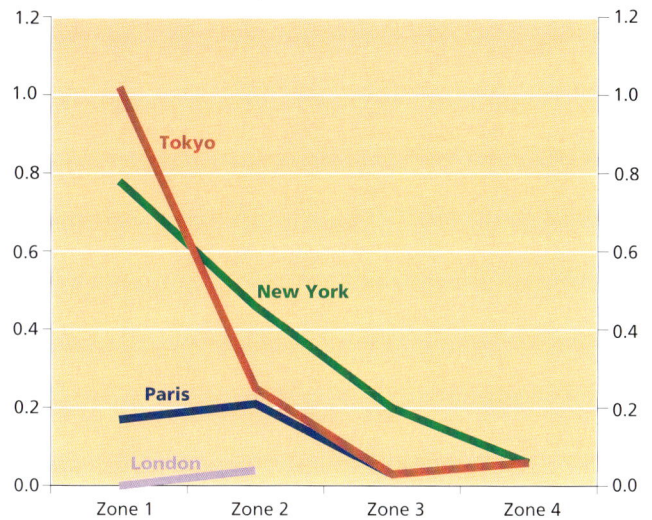

network. What differentiates Tokyo are its urban "expressways" in Zone 1 (43 kilometres for a density of 1.02 motorway kilometre per square kilometre of land area). Many of Tokyo's urban "expressways" run through relatively narrow streets or on top of canals and are elevated in several tiers. New York has only 8 kilometres of motorway in Zone 1, Paris 5, and London none.

In Zone 2, both New York and Paris have more than twice the motorway length of the other cities, but in Zone 2 Paris' motorway density is half that of New York's and about the same as Tokyo's. London has a low motorway density and, instead, facilitates vehicle movement from Zone 2 to Zone 1 by enforcing strict parking controls and optimising signals on nearly 500 kilometres of "Red Routes". In New York, Zone 2 motorways are generally radial, funnelling much regional traffic through New York City, across a limited number of crossings of the waterways that separate all the boroughs of the city (except Brooklyn to/from Queens). Of the 20 river crossings into Manhattan, 6 are tolled.

In Zone 3, New York and Paris have many more motorway kilometres than the other two cities, but when adjusted for area, New York has seven times the

motorway density of Paris and Tokyo. Many of the 1,343 kilometres of motorways in New York's Zones 1, 2 & 3 experience recurring congestion in the morning peak.

In Zone 4, New York again has by far the most motorway miles, but the density of New York's motorways is strikingly similar to that of London and Tokyo. Although London has a low density of motorways in Zones 3 & 4 it has a large number of dual carriageway roads.

Another significant difference among the four regions is that, while New York and London are not building any significant additions to the motorway system, both Paris and Tokyo are engaged in long-term programmes to build significant new routes, many orbital, such as Paris' A86 and the "central loop" of the urban expressways in Tokyo.

68   Table created by dividing figures in Table 24a by the figures in Table 4a.

London   The figure for London's Zone 4 is an aggregation of Zones 3 & 4.

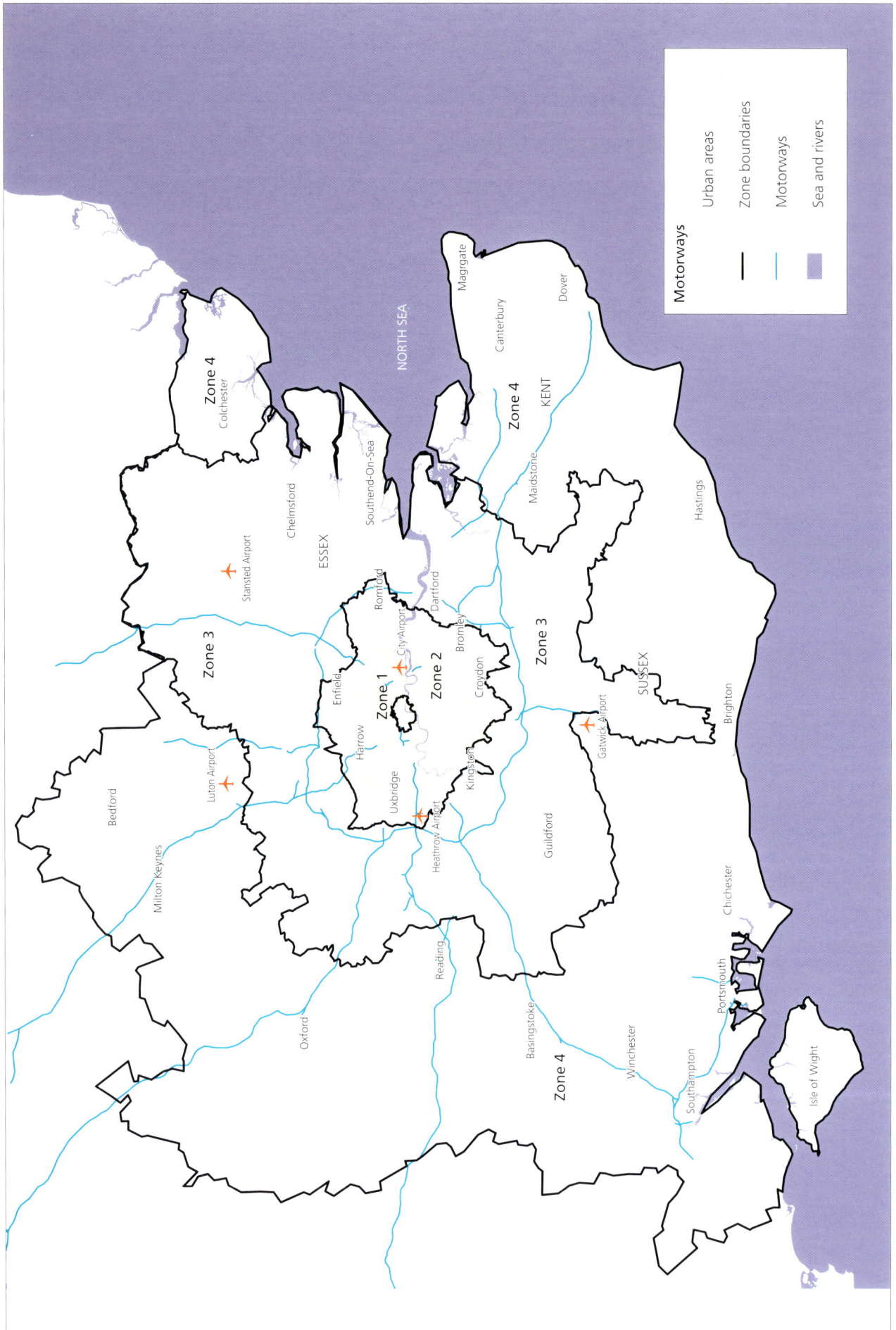

Scale 1cm = 14km

Motorways

—	Urban areas
	Zone boundaries
	Motorways
▨	Sea and rivers

NORTH SEA

Zone 4
Colchester

Chelmsford

ESSEX

Southend-On-Sea

Stansted Airport

Zone 3

Enfield

Romford

Dartford

City Airport

Zone 1

Zone 2

Bromley

Croydon

Harrow

Uxbridge

Kingston

Heathrow Airport

Maggrgate

Canterbury

Dover

Zone 4

KENT

Maidstone

Hastings

Zone 3

Brighton

SUSSEX

Gatwick Airport

Bedford

Milton Keynes

Luton Airport

Oxford

Reading

Basingstoke

Guildford

Winchester

Zone 4

Southampton

Portsmouth

Chichester

Isle of Wight

© Bartholomew's 1997, generated from Bartholomew's digital database: MM-1197-72

Scale 1cm = 14km

Map 12
Motorways - New York - the entire region (Zones 1,2,3 & 4)

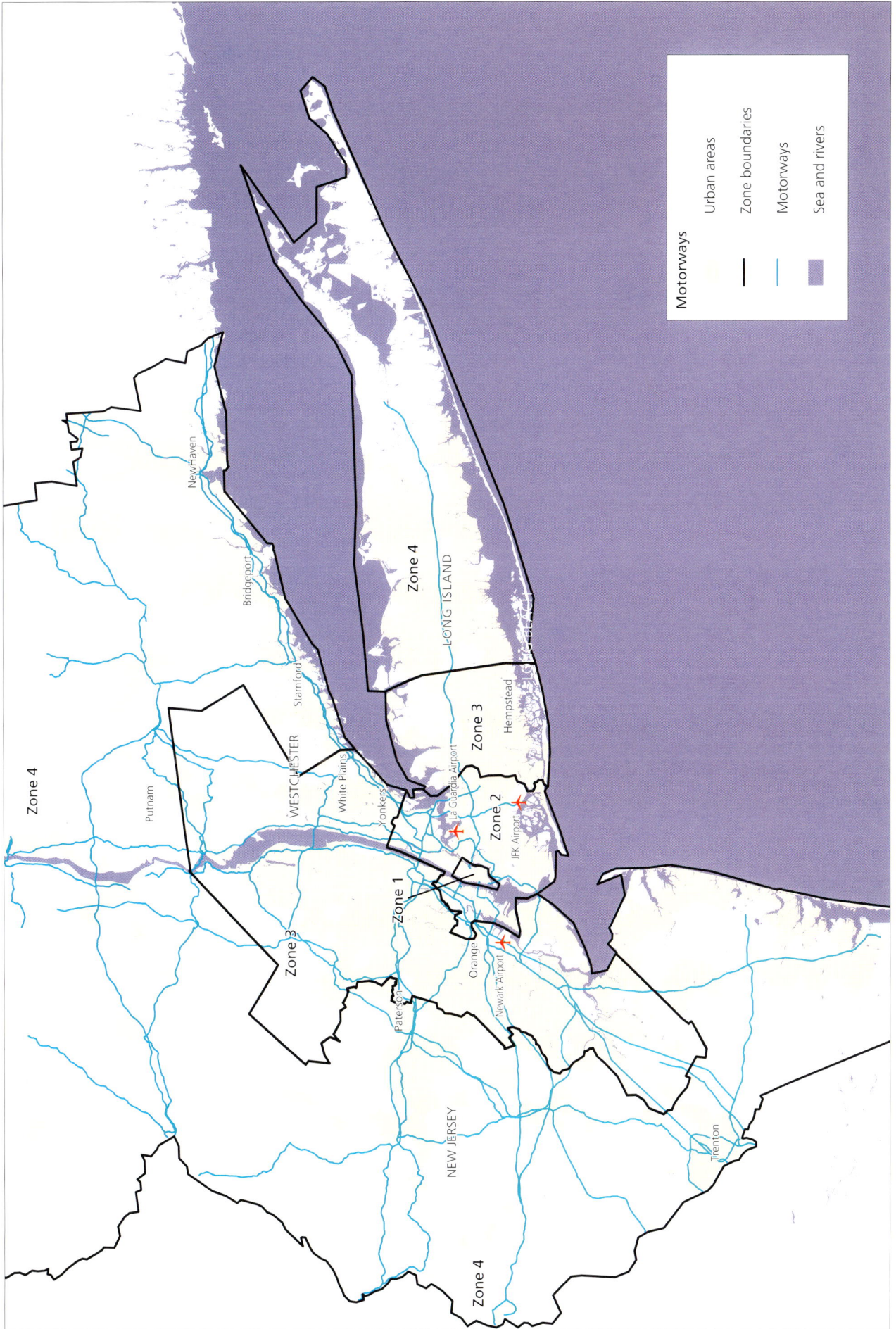

Motorways

Motorways	
	Urban areas
	Zone boundaries
	Motorways
	Sea and rivers

Zone 4

NewHaven

Bridgeport

Zone 4

Stamford

Putnam

WESTCHESTER

White Plains

Zone 4

LONG ISLAND

Yonkers

Hempstead

Zone 3

La Guardia Airport

Zone 2

JFK Airport

Zone 1

Zone 3

Paterson

Orange

Newark Airport

NEW JERSEY

Zone 4

Trenton

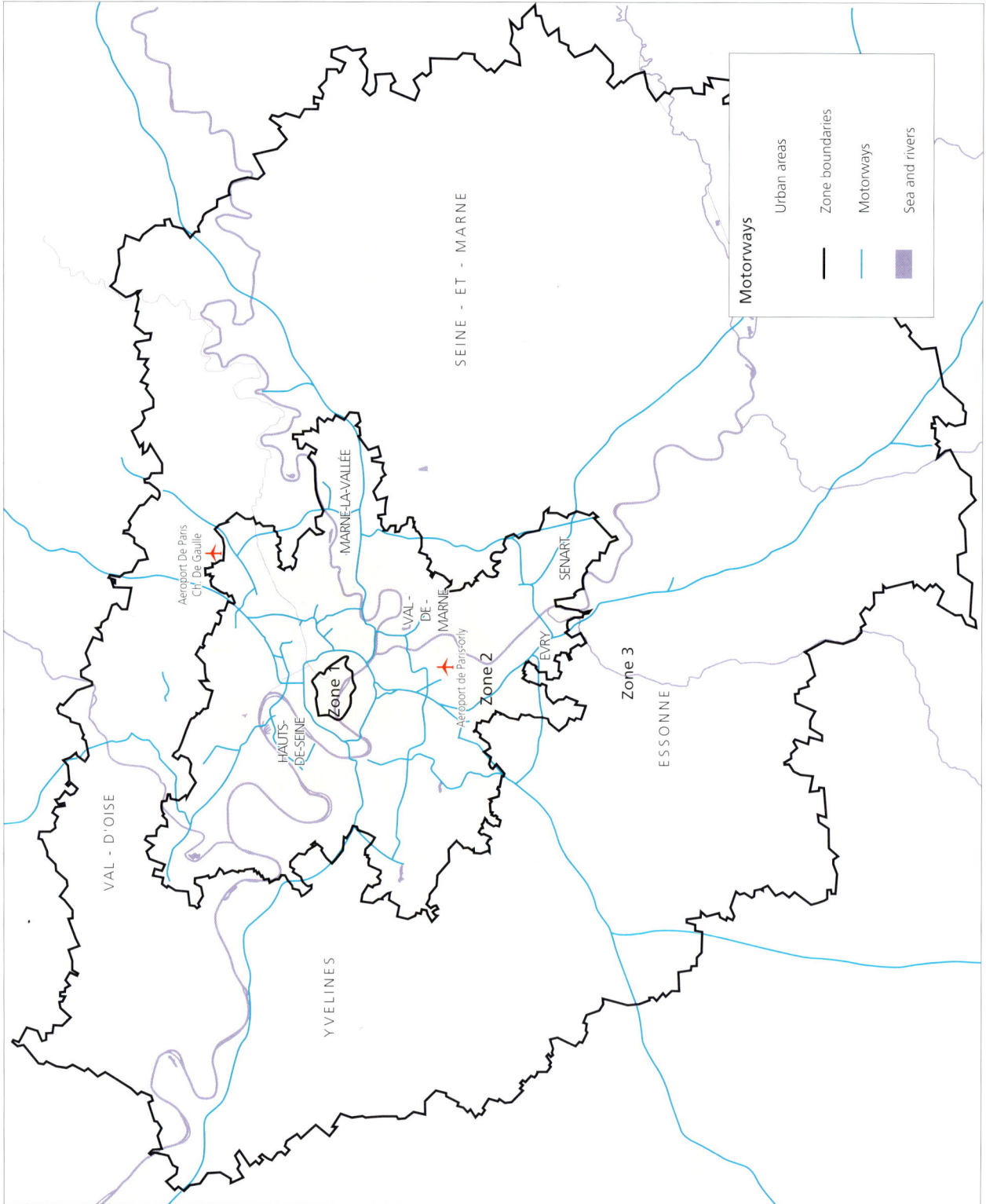

Map 12
Motorways - Paris - the entire region (Zones 1,2,3 &4)

Scale 1cm = 8km

Zone 1

Zone 2

Zone 3

SEINE - ET - MARNE

MARNE-LA-VALLÉE

VAL - DE - MARNE

HAUTS- DE-SEINE

VAL - D'OISE

YVELINES

ESSONNE

SENART

EVRY

Aeroport De Paris Ch. De Gaulle

Aeroport de Paris-Orly

Motorways

Urban areas

Zone boundaries

Motorways

Sea and rivers

Scale 1cm = 9.5km

Map 12
Motorways - Tokyo - the entire region (Zones 1, 2, 3 & 4)

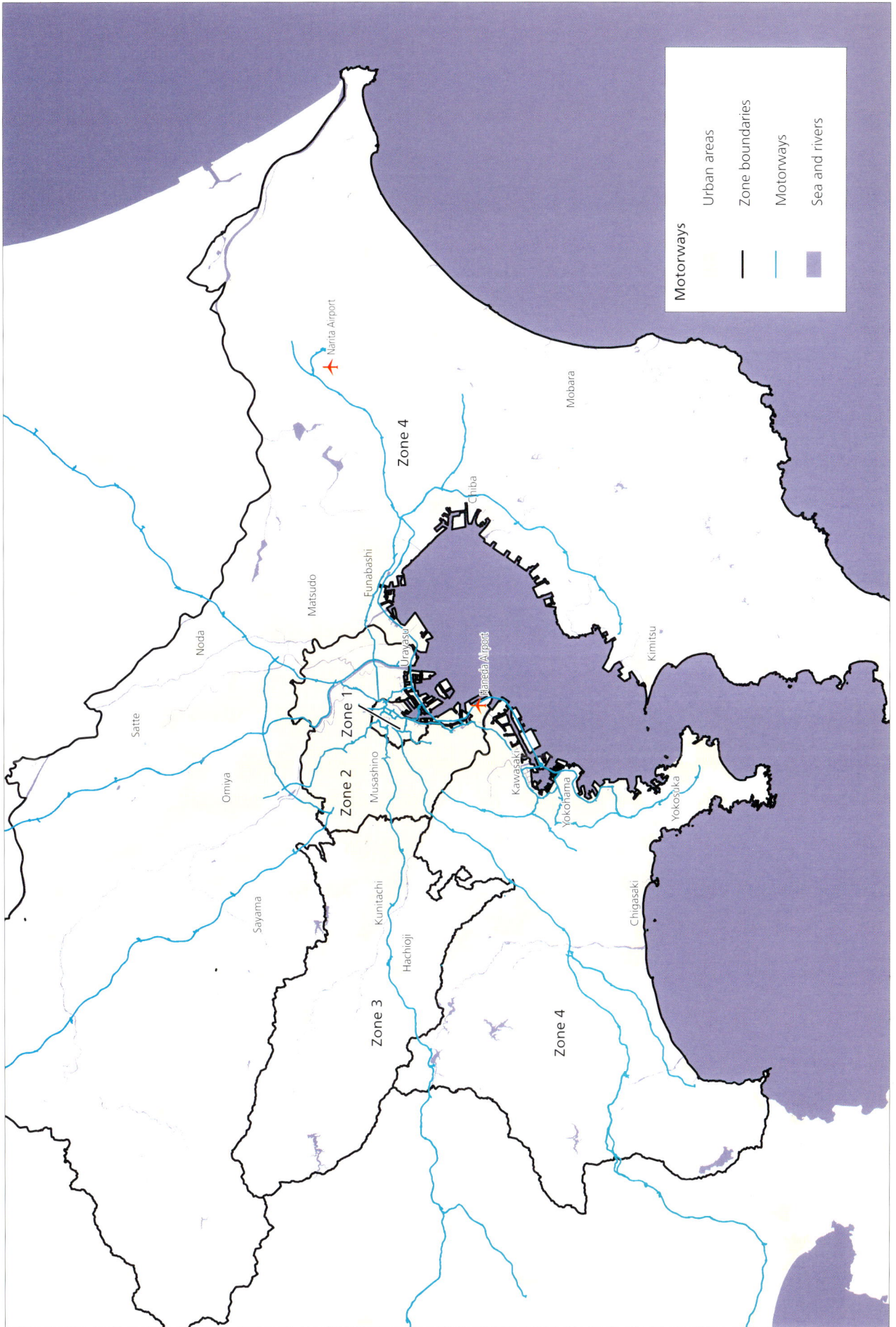

Motorways

Urban areas

Zone boundaries

Motorways

Sea and rivers

Narita Airport

Zone 4

Mobara

Chiba

Matsudo

Funabashi

Noda

Urayasu

Kimitsu

Satte

Zone 1

Haneda Airport

Omiya

Musashino

Kawasaki

Zone 2

Yokohama

Sayama

Yokosuka

Kunitachi

Zone 3

Hachioji

Chigasaki

Zone 4

4.4.2 Traffic accidents

The scourge of traffic accidents is one of the causes of diminution in the quality of life of the residents of the four world cities. This study compares the numbers of accidents and looks at the progress being made by each city to reduce both vehicular and pedestrian casualties.

The accident data reported is for the metropolitan area (Zones 1 & 2). Figures 12a to 12g show fatalities for car drivers, car passengers, cyclists, motorcyclists, lorry drivers and pedestrians. The reason for choosing fatalities is that it makes the data more comparable than injuries, which are measured in different ways and often remain unreported.

Nonetheless, there are still some definitional problems. In Tokyo deaths are attributed to a traffic accident only if they occur within 24 hours of the accident. Traffic accidents taking place on Tokyo's motorways are excluded from the data in figures 12a to 12g. The number of fatalities on Tokyo's motorways in Zones 1, 2 & 3 in 1994 was 21 [69]. By contrast, in New York, a fatality is recorded as being due to a traffic accident if the death is the result of an injury sustained within a year of the accident's having taken place. The equivalent period in London is 30 days. In Paris a fatality is recorded only if the person is found dead by the police at the accident site. Thus, the Parisian figures are somewhat an underestimate of the real level of fatalities.

The numbers of road accident fatalities experienced in Zones 1 & 2 of each city since 1984 are reported for six travel modes. Road accidents are also compared to population (table 5b), car ownership (tables 9a & 9b), traffic levels and distance travelled (tables 28 & 29). The results of this analysis are shown in table 26.

Figure 12a

Car drivers fatalities in Zones 1 & 2 since 1984[70]

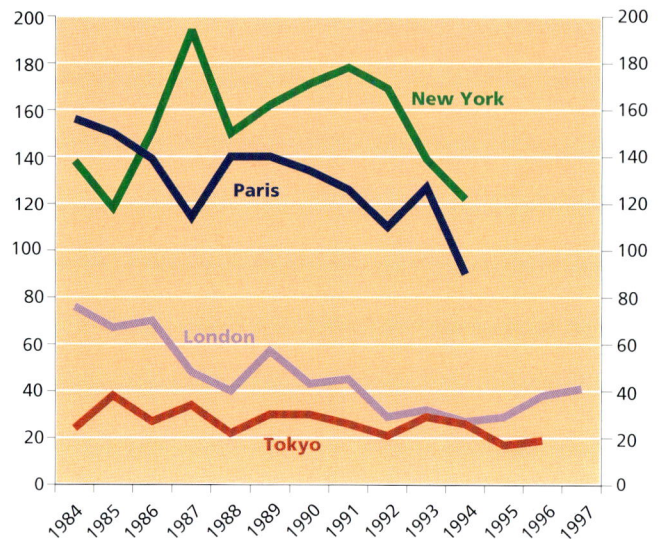

Metropolitan London (Zones 1 & 2) has demonstrated a steady decline in car driver fatalities from a high of 76 in 1984 to a low of 27 in 1994. Road safety is an important aspect of transport policy in Great Britain. In London, every borough has implemented road safety measures as well as extensive traffic calming measures. In Great Britain there is a national target of reducing all traffic accidents by a third by the year 2000 (using as a base the average between 1981 and 1985). Local authorities have to implement their own measures to meet the national standard locally.

Over the 11 year period shown in figure 12a, New York City has suffered car driver fatalities ranging from 118 in 1985 to 194 in 1987. The first of the City's four major transport goals is to "provide safe, efficient, and environmentally responsible movement of pedestrians, goods, and vehicular traffic on the City's streets and highways." In support of this goal, the New York City Department of Transportation has an Office of Safety

---

69 Motorway accident data is only available for Zones 1, 2 & 3. Of the 21 accidents reported in 1994, 4 involved car drivers or passengers, 3 motorcyclists, 11 lorry occupants and 3 pedestrians.

70 Tokyo   The data for drivers also includes passengers.

Figure 12b
Car passenger fatalities in Zones 1 & 2 since 1984 [71]

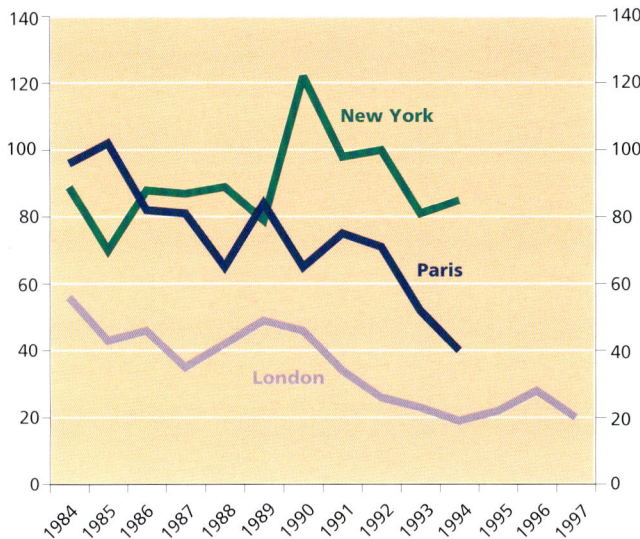

Figure 12c
Cyclist fatalities in Zones 1 & 2 since 1984

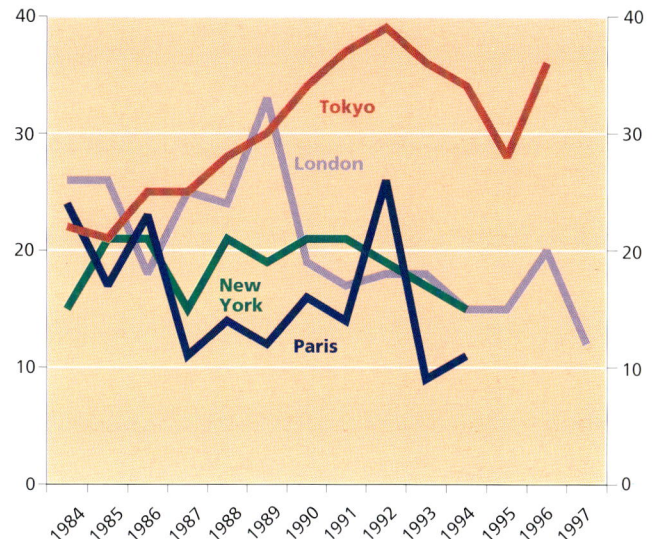

that carries out an extensive safety education programme for children and older citizens, which are essentially defence strategies for pedestrians. Driver safety is approached more as remedial engineering on roads that City or State studies have identified as deficient, based on analyses of accident data. These measures tend to be improvements in roadway geometry that can have the unintended effect of encouraging higher travel speeds. While in the last couple of years the number of fatalities has declined, this decline has not been dramatic, nor can it be predicted to be a trend, since it is well within the range of driver fatalities over the last decade. This difference in fatality statistics reveals a difference in traffic policies between London and New York. Whilst traffic calming and road safety remedial measures are being implemented all over London, in New York, an interest in traffic calming is just beginning, and local roads maintain a speed limit of 40 kilometres per hour, the minimum allowed under State law until 1998. New legislation in New York state allows municipalities to set limits of 24 kilometres per hour.

Paris' Zones 1 & 2 have also experienced a notable decline in driver casualties. Like London, traffic safety measures have been implemented as well as traffic calming and speed reduction measures.

The figures for Tokyo's Zones 1 & 2 have remained constant, but are already much lower than those of the other cities. Although as can be seen from table 28, there is considerably less car traffic in Tokyo's metropolitan area than the equivalent area of the other cities (eg. a quarter of that of Paris), Tokyo's traffic congestion and low speeds also mean that few accidents result in death.

The traffic fatality numbers in figure 12b suggest that car passengers are no more safe than are drivers. In London, with a concerted effort at slowing traffic and protecting motorists (and pedestrians), passenger fatalities in the past decade have been cut in half. In New York, the car passenger fatality figures have gone up and down without any discernible trend.

71   Tokyo   The data for drivers also includes passengers.

Figure 12d
Motorcyclist fatalities in Zones 1 & 2 since 1984

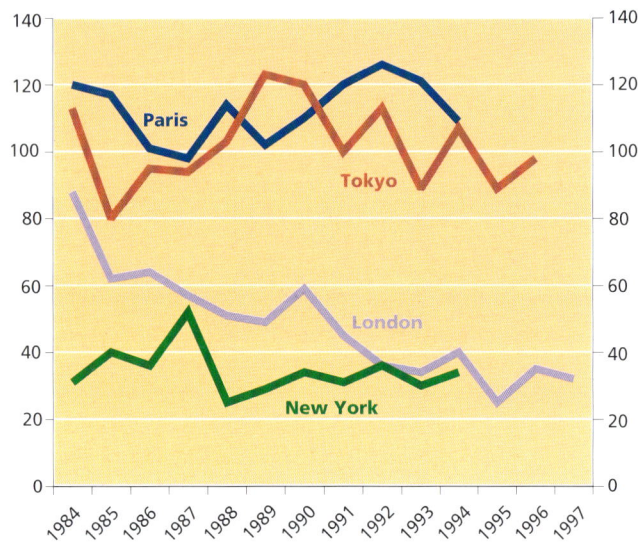

Figure 12e
Fatalities involving goods vehicle occupants in Zones 1 & 2 since 1984[72]

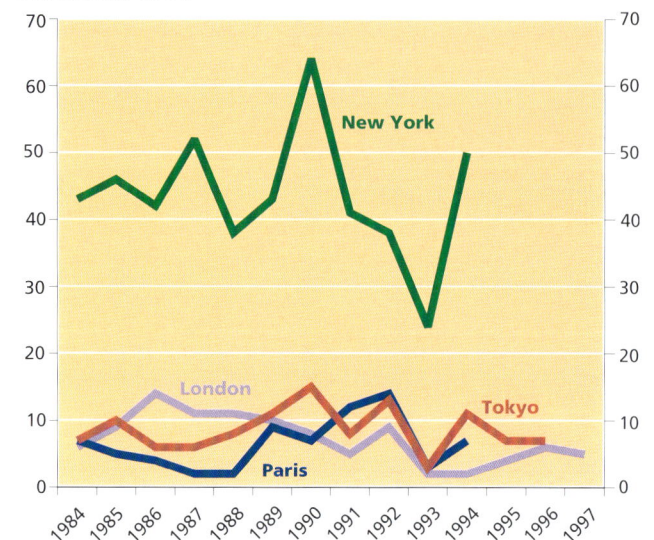

As with car driver and passenger fatalities, London has made some considerable gains in reducing cyclist fatalities. This is partly due to the construction of the London Cycle Network, a series of often segregated cycle lanes throughout the British capital. However, cycling in London has fallen significantly in the 1980s (there were 452,000 cycling trips in 1981 but only 312,000 in 1991). The number of cyclist fatalities remains slightly higher than in New York, where there has been no significant improvement in safety. There has been some improvement in Paris, but in Tokyo the trend has been worsening. In the Tokyo Metropolis (Zones 1, 2 & 3) one-third of the fatalities for cyclists involved the elderly (65 and over). Tokyo's high cycle accident rate can also be attributed to the absence of cycle lanes.

Motorcyclists are the ones who face the greatest risk of fatal accidents on the roads of the four cities. Their accident rates are disproportionate to the amount of travel they make.

38% of all traffic accidents that result in death in Tokyo involve a motorcyclist (and mopeds), over half of whom

are youngsters aged 15 to 24. Whilst little change has occurred in New York over the past ten years, it has to be borne in mind that very few people use motorcycles in Zones 1 & 2 in New York, compared to relatively large numbers of motorcyclists observed in London, Paris and Tokyo. Thus, proportional to the use of motorcycles, New York may actually be a very hazardous city for motorcyclists. Once again, the data reveals that London has made considerable strides in improving road safety and has reduced motorcyclist fatalities.

While the trend for lorry accidents in London has not been falling as consistently as have those for accidents involving car drivers and passengers, it is a distinct contrast to Paris, Tokyo and New York which appear to have made no progress at all (although Paris and Tokyo report very few lorry accidents).

All four cities, except New York, have distribution centres on their peripheries, where inter-city freight is re-loaded on to smaller lorries for in-city deliveries. Paris restricts movements to the city centre by heavy goods lorries. London has introduced a night-time city-wide

72   "Goods vehicle occupants" refers to drivers and passengers of lorries.

Figure 12f

Pedestrian fatalities in road accidents Zones 1 & 2 since 1984

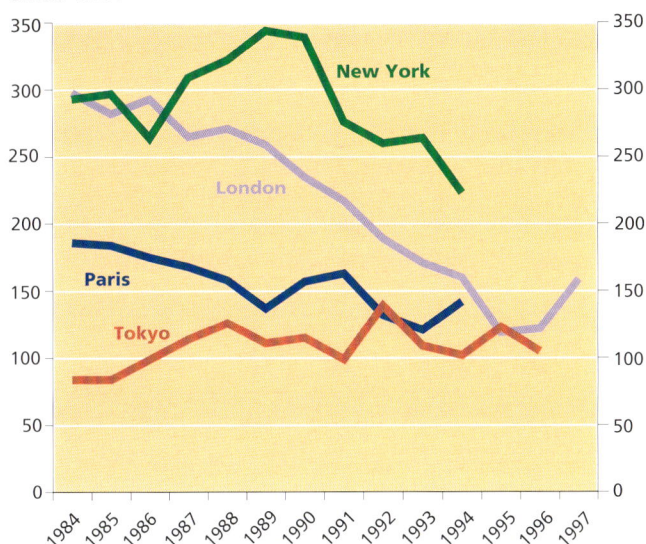

Figure 12g[73]

All fatalities due to road accidents in Zones 1 & 2 since 1984

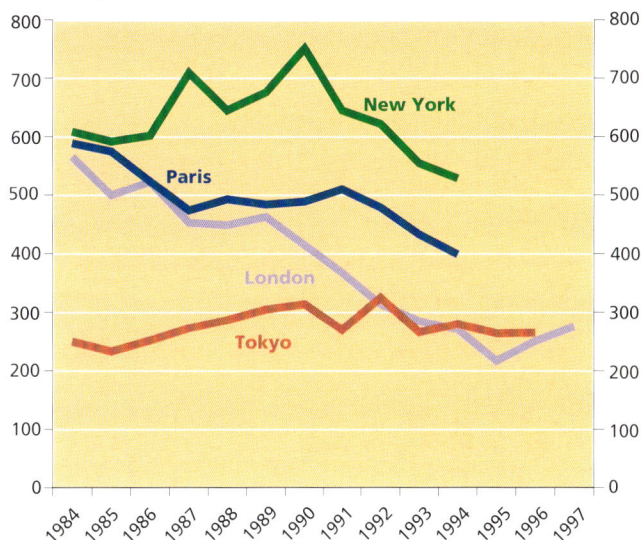

(Zones 1 & 2) lorry ban but it is not uniformly applied and most lorries can obtain exemption permits.

Only in Tokyo are pedestrian fatalities not showing any decline. However, the numbers are still considerably lower than those for the other cities. This is notable, considering the density of pedestrians on streets in central Tokyo. In the other cities, there have been decreases in pedestrian deaths. An effective measure in New York City and London has been the installation of red-light cameras that photograph the license plate of any vehicle that goes through a red light or exceeds the speed limit. In New York City with just 25 cameras in place in 1993, 250,000 violation notices were mailed to the owners of the offending vehicles. In London there are over 450 cameras in place. On many crossings throughout London there are barriers to prevent pedestrians crossing the road where it is deemed to be dangerous.

The progress that London and to a lesser extent New York and Paris have made, seems likely to continue as

pedestrian planning has begun to receive more significant funding and community groups throughout their cities push for traffic calming. For instance, the New York City Department of Transportation has recently formed an Office of Pedestrian Safety and Traffic Calming.

Overall, the accident fatality data reported in figures 12a to 12f show New York numbers going up and down without a clear trend. This is a striking contrast to London where accidents for car users and pedestrians have been cut in half since 1984 with a relatively steady rate of decline. London's fall in road accidents is due to concerted national and local policies to reduce accidents by defining targets and taking measures such as traffic calming and safety audits to reduce road speeds on residential roads. Paris figures are in a slower decline, whilst in Tokyo, which has the lowest level of accidents, they have remained broadly stable.

Overall, as can be seen from table 26, the four cities, with the exception of Tokyo, have seen a reduction in

73   For New York, Paris and Tokyo; the data is a summation of the data in figures 12a to 12f.

      For London the data in figure 12g are slightly higher than the summation of the data in figures 14a to 12f, as they also include taxi drivers and passengers as well as drivers and passengers of buses and coaches. In 1977 there were no fatalities for taxis and only 2 for bus passengers.

Table 26 [74]
All road accidents fatalities in Zones 1 & 2 in 1991 by population, car ownership, number of trips and person kilometres travelled

	London	New York	Paris	Tokyo
total number of fatalities	378	645	510	270
% change between 1984 and 1994	-52%	-13%	-32%	+12%
ROAD ACCIDENTS FATALITIES IN ZONES 1 & 2 PER:				
million inhabitants of Zones 1 & 2	55	86	58	33
million cars owned by inhabitants of Zones 1 & 2	158	358	161	173
billion car journeys within Zones 1 & 2	131	322	150	318
billion car kilometres travelled in Zones 1 & 2	18	24	28	n/a

fatal road accidents between 1984 and 1994. In London fatal accidents were cut by half.

The road accident fatality data have been compared to population (table 5b), car ownership (tables 9a & 9b) and traffic data (tables 28 & 29). The results of this analysis show that Tokyo, despite having fewer fatalities than the other cities, has a high accident record when compared to number of car journeys made. New York has the highest fatal accident record per journeys made.

London, with its committed policy of traffic safety, manages to have the lowest level of car accidents, both in terms of car ownership and total number of car journeys.

4.5 Infrastructure plans

Each of the four cities has a number of public transport or road schemes under construction or planned. Many schemes are in the planning phase, have uncertain funding and may never be built. This study reports on schemes which are either currently under construction or have secure funding.

4.5.1 London

London does not have a systematic plan for improvements to its transport system. There are several schemes which are currently being realised with diverse motivations, diverse sponsors and diverse funding mechanisms.

One major area of transport infrastructure improvement has come about through the redevelopment of Docklands (Zone 2) and the East Thames corridor (Zones 3 & 4). It is those areas that have seen most of London's new infrastructure since the 1980s.

74 The indicators of road safety provided in this table need to be interpreted with caution.

The accident data are those for 1991.

Population refers to residents of Zones 1 & 2 as reported in table 5b.

Car ownership data are extrapolated by amalgamating the figures of tables 9b and 5b. This is not quite accurate as Zone 1 data is missing - yet it is a robust estimate, since the population of Zone 1 is relatively small. For definitions, see table 9a.

Not all road accidents are car related, but these form a substantial proportion of the total number of accidents. It is thus interesting to look at accidents per car trip. Car trip figures have been taken from table 28. The figures available in table 28 are for a typical Monday to Friday. To obtain an annual estimate, the figures in table 28 were initially multiplied by 6 to cover a week (assuming that half the number of trips are made on Saturdays and Sundays) and then multiplied by 52 to cover the entire year. It has to be stressed that these figures are only indicative.

To obtain annual kilometres travelled, the figures derived from table 28 were multiplied by the average car journey distance reported in table 29. Again, it has to be stressed that these figures are only indicative.

The following schemes are under construction or have secured funding:

- The Jubilee metro line extension (Zones 1 & 2). This is the extension of the Jubilee line from central London, through Docklands to Stratford in east London. It will serve the Millennium Dome, the centrepiece for Britain's millennium celebrations. The scheme is under construction and should be completed by the year 2000.

- The Docklands Light Railway extension to Lewisham (Zone 2). This is the extension of the Docklands Light Railway line from Docklands to south of the river Thames to Lewisham in south-east London. The scheme, funded partly through private finance, is under construction and should be completed by the year 2000. It will be a much needed public transport link between Docklands and south London. There is also a minor scheme to link the Docklands Light Railway to City airport in the Royal Docks (Zone 2).

- Croydon Tramlink (Zone 2). A tram line is being constructed in south London in the Croydon area, partly using existing rail lines but also some streets.

- There are no major new roads being built in London. There are however a number of road improvement schemes:

  - The development of 315 miles of Red Routes (Zones 1 & 2). These schemes, which involve traffic management measures and on which parking controls are strictly enforced, are part of an evolving plan to improve traffic flows in Greater London.

  - Widening of the orbital M25 motorway in the south-west (Zone 3).

- Improvements to A406 North Circular Road (Zone 2).

- Improvements to the A13 that provide access from the M25 to Docklands and East London (Zone 2).

- The A12 linking Hackney Wick and the M11 (Zone 2).

Currently sizeable funds are being made available for the modernisation and improvement of the existing metro system. Part of these funds are expected to come from private sources.

4.5.2 New York

Like London, New York does not have a systematic rationale to its plans for new infrastructure. Under current national transport legislation, every state and metropolitan area must have a long-term plan related to land-use formulated with public participation. This long-term plan is supposed to be the basis for Transportation Improvement Programs for every state and metropolitan area. Transportation Improvement Programs establish priorities for transport investment. In the New York region, however, there is not one but 10 Metropolitan Planning Organisations, though two (one for southern New York and one for northern New Jersey) cover most of the region.

Of the total five-year financial commitment to transport in New York, 53% is dedicated to public transport and 47% is allocated to roads and bridges. For all transport, 90% of the funds is committed to rehabilitation and upgrading existing facilities and 10% is being invested in system expansion, although some increase in capacity will result from upgrades, e.g. wider motorway lanes and more efficient track signalling.

The following schemes are under construction or have secured funding:

- A 22 kilometre light rail system in Hudson County (Zone 2), just across the Hudson River from Manhattan, and, beginning in 1998, construction of a 13 kilometre, 11 station extension of the light rail line spur from Newark to Elizabeth (Zone 3).

- An 8 kilometre extension of Metro North regional rail in Dutchess County, New York (Zone 4).

- A 2.4 kilometre metro tunnel connection in Queens (Zone 2) to provide more through-running capacity on the existing metro lines.

- Improvements to the rail system related to making New York's airports, John F. Kennedy in the New York suburb of Jamaica, east of Manhattan, and Newark in New Jersey, better connected to the region's rail and metro systems:

    - A rail link to Newark airport in Union County, New Jersey (Zone 3).

    - A rail link from the Long Island Railroad's Jamaica station to John F. Kennedy Airport, Queens County, New York (Zone 2).

- Over the next three decades, the New York region is faced with replacing or rebuilding thousands of kilometres of motorways and arterial roadways due to age and/or inadequate maintenance. As in London no new roads are being built, but there are numerous road improvement or reconstruction projects which are being undertaken. The major projects with secured funding scheduled for the region over the next five years include:

    - Improvement to the orbital Cross Westchester Expressway I-287 (Zone 3).

- Completion of Route 9A on the west side of Manhattan with limited signalised intersections alongside a new Hudson River Park (Zone 1).

- Reconstruction of parts of the Major Deegan Expressway (Zone 2).

- Reconstruction of several interchanges of the Long Island Expressway (I-495), Nassau/Suffolk counties (Zone 2).

- Reconstruction of the elevated Gowanus Expressway (Brooklyn) (Zone 2).

- Major highway interchanges, Garden State Parkway (Bergen), and routes 1 and 18 (Middlesex) (Zone 3).

- New Jersey's turnpike widening and interchange improvements, (Somerset, Middlesex) (Zones 3 & 4).

- Reconstruction of inter-state 95 (Fairfield, New Haven) (Zone 4).

4.5.3 Paris

Transport infrastructure projects are based on the region's structure plan, the Schéma Directeur d'Aménagement et d'Urbanisme, and the spending contracts between the government and the Région d'Ile-de-France (we are currently in the 11th contract covering 1994 to 1998).

The following schemes are the main ones currently under construction:

- A new line E (EOLE) of the Réseau Express Régional (Zones 1 & 2), planned to start operations in 1999. This is a 4 kilometre tunnel linking regional rail lines currently terminating at St. Lazare and Gare du Nord/Gare de l'Est.

- A new automatic east-to-west metro line METEOR (Zones 1 & 2), designed to relieve congestion on line A of the Réseau Express Régional (an 8 kilometre section will be operational in 1998).

- A 1.4 kilometre extension of line 13 of the Metro in St. Denis (Zone 2). Its objective is to serve the university and it is due to open in 1998.

- The northern section of the Francilienne (Zone 2). This new road will link Charles de Gaulle airport with the new town of Cergy-Pontoise from 2001.

- The western section of motorway A86 (Zone 2). This road is being constructed with private finance and contains a 12.5 kilometre underground section. It is due to open in 2001/02.

4.5.4   Tokyo

There are a large number of schemes being built in Tokyo which are more ambitious than those of the other cities. The plans for the railways are:

Metro:

- An extension of the Mita line (between Mita and Seishokomae - 1.6 kilometres).

- An extension of the Nanboku line (between Meguro and Tameikesanno - 5.2 kilometres).

- An extension of the Hanzomon line (between Suitengu-mae and Oshiage - 5.9 kilometres).

- Line no. 12. Construction work started on this line in 1986 and the first part became operational in 1992. A radial section (between Shinjuku and Nerima - 9.1 kilometres), was completed in 1997. Now an orbital section (28.8 kilometres) is being constructed, and is due to be completed by 2000.

- A new metro line in Saitama (Zone 4), the Saitama Rapid Transit line (8.4 kilometres).

- A new metro line in Kanagawa prefecture (Zone 4), line MM21 (4.3 kilometres).

- An extension of the Yokohama Rapid Transit line 1 (in Zone 4 - 7.4 kilometres)

Regional rail:

- The New Joban line (between Akihabara and Tsukuba - 58.3 kilometres), to be completed by 2005. Its purpose is to relieve congestion on existing lines and help to further develop the north-eastern part of the Tokyo Metropolitan Region.

- The extension of the Tokyo Waterfront Area Rapid Transit (between Tokyo Teleport and Osaki - 7.3 kilometres). This line is part of the water-front area development. The line is due to be completed by 2000.

- Furthermore, there are minor extensions to existing regional rail lines, such as 3.8 kilometres to the Chiba New Town line, or the 3.1 kilometre extension to Sotetsu Izumino line in Kanagawa prefecture.

Monorail and "new transit systems":

- The Tama Urban Monorail (between Tama Centre and Kamikitadai - 16.2 kilometres). This line is meant to aid development of the Tama area. The first part is due to become operational in 1998 and the remainder is due for completion in 1999.

- A 1.7 kilometre extension of the Chiba monorail from Chiba to Kenchomae, to be completed by 1999.

- A small 0.7 kilometre extension to the Tokyo monorail (from Haneda Airport to the north-east Terminal).

- The Nippori - Toneri line (between Nippori and Minumadai Shinsui Park - 9.8 kilometres). This line is aimed at improving public transport in the north-eastern part of Zones 1 & 2.

The plans for roads are based on improving orbital movement, with construction of roads such as the central loop of the urban expressways. Because of environmental concern and the high cost of land, sections of the new urban expressways are to be built underground in tunnels. In the meantime numerous split level crossings are also being built between roads and between roads and railway lines.

4.6   Travel patterns

All four cities are characterised by heavy commuting to the city centre, mainly by metro and regional rail services. In the suburbs and further out, the patterns of travel are different. Although the car is the dominant mode for trips in Zones 3 & 4 in all cities, public transport retains a role in London's and Paris' outer Zones and even more so in Tokyo.

This section concentrates on commuting flows to the central area (Zone 1) and analyses travel data of journeys made in the cities' metropolitan areas (Zones 1 & 2). Journeys are defined by main mode excluding walking. In London, New York and Paris, the dominant mode for multi-modal journeys is defined as that of the greatest length. Tokyo uses instead a hierarchical structure for assigning mode to multi-modal journeys, rail being the dominant mode, followed by bus, then car and lastly, motorcycle.

Due to the variety of ways in which the four cities report walking trips, these are not included in the tables, although walking represents a significant portion of the trips in Zones 1 & 2 in all the cities. Residents of Zones 1 and 2 in Tokyo make a daily total of 5.6 million journeys on foot. In London, in 1991, four million trips were made daily in Zones 1 & 2, entirely on foot. In New York, survey results show that at least three million people in Zones 1 & 2 travel daily by walking the entire way between their origin and destination.

The data for tables 27, 28, 29 and 31 on the number of journeys, journey origins and destinations, journey lengths, journey modes and journey purposes come from travel surveys in the four cities. These are:

London   Data for London are derived from the 1991 London Area Transport Survey which carried out by the Department of Transport and all the London boroughs through the London Research Centre. The main results of the survey were published in "*Travel in London*" (London Research Centre & Department of Transport, 1994). The

1991 London Area Transport Survey collected detailed data for all movements within the M25 motorway, an area slightly larger than Greater London (Zones 1 & 2). Travel data for residents of Greater London were gathered through an individual household interviews and the completion of a one day travel diary. Over 160,000 people were interviewed. There were also roadside and on-board surveys carried out on the metro and other rail services. In total, these yielded over 1.5 million interviews for residents, visitors and commuters to London.

New York For travel into Zone 1, the 1990 "Hub-Bound Study" was used. This is an annual cordon count by the New York Metropolitan Transportation Council of all persons and vehicles entering and leaving the Manhattan central business district. To separate resident from non-resident trips, these numbers were adjusted using origin-destination data reported by the New York Metropolitan Transportation Council for 1980 and, for work trips only, by the United States census of 1990. Non-work trips are estimated by extrapolating from the New York sample drawn from the 1990 Nation-wide Personal Transportation Survey. Forecasts come from "*Access to the Region's Core*" (1995), an interim report of a major inter-agency planning study. Other data used in this analysis were extracted from the New York Metropolitan Transportation Council's

"*Regional Transportation Report*" of February 1996.

Paris The data for Paris come from the Enquête Globale des Transports which was last carried out in 1991. The Enquête Globale des Transports is a household based survey undertaken to complement every census of population. In 1991, data was collected on 16,000 households. It is carried out by the National Statistical Institute on behalf of the Direction Régionale de l'Équipement and is financed by numerous stake-holders in the region.

Tokyo Data for Tokyo come from the third "Person Trip Survey" of 1990. This survey was undertaken by the Tokyo Metropolitan Region Transport Planning Commission [75]. The survey was conducted by interviewing 820,000 persons in 300,000 households in Zones 1, 2, 3 & 4 and the southern part of Ibaraki prefecture. Each household was visited by a surveyor who handed out a one-day trip diary in the form of a questionnaire. The response rate was 81.5%.

4.6.1 Travel into the central area

The four cities exhibit striking differences in travel patterns to the core. Tokyo has by far the largest commuting population in the morning peak, just under two million people. Yet New York has the highest number of people going into the central area over a 24

---

[75] The Tokyo Metropolitan Region Transport Planning Commission comprises the Ministry of Construction; the Tokyo Metropolitan Government; prefectural governments of Kanagawa, Saitama, Chiba and Ibaraki; municipal governments of Yokohama, Kawasaki and Chiba; the Housing and Urban Development Corporation; the Japan Highway Public Corporation; and the Metropolitan Expressway Public Corporation.

Transport structure

Table 27a [76]

Number of persons entering the central area (Zone 1) daily (24 hours Monday to Friday) by main mode of travel - excluding those on foot

		London	New York	Paris	Tokyo
Car	Residents of Zones 1 & 2	340,000	680,000	630,000	200,000
	Residents outside Zones 1 & 2	80,000	350,000	30,000	130,000
	Total	420,000	1,030,000	660,000	330,000
	%	25%	32%	28%	11%
Metro	Residents of Zones 1 & 2	500,000	1,660,000	860,000	
	Residents outside Zones 1 & 2	110,000	50,000	5,000	included in "Rail"
	Total	610,000	1,710,000	865,000	
	%	35%	54%	37%	
Rail	Residents of Zones 1 & 2	290,000	35,000	420,000	1,080,000
	Residents outside Zones 1 & 2	230,000	190,000	60,000	1,490,000
	Total	520,000	225,000	480,000	2,570,000
	%	30%	7%	21%	86%
Bus	Residents of Zones 1 & 2	130,000	100,000	210,000	30,000
	Residents outside Zones 1 & 2	-	120,000	-	5,000
	Total	130,000	220,000	210,000	35,000
	%	7%	7%	9%	1%
Motorcycle	Residents of Zones 1 & 2	20,000		60,000	20,000
	Residents outside Zones 1 & 2	-	included in "Car"	5,000	5,000
	Total	20,000		65,000	25,000
	%	1%		3%	1%
Total (may include other modes)	Residents of Zones 1 & 2	1,320,000	2,475,000	2,215,000	1,350,000
	Residents outside Zones 1 & 2	420,000	710,000	100,000	1,640,000
	Total	1,700,000	3,185,000	2,315,000	2,990,000
	% of other modes	2%	0%	2%	1%

76   The figures include both residents of Zone 1 and non-residents. However trips made entirely within Zone 1 are not included in the data.

London   The only data available for bus travel come from the household interview survey of the 1991 London Area Transport Survey, and relate only to residents of Zones 1 & 2. It is assumed that residents of Zones 3 & 4 make very few main mode bus trips in Zones 1 & 2.

New York   The bus data include commuter coaches.

Tokyo   The metro figures include rail figures.

Monorail is in the "other modes" category.

Figure 13a
Number of persons entering the central area (Zone 1) daily (24 hours Monday to Friday) by main mode of travel - excluding those on foot

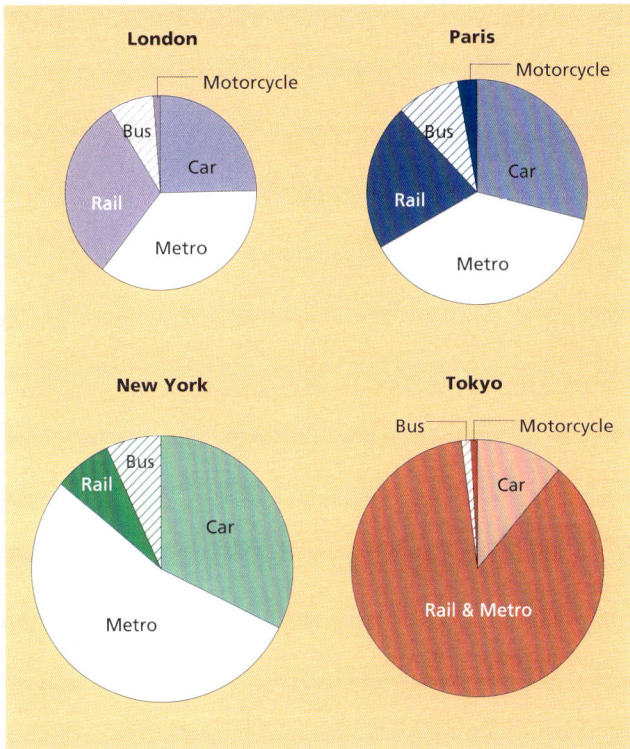

Figure 13b
Number of persons entering the central area (Zone 1) daily in the Monday to Friday morning peak (07:00 - 09:59) by main mode of travel - excluding those on foot

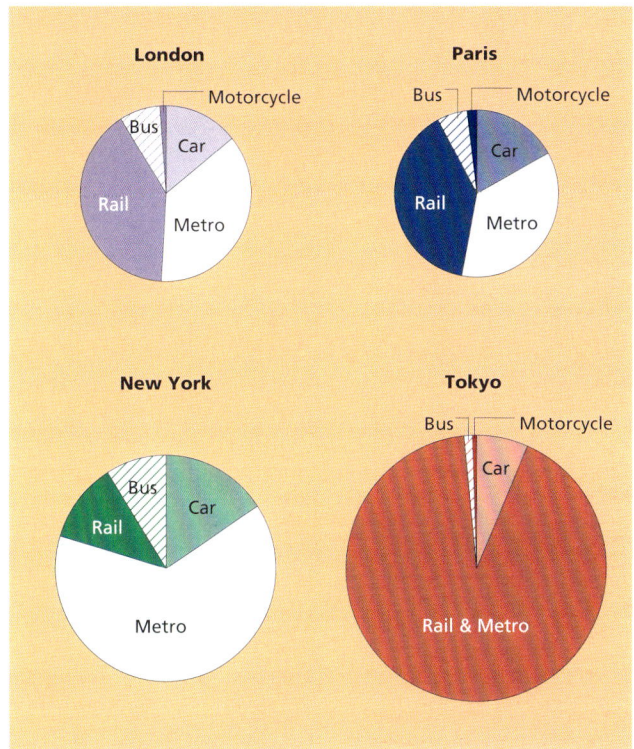

hour period. This indicates that the attraction of Manhattan is far more than that of employment.

The percentage of the total day travel to the core that occurs in the morning peak period is very different in the four cities:

- London   50%
- New York   44%
- Paris   33%
- Tokyo   65%

This indicates that central Tokyo is predominantly a work location for commuters living outside, while Paris, on the other hand, with its large residential population, sees travel to and from the centre occurring at all times.

In Tokyo, over 90% of morning commuters arrive by train or metro. Whilst rail and metro operate frequently

and punctually, car travel times are unpredictable and parking can be unavailable. In the other cities, the proportion commuting by regional rail or metro is 76% for London, 75% for New York and 75% for Paris. Commuting to the city centre by car is uncommon. In no city is it more than 17% of the total.

It is important to note that most Japanese companies bear their employees' commuting expenses (In 1995, 86% of companies paid the total amount of their employees' commuting expenses). For this reason, the level of public transport fares does not seem to influence commuters' choice of residential location. What matters most to them are land prices and not the length of their daily commuting journeys. In Paris employers are obliged by law to pay half the commuting costs of their employees, but only within the Ile-de-France region (within Zones 1, 2 & 3).

Transport structure

Table 27b [77]
Number of persons entering the central area (Zone 1) daily in the Monday to Friday morning peak (07:00 - 09:59) by main mode of travel - excluding those on foot

		London	New York	Paris	Tokyo
Car	Residents of Zones 1 & 2	100,000	140,000	120,000	85,000
	Residents outside Zones 1 & 2	20,000	80,000	10,000	40,000
	Total	120,000	220,000	130,000	125,000
	%	14%	16%	17%	6%
Metro	Residents of Zones 1 & 2	290,000	856,000	275,000	included in "Rail"
	Residents outside Zones 1 & 2	20,000	30,000	-	
	Total	310,000	895,000	275,000	
	%	36%	64%	36%	
Rail	Residents of Zones 1 & 2	180,000	30,000	250,000	780,000
	Residents outside Zones 1 & 2	160,000	130,000	50,000	1,000,000
	Total	340,000	160,000	300,000	1,780,000
	%	40%	11%	39%	91%
Bus	Residents of Zones 1 & 2	65,000	50,000	45,000	20,000
	Residents outside Zones 1 & 2	-	75,000	0	-
	Total	65,000	125,000	45,000	20,000
	%	8%	9%	6%	1%
Motorcycle	Residents of Zones 1 & 2	10,000	included in "Car"	15,000	10,000
	Residents outside Zones 1 & 2	-		0	-
	Total	10,000		15,000	10,000
	%	1%		2%	1%
Total (may include other modes)	Residents of Zones 1 & 2	655,000	1,185,000	705,000	900,000
	Residents outside Zones 1 & 2	200,000	215,000	60,000	1,050,00
	Total	855,000	1,400,000	765,000	1,950,000
	% of other modes	1%	0%	0%	1%

77   For definitions, see table 27a.

Table 28 [78]

Daily, 24 hours Monday to Friday motorised journeys made entirely within the metropolitan area (journeys that start and end within Zones 1 & 2) by main mode of travel

	London	New York	Paris	Tokyo
Car	9,020,000	6,410,000	10,910,000	2,720,000
	64%	51%	65%	27%
Metro	1,870,000	3,550,000	2,280,000	included in "Rail"
	13%	28%	14%	
Rail	800,000	140,000	2,110,000	5,760,000
	6%	1%	12%	58%
Bus	1,850,000	1,860,000	1,590,000	630,000
	13%	15%	9%	6%
Motorcycles	140,000	10,000	n/a	510,000
	1%	0%	n/a	5%
Total (may include other modes)	14,140,000	12,660,000	16,890,000	9,990,000
% of other modes	3%	5%	0%	4%

Figure 14

Daily, 24 hours Monday to Friday motorised journeys made entirely within the metropolitan area (journeys that start and end within Zones 1 & 2) by main mode of travel

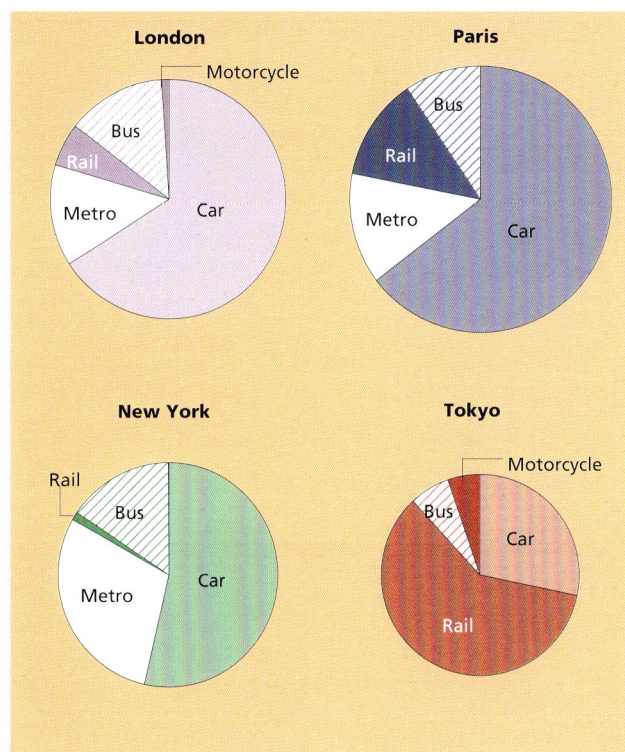

4.6.2   Travel within the metropolitan area

Tokyo has the lowest number of people travelling, in general by motorised modes, within Zones 1 & 2. More people travel by metro and train within Tokyo's metropolitan area (58% of all trips) than in the metropolitan areas of the other cities. London and Paris are the most motorised of the four cities with cars accounting for 64% and 65% respectively of all trips. In London and New York, bus use is also significant, attracting over 15% of all motorised travel in Zones 1 & 2. The high level of bus use in New York's Zones 1 & 2 is unexpected in view of the irregularity of service and the absence of fare transfers (at the time this data was collected in 1995). When free fare transfers were introduced between metro and bus in July 1997, bus ridership jumped by 17% in the first month.

The cost of public transport and the type of ticketing can have an effect on the level of mobility and journey patterns. The costs of public transport vary between the four cities. In a study by the London Research Centre (the *International Fares Comparison Study* of 1995, summarised in table 30), New York was the most expensive city for public transport out of a world sample of 15. Meanwhile, the cost of driving in New York is by far the cheapest of the four cities.

---

78   For definitions, see table 27a.

Data in table 28 are slightly greater than the origin-destination matrices presented in table 31a, because in table 28 all modes are counted, while table 31a is comprised of car, regional rail, metro and bus only.

Transport structure

Table 29 [79]

Average journey length of residents of the metropolitan area (Zones 1 & 2) by main mode (in kilometres "straight line")

	London	New York	Paris	Tokyo
Car	7.1	13.2	5.4	n/a
Metro	8.7	8.7	5.0	n/a
Rail	20.5	n/a	13.7	n/a
Bus	4.0	4.4	3.4	n/a
Walk	1.1	1.0	0.5	n/a
Bicycles	2.9	3.1	included in "motorcycles"	n/a
Motorcycles	7.6	n/a	3.6	n/a
Taxis	4.6	8.4	5.3	n/a

Table 30 [80]

Average weekly costs of public transport in Zones 1 & 2 in 1995 in US $

City	Working age	Retirement age	11 - 15 year olds	Overall
	1995 exchange rate	1995 exchange rate	1995 exchange rate	weighted at purchasing power parity
London	12.01	0.15	8.29	8.56
New York	14.70	5.06	8.29	11.73
Paris	10.78	5.08	14.19	7.03
Tokyo	19.94	13.76	18.09	8.27

79   For definitions, see table 27a.

Walk trips cannot be readily compared due to differing definitions of "walk" and cut-off points of short walk trips.

New York	The New York survey data contain very few rail users and motorcycle users to give robust enough figures.
Paris	Motorcycle data include bicycle.
Tokyo	Data are unavailable as the "Person Trip Survey" does not measure journey length.

80   The data in this table are from a study by the London Research Centre, *International Fares Comparison Study*, last updated in 1995 (Focas & Brown, 1995).

The analysis was based upon a segmentation of the London travel market which was applied to the other cities. It applies only to the users of public transport.

The travel market was divided into eight broad groups defined by their age, area of residence and intensity of use of public transport. Each of these eight groups was analysed to define a 'package' of public transport journeys which was broadly typical. The eight packages of journeys were then priced on the basis of the best available public transport fare including monthly or weekly discounted season tickets, railcards and/or 'strip' tickets, such as the Parisian "carnet". The fares for each journey package, in each city, were combined into a single overall index of fares by the use of weights, derived from London's travel market.

The figures in the table do not take into account reimbursements systems, such as the one in Paris where salaried workers have half their season ticket 'Carte Orange' refunded by their employer. Many employees in Tokyo have their entire commuting fare paid by their employer.

The result of this analysis is, therefore, an assessment of how much it would cost in other cities to make the journeys that Londoners actually make, assuming that travellers use the most favourable fare available. Note that this is not necessarily the same as assessing how much other cities' residents in fact pay for the journeys they actually make.

The figures were correct for 1995 and calculated in UK £. These were then converted to US $.

The data in table 30 present the average weekly cost of travel for public transport users in all four cities based on the travel patterns made in London. London offers free travel to nearly all senior citizens but still has an overall high cost for the user of public transport. New York is the most expensive city for public transport, not having comprehensive travel passes for all transport modes, as has London with the "Travelcard" and Paris with the "Carte Orange". But, since 1995, New York has introduced the "MetroCard" giving access to both Metropolitan Transit Authority's buses and metro, which will have had the effect of somewhat reducing the overall fare burden for passengers. Regional rail does not take part in the "MetroCard" scheme.

It must also be remembered that most employees in Paris and Tokyo have part of their public transport costs reimbursed by their employer. This is not reflected in table 30, but further accentuates the high cost to the user of public transport in New York and London.

Since 1995 public transport fares in London have increased above inflation levels, while in New York the introduction of the free transfer between the Metropolitan Transit Authority's buses and metro and discount fares for frequent users will have had the effect of reducing the overall fare for passengers and increasing public transport use.

4.6.3   Origin-destination matrices

The pattern of travel within the four cities is different for the different modes. Clearly, metro and regional rail are designed to serve more densely developed areas, while car travel dominates in less densely developed areas. London, New York and Tokyo have a more radial orientation of their public transport trips than does Paris.

The origin-destination matrices reveal the level of car dependence within New York's Zones 3 & 4, where car travel makes up 97% and 99% of all trips, respectively.

Car travel in the New York region also tends to remain in the Zone where it originates. For example, nearly 15 million vehicle trips a day begin and end in Zone 3; nearly 12 million trips begin and end in Zone 4. This represents more than 90% of all car travel within each Zone. The same pattern, although less extreme, can be observed in Paris and London.

Tokyo is slightly different. While car travel dominates in Zones 3 & 4, like New York, with just under 12 million journeys, the majority of journeys in Zone 2 are undertaken by public transport. In all cities the majority of trips within and to and from Zone 1 are by metro or regional rail. What is quite striking is the amount of rail trips with both origins and destinations in Tokyo's Zone 4, nearly four and a half million, compared to only 9,000 in New York. This is due to Tokyo's punctual, reliable and frequent rail services with numerous non-radial rail lines - as well as the concentration of employment, housing and retail developments adjacent or close to railway stations. Although the number of journeys by bus within Tokyo's Zones 3 & 4 is relatively small compared to those by rail, especially related to the number of bus routes (see table 20), this is an underestimate of bus use, because buses are often used as feeder routes to railway stations - and all bus-rail or bus-metro journeys are counted as rail journeys in Tokyo.

A major reason for the patterns of car use, in addition to the density of origins and destinations and availability of public transport, is the ease of parking. For instance, while parking capacity is abundant and free nearly everywhere in New York's Zones 3 & 4, except at rail stations, in New York's Zone 1, parking off-street is very costly, and parking on-street is severely restricted before 19:00 in most areas. On the other hand, motorists even from outside Zones 1 & 2 are able to park for free on the street in most residential areas of Zone 2. By contrast in London and Paris non-residents are charged for on-street parking in many areas of Zones 1 & 2, more than residents may be charged. But like New York, parking in central London is severely restricted, time

Transport structure

Origin-Destination matrices for daily car and public transport journeys (person trips - 24 hrs Monday to Friday)

Origin	Destination	Zone 1	Zone 2	Zone 3	Zone 4
London	Zone 1	440,000	1,210,000	300,000	-
	Zone 2	1,310,000	10,340,000	600,000	-
	Zones 3 & 4	290,000	590,000	21,940,000	-
New York	Zones 1 & 2	n/a	11,955,000	1,547,000	300,000
	Zone 3	n/a	1,557,000	15,288,000	734,000
	Zone 4	n/a	292,000	766,000	11,926,000
Paris	Zone 1	619,000	1,497,000	99,000	-
	Zone 2	1,054,000	12,720,000	829,000	-
	Zone 3	96,000	825,000	2,712,000	-
	Zone 4	-	-	-	-
Tokyo	Zone 1	665,000	1,415,000	246,000	1,153,000
	Zone 2	1,438,000	5,598,000	643,000	2,063,000
	Zone 3	260,000	644,000	2,515,000	454,000
	Zone 4	1,195,000	2,069,000	456,000	17,422,000

81   The figures in tables 31a to 31f may be at slight variance with those in table 28. This is due to differences in defining main mode and inclusion of "other" modes. See definitions in table 27a.

The main mode is the mode on which the longest stage of a trip took place.

London   Data shown for "Zone 3" is for "Zones 3 & 4" combined.

The data for all cells, except for the cell, origin "Zones 3 & 4" to destination "Zones 3 & 4", come from the household interview survey of the 1991 London Area Transport Survey. The data for the cell, origin "Zones 3 & 4" to destination "Zones 3 & 4", come from the annual National Travel Survey and relate to a daily average of 1992 and 1996 (including Saturdays and Sundays).

New York   The New York public transport origin-destination data have been estimated from the 1990 journey-to-work question in the census and other sources. The result is that the public transport data are symmetrical.

The last major origin-destination study was completed in 1963; others should be completed by 1998. Specialised origin-destination studies have been undertaken by the Metropolitan Transportation Authority and others, but they are not analysed. It has been necessary for this study, therefore, to estimate origin-destinations by mode based on available information. For each of the following tables, origin-destinations have been estimated from available data provided by the New York Metropolitan Transportation Council, combined with work trip origin-destinations developed from United States census data for 1980 and 1990.

The car journey data are estimates based on origin-destination data of 1980 and updated from 1990 trip end data supplied by the New York Metropolitan Transportation Council.

The Zone 1 public transport trips are combined with Zone 2 trips. This affects tables 31a, 31c, 31d, 31e and 31f. Data in these tables shown as either "Zones 1 & 2" or "Zone 1" are in fact an aggregate of Zones 1 & 2. The public transport data are estimates based on origin-destination data of 1980 and updated from work trips of the 1990 United States census and public transport travel data supplied by the New York Metropolitan Transportation Council, "*1995 Regional Transport Report*", February 1996.

Tokyo   The data for Tokyo combine metro and regional rail data, and are shown in table 31e.

The public transport trip matrix, 29c, is a combination of bus and rail.

The Tokyo "regional rail" figures in table 31e include monorail, metro and regional rail.

Table 31b [82]
Origin-Destination matrices for daily car journeys (passenger & driver trips - 24 hrs Monday to Friday)

Origin ↓	Destination →	Zone 1	Zone 2	Zone 3	Zone 4
London	Zone 1	140,000	330,000	10,000	-
	Zone 2	340,000	7,940,000	410,000	-
	Zones 3 & 4	10,000	420,000	19,480,000	-
New York	Zone 1	166,000	615,000	227,000	67,000
	Zone 2	649,000	4,980,000	842,000	119,000
	Zone 3	255,000	824,000	14,854,000	718,000
	Zone 4	65,000	113,000	751,00	11,812,000
Paris	Zone 1	201,000	432,000	29,000	-
	Zone 2	429,000	9,396,000	670,000	-
	Zone 3	26,000	655,000	2,429,000	-
Tokyo	Zone 1	218,000	229,000	19,000	78,000
	Zone 2	231,000	2,044,000	120,000	480,000
	Zone 3	18,000	118,000	1,616,000	189,000
	Zone 4	72,000	476,000	190,000	11,938,000

82   For overall definitions, see table 31a.

Transport structure

Table 31c [83]
Origin-Destination matrices for daily public transport journeys (passenger trips - 24 hrs Monday to Friday)

Origin ↓	Destination →	Zone 1	Zone 2	Zone 3	Zone 4
London	Zone 1	300,000	880,000	290,000	-
	Zone 2	970,000	2,370,000	190,000	-
	Zones 3 & 4	280,000	170,000	1,080,000	-
New York	Zones 1 & 2	n/a	5,545,000	478,000	114,000
	Zone 3	n/a	478,000	434,000	15,500
	Zone 4	n/a	114,000	15,500	114,000
Paris	Zone 1	418,000	1,065,000	70,000	-
	Zone 2	1,075,000	3,324,000	159,000	-
	Zone 3	70,000	170,000	283,000	-
Tokyo	Zone 1	447,000	1,186,000	227,000	1,075,000
	Zone 2	1,207,000	3,554,000	523,000	1,583,000
	Zone 3	242,000	526,000	899,000	265,000
	Zone 4	1,123,000	1,593,000	266,000	5,484,000

Table 31d [84]
Origin-Destination matrices for daily metro journeys (passenger trips - 24 hrs Monday to Friday)

Origin ↓	Destination →	Zone 1	Zone 2	Zone 3	Zone 4
London	Zone 1	240,000	480,000	50,000	-
	Zone 2	580,000	570,000	30,000	-
	Zones 3 & 4	30,000	20,000	-	-
New York	Zones 1 & 2	-	3,548,000	77,000	7,000
	Zone 3	-	77,000	8,000	-
	Zone 4	-	7,000	-	-
Paris	Zone 1	297,000	549,000	4,000	-
	Zone 2	567,000	858,000	8,000	-
	Zone 3	4,000	11,000	200	-
Tokyo			included in "regional rail"		

83   For overall definitions, see table 31a.

84   For overall definitions, see table 31a.

Table 31e [85]
Origin-Destination matrices for daily regional rail journeys (passenger trips - 24 hrs Monday to Friday)

Origin ↓	Destination →	Zone 1	Zone 2	Zone 3	Zone 4
London	Zone 1	10,000	270,000	240,000	-
	Zone 2	270,000	250,000	120,000	-
	Zones 3 & 4	250,000	110,000	165,000	-
New York	Zones 1 & 2	-	141,000	171,000	71,000
	Zone 3	-	171,000	26,000	6,000
	Zone 4	-	71,000	6,000	9,000
Paris	Zone 1	13,000	400,000	64,000	-
	Zone 2	407,000	1,238,000	112,000	-
	Zone 3	64,000	122,000	42,000	-
Tokyo	Zone 1	408,000	1,152,000	226,000	1,073,000
	Zone 2	1,175,000	3,031,000	509,000	1,569,000
	Zone 3	241,000	513,000	660,000	259,000
	Zone 4	1,121,000	1,580,000	260,000	4,418,000

85   For overall definitions, see table 31a.

Transport structure

Table 31f [86]

Origin-Destination matrices for daily bus journeys (passenger trips - 24 hrs Monday to Friday)

Origin ↓	Destination →	Zone 1	Zone 2	Zone 3	Zone 4
London	Zone 1	50,000	130,000	-	-
	Zone 2	120,000	1,550,000	40,000	-
	Zones 3 & 4	-	40,000	918,000	-
New York	Zones 1 & 2	-	1,856,000	230,000	36,000
	Zone 3	-	230,000	400,000	9,500
	Zone 4	-	36,000	9,500	105,000
Paris	Zone 1	108,000	118,000	1,000	-
	Zone 2	101,000	1,228,000	39,000	-
	Zone 3	2,000	38,000	241,000	-
	Zone 4	-	-	-	-
Tokyo	Zone 1	39,000	35,000	1,000	2,000
	Zone 2	33,000	525,000	14,000	14,000
	Zone 3	1,000	13,000	239,000	6,000
	Zone 4	2,000	13,000	6,000	1,078,000

86   For overall definitions, see table 31a

limited and costly. Planning requirements in many areas of the New York region (in Zones 3 & 4) often require the provision of ample off-street parking for employees and visitors. In Tokyo there is a specific requirement to have an off-street parking space in order to obtain a permit to purchase a car.

4.7   International connectivity and access to airports

To maintain a world city status, attract tourism and inward investment, London, Paris, New York and Tokyo have to be well connected internationally. That means having easy and quick access to airports and direct connections to a large number of other cities world-wide. In this study, both types of connections are examined.

All the four cities have more than one airport serving the metropolis: Paris and Tokyo have two; New York, three; and London, five, including an inner city short-take-off-and-landing airport. In some cities, there are also some minor regional airports in the outer periphery (Zone 4) such as Southampton near the south coast of England. These have been excluded from the analysis.

4.7.1   Access to airports

London has more airports than the other three cities and more passengers pass through them than pass through the airports of any other city in the world. Heathrow, in London's Zone 2, is the world's fourth busiest airport in terms of number of passengers (54 million); see table 35. It is operating at near full capacity. At present there are plans under a public inquiry to build a fifth terminal to increase further the number of passengers that can use it. Heathrow is connected to London via the rather slow Piccadilly metro line, (which takes about an hour to the city centre) and a fast non-stop regional express line to Paddington station in Zone 1. BAA, the airport owner,

is taking measures to encourage public transport access to the airport both for passengers and staff. It built the express line to Paddington. Gatwick airport to the south of London (Zone 3), is also growing in stature as a major international airport, and is well connected by regional rail routes to many parts of the south-east of England, as well as by two direct services to central London. The smaller airports of Luton (Zone 4) and Stansted (Zone 3) are also experiencing strong growth especially with the new "no frills" carriers that have established services following the deregulation of European aviation. However, these airports have more limited accessibility, although Stansted has a direct half hourly train service. London City airport (Zone 2) built on one of the old wharves of London's docks, is a short-take-off-and-landing airport (stolport). It serves mainly business destinations in Europe. It is only 10 kilometres from the city centre, but is not well connected to public transport. Many business people using this airport access the airport by taxi.

Overall, New York comes a close second to London in number of passengers going through its airports. New York has three major airports, two in Zone 2 and one in Zone 3. La Guardia airport, which ranks 35th internationally in terms of passengers (23 million) is in northern Queens. It is about a half hour car or taxi trip from midtown Manhattan and, servicing domestic routes, is heavily used by business travellers. Kennedy Airport, in southern Queens, about an hour by car from Manhattan, serves largely international travellers. New York's third airport, Newark, is in an industrial area of Zone 3. Although it is in New Jersey, it is only about a half hour ride from Manhattan's core. It serves both domestic and international flights, and has become the fastest growing airport in the region. All three airports are reached nearly entirely by car, taxi and limousine from Zones 3 & 4. All are served by bus from Manhattan. An on-airport monorail, which began servicing remote parking at Newark Airport in 1996, is planned to connect to the regional rail service to Midtown Manhattan. Direct rail access to La Guardia and Kennedy airports, a high priority for New York's

Transport structure

Table 32
Access to airports from the city centre

Airport No. of Terminals Distance from City Centre (straight line) in kilometres	Public Transport Connections	Frequency of service	Average Access Time to City Centre
London - Heathrow Terminals: 4 Distance: 23 kilometres	**Metro -** Piccadilly line	every 5 minutes	about 50 to 60 minutes
	Bus - "Airbus" to Victoria	every 30 minutes	about 60 to 75 minutes
	Coach - to Victoria station	every 30 minutes	about 35 to 60 minutes
	Regional Rail - Heathrow Express to Paddington station	every 15 minutes	15 to 21 minutes
London - Gatwick Terminals: 2 Distance: 48 kilometres	**Regional Rail -** "Gatwick Express" and "Connex South Central" to Victoria Station, and "Thameslink" to 5 stations in central London	every 5 to 10 minutes (hourly between midnight and 06:00)	30 to 45 minutes (depending on the train operator)
	Coach - to Victoria station	hourly	about 75 minutes
London - Stansted Terminals: 1 Distance: 64 kilometres	**Regional Rail -** "WAGN" train to Liverpool Street station	every 30 minutes	45 minutes
	Coach - to Victoria station	every 60 minutes	about 60 to 80 minutes
London - Luton Terminals: 1 Distance: 52 kilometres	**Regional Rail -** Shuttle Bus to Luton station, then "Thameslink" train to 5 stations in central London	Shuttle Bus every 5 minutes and "Thameslink" trains every 5 to 15 minutes	40 to 60 minutes
	Coach - to Victoria station	every 60 minutes	about 85 to 100 minutes
London - City Terminals: 1 Distance: 10 kilometres	**Bus & Metro -** Bus 473 to Plaistow station, then District line to Monument station	bus 473 every 12 minutes & District line every 5 minutes	about 40 to 45 minutes
	Bus - London City Airport Shuttle bus to Liverpool Street station	every 10 minutes	about 25 to 30 minutes
	Regional Rail & Metro - Walk to Silvertown station (300 metres), then "Silverlink" train to West Ham station, then District line to Embankment station	the "Silverlink" train every 20 minutes & District line every 5 minutes	about 60 minutes
New York - JFK Terminals: 11 Distance: 21 kilometres	**Bus & Metro -** Shuttle-bus to Howard Beach station, then A line to Manhattan	every 20 minutes	about 75 minutes
	Bus - to Port Authority bus terminal to Grand Central station	every 30 minutes	about 60 minutes

Airport No. of Terminals Distance from City Centre (straight line) in kilometres	Public Transport Connections	Frequency of service	Average Access Time to City Centre
New York - Newark Terminals: 3 Distance: 26 kilometres	**Bus -** to Port Authority bus terminal, Grand Central station or World Trade Centre	every 20 minutes	about 40 minutes
New York - La Guardia Terminals: 4 Distance: 13 kilometres	**Bus & Metro -** Q33 bus to Roosevelt Avenue station, then E or No.7 line to Manhattan	every 10 minutes	about 60 minutes
	Bus - to Port Authority bus terminal or Grand Central station	every 30 minutes	about 45 minutes
Paris - Charles de Gaulle Terminals: 6*[87] Distance: 26 kilometres	**Regional Rail -** Reseau Express Regional line B (Shuttle-bus connection for "aerogare" 1)	every 7.5 minutes during the day	29 to 38 minutes
	Bus - Air France bus or "Roissybus"	every 15 minutes	about 45 minutes
Paris - Orly Terminals: 2 Distance: 14 kilometres	**Regional Rail -** Reseau Express Regional line B with connection by either the automated train "Orly VAL" or a shuttle-bus	every 4 to 5 minutes in the peak and 7.5 minutes up to 21:00, thereafter every 15 minutes	about 25 to 30 minutes
	Bus - numerous bus services by different operators	about very 5 minutes	about 20 to 35 minutes
Tokyo - Haneda Terminals: 2 Distance: 19 kilometres	**Monorail -** to Hamamatsucho station	every 4 to 5 minutes	23 minutes
	Regional Rail - "Keihin" train line	every 6 to 10 minutes	40 minutes
	Bus - Shuttle-bus to Japan Railways Tokyo or Shinjuku stations	every 15 to 35 minutes	45 to 50 minutes
Tokyo - Narita: Terminals: 2 Distance: 66 kilometres	**Regional Rail -** Japan Railways Shuttle-express train and the Keisei Shuttle Skyliner train	every 15 to 60 minutes	55 to 64 minutes
	Bus - Shuttle-bus to Tokyo City Air Terminal or Japan Railways Sinjuku or Ikebukuro stations	about every 10 to 60 minutes	about 80 to 85 minutes

87   Charles de Gaulle airport has two main terminals: "aerogare 1" and "aerogare 2". "Aerogare 2" has four terminals, A, B, C, and D. Furthermore, there is a very small "T9" terminal.

business leadership, has been under discussion for three decades. The current airport access plan is to build a monorail from Kennedy airport (for an estimated $1,000 million) to connect to a regional rail hub at Jamaica station on the Long Island Railroad, located in Zone 2. In 1996, a premium, high speed ferry service was introduced from the east side of Manhattan to La Guardia airport.

Although Paris ranks seventh in the world in terms of air passengers, it comes second (after London) for international passengers going through its airports; see table 35. Access to Paris' two airports is relatively fast and convenient. Orly airport is only 14 kilometres from the city centre while Charles de Gaulle is at 26 kilometres. It is possible to reach both airports by public transport within half an hour from Zone 1. Yet there are still problems. The main one is that line B of the Réseau Express Régional that connects the airports to the city centre can be difficult to use at peak times and has no dedicated on-board facilities for airport passengers. Furthermore, it links directly only to terminal 2 of Charles de Gaulle airport. For terminal 1 there is the need to change on to a shuttle-bus and for Orly on to an automated rail system, the OrlyVAL. It is the policy of the Région to augment the percentage of people going to or from the airports by public transport from the current 30% to at least 40%; this is to be achieved by increasing the frequency of service on line B of the Réseau Express Régional.

After London and New York, Tokyo is the city with the greatest number of air travellers. Both Tokyo's airports are operating at full capacity. Narita, Tokyo's international airport, was opened in 1978 (after a decade of strong local opposition) with only one runway. A second runway has been planned. Negotiations with various land owners, farmers and other interest groups are taking place. However, it has also been the focus of local and environmental opposition. In the Tokyo Metropolitan Region, it is estimated that even with the completion of the current expansion of Haneda airport, its capacity will be reached early in the 21st century. The

7th Five Year Plan for Airport Construction (1996-2000), approved by the Cabinet in December 1996, stipulated that construction of hub airports in metropolitan regions receive first priority. Nonetheless, no new airport is being built or planned. Instead, some of the pressure is being taken from Tokyo by the completion and operation of the new Kansai airport near Osaka. Both Haneda and Narita airports are linked by rail to the city centre.

4.7.2 International connectivity

In terms of international connectivity, all cities are well connected. Charles de Gaulle airport in north-east Paris, serves 210 destinations, more than any other airport in the four cities, but only 117 of these were served at least once a day. However, Newark in New Jersey is the airport serving the greatest number of destinations with at least one flight per day, 122, with Heathrow and John F. Kennedy in New York coming close joint second with 115. Paris is the world's best connected city serving overall 272 destinations with its two airports. Tokyo is the least well connected of the four cities with only 114 destinations. Tokyo's situation is further exacerbated by the fact that its two airports are already operating close to capacity and have little possibility of expansion. New York offers the greatest choice of destinations with at least a daily flight, with 184 destinations, yet 107 of those are in North America. Tokyo is far behind the other cities with only 77 daily destinations.

Each city serves as a gateway to destinations in its continent. New York serves more places in North and South America than the other cities and Tokyo more places in Asia. Paris connects to more places in Europe than does London. Africa is best served by Paris and Oceania by Tokyo.

Despite not being as well connected as Paris, London still sees more passengers pass through its airports than any other city in the world.

Table 33a [88]
Destinations served by air daily or more frequently

	Africa	Middle-East	Asia	Europe	North America	South America	Oceania/Pacific	Total
Heathrow	3	10	12	71	15	0	4	115
Gatwick	2	2	0	69	19	1	0	93
Stansted	0	0	0	25	0	0	0	25
Luton	0	0	0	16	0	0	0	16
City	0	0	0	9	0	0	0	9
All London	4	10	12	102	28	1	4	161
JFK	2	1	6	29	48	29	0	115
Newark	0	0	1	19	83	19	0	122
La Guardia	0	0	0	0	80	9	0	89
All New York	2	1	7	33	107	34	0	184
Charles de Gaulle	6	3	5	85	14	4	0	117
Orly	4	1	0	46	6	2	0	59
All Paris	10	3	5	103	16	6	0	143
Narita	0	0	15	6	11	0	7	39
Haneda	0	0	42	0	0	0	0	42
All Tokyo	0	0	53	6	11	0	7	77

Figure 15a
Destinations served by air daily or more frequently

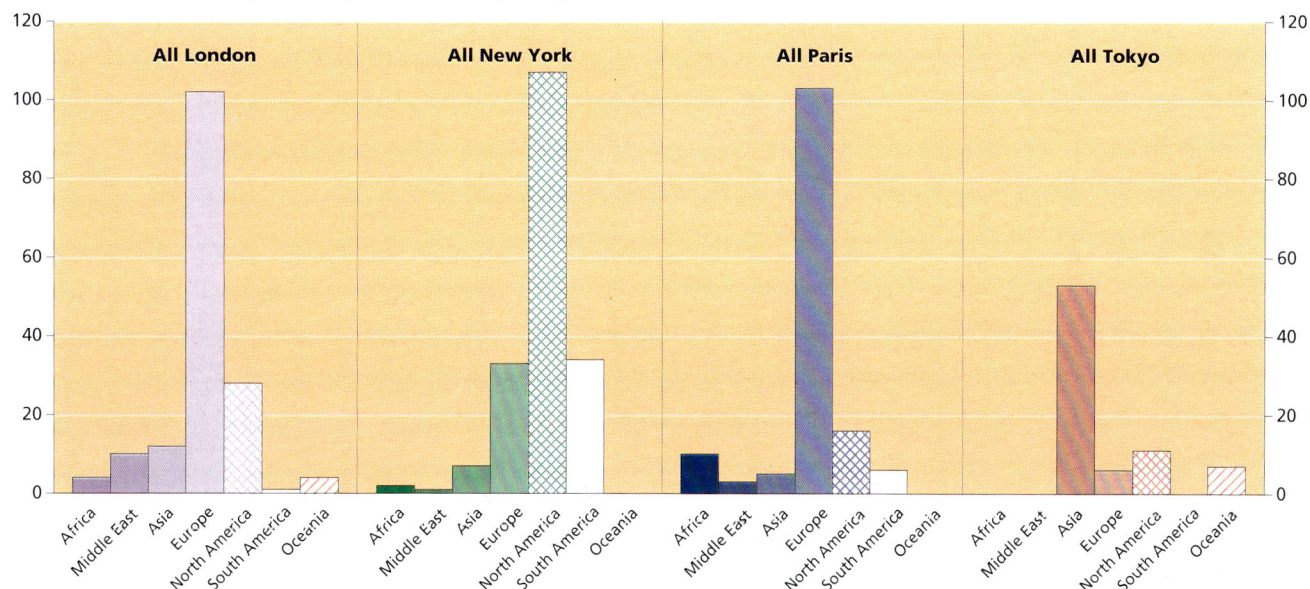

88   Source: OAG World Airways Guide - April 1998.

Table 33b [89]

Destinations served by air (irrespective of frequency)

	Africa	Middle East	Asia	Europe	North America	South America	Oceania/ Pacific	Total
Heathrow	19	17	27	87	16	10	5	181
Gatwick	10	6	7	101	20	23	0	167
Stansted	0	1	0	35	1	0	0	37
Luton	1	0	0	22	0	0	0	23
City	0	0	0	17	0	0	0	17
All London	25	18	30	134	30	24	5	266
JFK	8	7	15	40	53	35	0	158
Newark	0	1	4	22	97	27	0	147
La Guardia	0	0	0	0	102	12	0	114
All New York	8	7	15	43	121	46	0	240
Charles de Gaulle	31	15	22	111	14	15	2	210
Orly	15	5	3	68	7	12	11	113
All Paris	43	16	23	148	16	23	3	272
Narita	1	1	28	15	14	4	13	76
Haneda	0	0	42	0	0	0	0	42
All Tokyo	1	1	66	15	14	4	13	114

Figure 15b
Destinations served by air (irrespective of frequency)

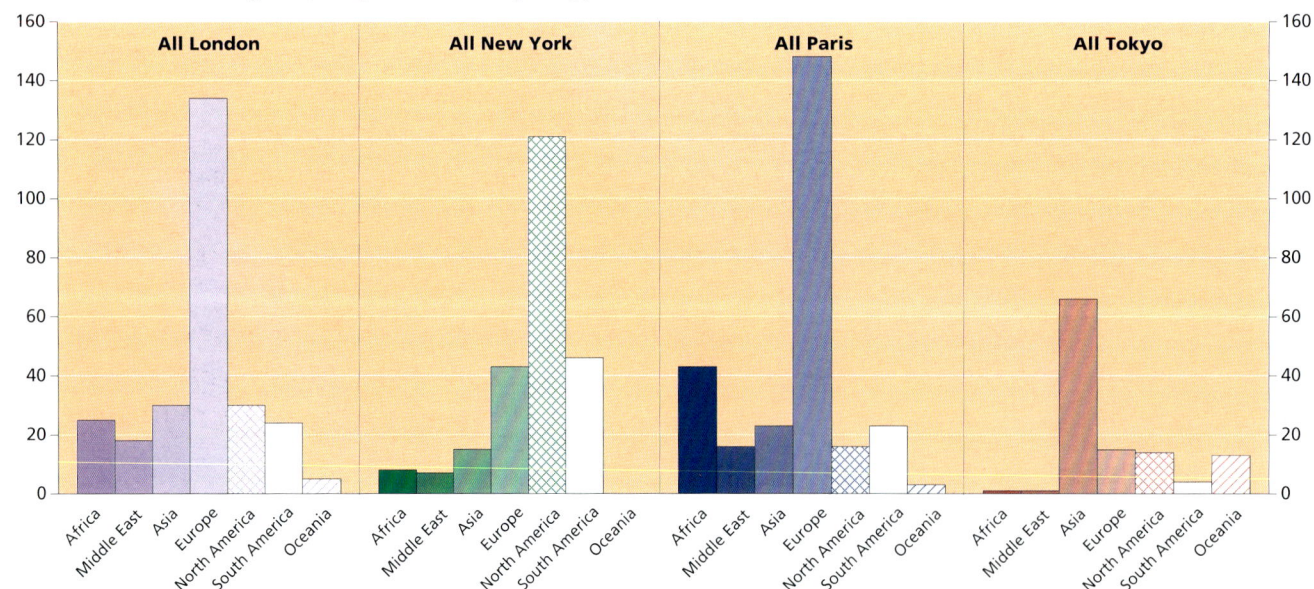

89   Source: OAG World Airways Guide - April 1998.

Table 34 [90]
Airport passenger and freight in 1995

	All passengers (millions)	All passengers (world ranking of airports and cities)	International passengers (millions)	International passengers (world ranking of airports and cities)	Freight & mail (million (tons)
London Heathrow	54	4th	47	1st	1.1
London Gatwick	22	30th	21	8th	0.2
London Stansted	4	-	3	-	0.1
London Luton	2	-	2	-	>0.0
London City	>1	-	>1	-	>0.0
All London	82	1st	73	1st	1.4
New York John F. Kennedy	30	12th	17	10th	1.6
New York Newark	27	20th	4	-	0.9
New York La Guardia	23	35th	1	-	0.1
All New York	80	2nd	22	8th	2.6
Paris Charles de Gaulle	28	14th	26	4th	0.9
Paris Orly	27	19th	11	19th	0.3
All Paris	55	7th	37	2nd	1.1
Tokyo Haneda	46	6th	1	-	0.7
Tokyo Narita	24	25th	23	5th	1.6
All Tokyo	70	3rd	24	6th	2.3

The advent of high-speed trains is attracting travellers away from airlines. Paris is at the forefront with the construction of the high speed "TGV" (trains à grande vitesse) network. Not only does this reach many parts of France but it also extends to Belgium, Holland, Germany and Switzerland.

Tokyo has an established network of its "bullet" high-speed trains linking destinations both north and west of the capital.

London is linked to Paris and Brussels through the Channel Tunnel rail link through which run the high-speed Eurostar trains. But while they run at high speeds on new track in Belgium and France, no new track has yet been built in England, thus reducing their speed on the English portion of the journey. There are plans for the construction of new track from the Channel Tunnel to London involving the private sector.

New York also does not have a high-speed network. But currently the Boston-New York-Washington rail corridor is being upgraded to permit the running of high-speed tilting trains.

90   Source: Airline Business, December 1996, and Civil Aviation Authority in the Great Britain

Conclusions

Content

5.   Conclusions

The purpose of this report is to compare transport structures and travel patterns in the four cities and from these comparisons draw out some ideas that can be exchanged to improve the way travel is carried out and its environmental and economic costs minimised. There may be lessons for other large metropolises too. The conclusions are those of the editor (but with significant input from the other cities). They are not a summary of the report but suggestions about policy, based on a thorough analysis of the data in the report.

In drawing conclusions, the main influences have been a policy framework of sustainability, protection of the environment and the enhancement of quality of life. Increasingly, public policies are moving towards these goals in transport, for instance with recent White Papers, in the United Kingdom, *New Deal for Transport*, and in the European Union, *Fair Payment for Infrastructure Use*, both of which aim to make transport more environmentally accountable. The hitherto, free and unfettered use of cars is brought into question [91].

The main transport issues that emerge are how best to bring people to business, leisure and retail centres and how to facilitate travel to work or social activities during the day in a sustainable manner. National, regional and local governments can act along two policy paths:

- direct land-use planning to meet sustainable transport and mobility requirements

- improving the efficiency of the region's transport systems (especially public transport).

Both policy paths are important, but land-use will have longer term effects.

The conclusions do not aim to be prescriptive for the four cities but rather to identify aspects of good practice and suggest where there may be transferable lessons. The conclusions should:

- acquaint the general reader with what the study participants have learnt

- encourage the readers to look for their own conclusions.

The report itself provides a strong database which, if maintained, will allow each city to track the other cities' efforts to deal with their common problems.

5.1   Why compare?

This is a comparative study of the world's four foremost cities, London, New York, Paris and Tokyo, and the transport systems that support their cultural and financial world leadership. Here, the term "cities" applies to the large urbanised regions that operate as economic, rather than administrative, units, as all have multiple layers of government. In this study, the cities are divided into comparable and roughly concentric zones: Zone 1, is the city centre; Zones 1&2, are the metropolitan area; and Zones 1,2,3&4, compose the entire region.

All four cities have extensive public transport systems and road networks. Also all four have experienced and are still experiencing centrifugal forces of development from the centre. Although they have for many decades seen an expansion of their suburbs, in recent times there has been a dramatic growth in exurbia, the hinterlands of the cities beyond their suburbs. This growth has been largely car dependent (with the exception of Tokyo, whose growth has been delineated by the expansion and extension of regional rail lines).

Comparisons of transport systems and policies among the four principal centres of the global economy

---

91   The European Commission argues in the Green Paper, *Citizens' Network*, (European Commission, 1996), that the adverse effects caused by the increasing use of the private car can only be solved by "reinforcing public transport services". Public transport is not seen just as a solution to dealing with these noxious "externalities" but also as a form of social policy.

Conclusions

(London, New York, Paris and Tokyo) can provide leads to improving policies and programmes in each of the cities despite cultural and governmental differences.

5.1.1 Common goals

In their quest to remain the principal and leading centres in the world economy, and at the same time provide a high quality environment for their citizens and visitors, the four cities have largely similar transport needs and the same transport goals:

- to retain a city centre that can compete in convenience, efficiency and variety of services, skills and opportunities in the contest to be headquarters of the global economy, and that is efficiently serviced by public transport

- to minimise the sprawl of urbanisation in the countryside without inhibiting new housing, leisure, retailing and employment developments

- to meet residents', workers' and visitors' travel needs and maximise the efficiency of the transport system while reducing the environmental damage now being done, mainly by cars and lorries

- to improve the quality of the travelling environment for passengers of public transport

- to avoid further polluting and degrading of the environment, by minimising unnecessary car travel without inhibiting the access that people want.

5.1.2 A common strength

The magnetism and the raison d'être of the economies of these four metropolitan regions are largely based on the vibrancy of their city centres (Zone 1 in this study).

Into these tiny areas, ranging from 23 to 42 square kilometres, pour between 0.8 and 2.0 million people daily within the 3 hour morning peak period.

City centres are no longer needed for manufacturing or routine paperwork. That leaves them primarily as locations where transactions occur that are best done when people face each other across a table or happen upon each other in the street, restaurant or club. The electronic revolution may suggest that it has become unnecessary for people to meet face to face in order to do business, but activities in the centres of all four of these cities are growing. Apparently there is no substitute for people getting together, and not just for business. Tourism, a wide range of entertainment, high quality education and retailing are also important elements in the economies of these cities. They contribute to the attractiveness of the cities for the highly talented personnel needed for global business leadership, and some contribute directly to business, higher education and the arts. The complexity of contemporary business requires increasing contacts between different kinds of experts meeting in shifting groups throughout the day. Continuing high levels of employment are projected for all four regions' central business districts despite a high premium to locate there. Businesses pay high rents to be in the centre (in Tokyo high enough to drive out residents) in order to share in the rich rewards of the profitable global economy.

Transport is a key element in making these regions efficient both for work, recreation and other activities. A poorly performing transport system not only costs enormous sums to businesses in lost productivity but also aggravates, irritates and reduces the quality of life of the travelling public. In all four cities many employees commute long distances, often jammed on to crowded trains or moving slowly and uncertainly on congested highways. This can also throw into question the primacy of the cities as world locations for business and tourism. All four cities require comprehensive, efficient and high quality transport systems that serve the changing needs both of their city centres and their entire regions.

New developments at Marne-la-Vallee new town in the outskirts of Paris

5.2 Integrating transport and land-use

All four metropolises have expanded outward in the last half century, although Paris has remained the most compact. The centrifugal effect of development from the centre has been progressing in all four cities. Tokyo and Paris have accomplished their population and employment shifts by design, through development focused around public transport. London, and more so New York, have seen a scatter of low density and car dependent developments throughout their regions. These vary from small scale developments to large shopping centres situated near motorway junctions, such as Lakeside in Essex (London).

Table 35 [92]
Changes in population since 1970 in the metropolitan area (Zones 1 & 2) and in the rest of the region (Zones 3 & 4)

	London	New York	Paris	Tokyo
Zones 1 & 2	-5%	+4%	+8%	-10%
Zones 3 & 4	+16%	+11%	+73%	+61%

Nonetheless, all four cities still retain a high density core of residents and more importantly of employment.

Current thinking and the results of this study suggest that there are five main areas of land-use planning that the four cities can concentrate on to create sustainable, prosperous and high quality habitats:

- retaining the high population and employment densities of the city centre including a large range of services

- decentralising activities not necessary in the city centre to other, or new, peripheral high density locations

- clustering residences, businesses and services around transport nodes to encourage the use of public transport

- saving the countryside from the haphazard sprawl of car-dependent developments

- promoting policies that reduce car-use and increase the attractiveness of other forms of transport, such as walking and cycling, to improve the quality of life in the cities.

5.2.1 Retaining a vibrant high density city centre

Having a high density of activities in the centre makes possible a variety of activity within a short period of time. Even on foot or by bicycle, a person in a large compact city centre can, during the day, meet many people more quickly than can a suburban worker using a car. A large compact city centre also creates conditions that lead commuters to choose public transport to travel to work, ie, roads are congested, parking is expensive and hard to find and the compactness makes public transport convenient.

92   This table has been constructed using the data of figures 3c, 3d and 3f. The data for the four cities, except Paris, are for either 1970 or 1971 and 1995 or 1996. The Paris data are for 1968 and 1990. The Parisian outer area is only Zone 3.

Conclusions

Manhattan's central business district (Zone 1) has the highest concentration of employment of the four cities, at 85,550 jobs per square kilometre. This enables those employed in Manhattan to undertake numerous transactions which are close together, by walking or taking a short taxi, metro or bus trip during the day. New York and Paris retain large numbers of residents in their central area (Zone 1): 543,000 in New York and 622,000 in Paris - more than twice the number of residents in London's and Tokyo's central areas. Thus New York and Paris retain many short commuting trips, a large number on foot.

New York's Zone 1 population has dropped only 16% since 1950 compared with population losses in the other three cities' Zone 1 of over 30%. However over the past decade in the Zone 1 of all cities except Tokyo, population has stabilised or shown a small increase, even with very high property values. In central London and in Lower Manhattan (Wall Street area) office buildings are being converted for housing.

To retain the vibrancy of the city centre, these cities need to plan for high density employment and for other services that attract visitors from throughout the region and further afield. The cities can encourage retailing, entertainment and other services to locate in Zone 1. Furthermore, the greater the ratio of off-peak to peak passenger numbers the greater the 'spread' of fixed costs on the system and the lower the average cost per passenger.

A possible measure of Zone 1 attraction for purposes other than work is the number of people arriving in non-commuting hours. Of course, some off-peak visitors come to do business, e.g., from planned sub-centres like Paris' La Défense. But it is likely that many non-peak visitors come for entertainment, education or shopping. Comparing the number and percentage of people who enter Zone 1 outside the morning rush hours (07:00 to 10:00), New York has by far the most, 1.8 million a day entering outside commuter hours (56% of the total), but Paris has the highest percentage

of off-peak entrants, 67%. Tokyo has just over 1 million entrants outside commuter hours but they are only 35% of the daily total. London, instead, has the fewest non-commuter entrants at 845,000, though they form 50% of the daily total.

London, New York, and to some extent, Paris, are developing services that remain open at off-peak times and often throughout the day and night, turning the core of the metropolises into "24 hour cities"; this is not only for tourism and leisure activities but also for global business needs requiring communication with people in different time zones. New York has a 24 hour metro service on nearly all lines. Public transport needs to reflect the changes to meet the challenge of the "24 hour city" by providing efficient off-peak services in a safe environment.

5.2.2   Decentralising non-core activities

The four cities are decentralising activities that do not have daily relations with other activities in the centre. One purpose of decentralising is to reduce congestion, transport costs and high land values in the centre. The policy of moving the national capital out of Tokyo is partly in order to reduce the high level of congestion in the city centre. All four cities have developed close-in business clusters, easily reached from Zone 1 but not in the centre: such as Docklands in London (primarily serving the financial and publishing sectors), La Défense in Paris (a government and business district), Brooklyn City-Centre in New York (an education, business and government sub-centre), and Shinjuku in Tokyo (also a government and business centre). They are all tied to Zone 1 with high-frequency rail services. Docklands even has its own regional airport.

A second purpose of decentralising is to reduce commuting time and congestion by creating business sub-centres outside Zone 1. Paris and Tokyo are moving people and services to new towns or sub-centres in Zones 2 & 3, and Tokyo has designated "business core" cities in both Zones 3 & 4 to receive added activities decentralised from central Tokyo but with good rail connections to the centre. The Tokyo Metropolitan Government has set for itself the fundamental task of redressing the balance between the night-time population and the day-time working population in the central area of Tokyo, to transform the Tokyo metropolis from a centralised structure into a multi-centred structure that "balances work and home".

5.2.3 Clustering residences, businesses and services around transport nodes

Paris and Tokyo have planning mechanisms and policies that limit car-use by clustering residences, businesses and services around regional rail stations and metro stations where additional capacity exists. Both have powerful land-use plans that keep housing and jobs in locations that can rely on public transport. Japan subsidises developments that build housing and improve railroads simultaneously. Tokyo's Zone 4, an area beyond the suburbs but developing fast, retains over 31% of all trips within that Zone on public transport by clustering jobs, services and housing and providing a highly reliable regional rail system. By contrast within New York's Zone 4 only 0.95% of trips are made by public transport.

The focusing of housing around services, jobs and public transport can effectively reduce the need to drive even at much lower densities. The importance of clustering compared to overall density is illustrated by comparing London's and New York's Zones 3 & 4. Both have about the same overall density but more of the population in London's Zones 3 & 4 live in towns and villages. One result is that whilst 98% of trips within that area (Zones 3 & 4) are made by car in New York, the figure for London is 89%. Few of New York's Zone 3 & 4 residences are clustered around rail stations or bus hubs and most of the population is spread and scattered, in a way that is unrelated to public transport.

The level of clustering jobs and population can be assumed to be inversely proportional to the level of household car ownership. In New York's Zone 4, where almost all trips must be by car because homes, jobs and services are not clustered, most households have two or more cars (1.86 vehicles per household). This contrasts with London and Tokyo that have respectively 1.08 and 1.05 cars per household in their Zone 4.

5.2.4 Saving the countryside

A dense business core and sub-centres are essential to keep overall regional development compact and save open countryside. Yet as can be seen from table 35, in all four cities, growth is happening in Zones 3 & 4, often encroaching on the countryside.

Outside the metropolitan area (Zones 1 & 2), New York has over 12 million residents scattered over more than 32,000 square kilometres. In Zone 4 average residential density is as low as 230 persons per square kilometre. New York has allowed car-dependent office, retail and housing complexes to develop. Many of these are only accessible by car. Shops may be clustered in out-of-town centres, but their layout may make walking between them nearly impossible. A shopper will often have to drive from one car-park to another to visit more than one shop.

Such an unplanned spread of housing and other business developments through the region has the effect of dissolving the distinction between town and country with the whole region becoming an amorphous low density exurbia scarred by a web of large roads. These have the effect of increasing and spreading pollution as well as destroying natural habitats.

After the Second World War, London planned to limit its spread by preserving a green-belt (on the border between Zones 2 & 3), with towns beyond the green belt whose economies would be little related to the centre's. Data in this study confirm that this did not work as planned. Although the green-belt has remained largely rural, unchecked development has leap-frogged it to the rest of the south-east of England. London's Zones 3 & 4 now contain over 10.5 million residents and just under 4.5 million jobs. These are the areas that are showing the highest rates of growth in population and jobs. Furthermore, just under a million people cross the green-belt on a typical day to enter metropolitan London (Zones 1 & 2).

Paris and Tokyo, with their interventionist regional structure plans and their investment in regional rail, have managed, through the creation of "new towns", "poles of development" and "business core cities", to create high density towns and cities, causing little loss of the countryside. London's looser planning system, based on advice, has allowed a spread of development throughout the south-east of England, much of it car dependent. New York, without an official regional plan and land-use powers devolved to municipalities, has been unable or/and unwilling to control the spread of developments throughout the region.

5.2.5   *Walking and cycling*

Walking is an essential part of both a healthy lifestyle and the metropolitan transport system, but it is scarcely studied as part of transport planning. Overall, there is too little research in the four cities relating walking to building space, into allocating space appropriately between pedestrians and motorists or into providing conditions that encourage people to walk. There are a few exceptions, such as the London Planning Advisory Committee's call for a strategic plan for walking, *Advice on a Walking Strategy for London* (1997). In this study walking trips often had to be omitted because data were either unavailable or inconsistent.

Policies to encourage walking need also to address the issue of the large number of people injured or killed in traffic accidents. About 150 pedestrians are currently

killed a year by cars on the streets in each city's metropolitan area (Zones 1 & 2) in London, Paris and Tokyo whilst in New York the figures are consistently over 200.

5.2.6   *Measures the cities might consider to improve transport and land-use planning*

Based on all these land-use/transport observations, there are policy implications that can be drawn out for further investigation by the cities.

Vibrant city centres

- Whilst New York and Paris have over 500,000 inhabitants in their city centres (Zone 1), London and Tokyo have less than half and could consider further measures to promote more housing in Zone 1.

- To achieve a balance of employment, residents and services in the city centre, Tokyo might consider inducing more leisure, retail and education facilities in or very near Zone 1 to draw people to use them, especially at off-peak times.

Decentralisation

- Decentralising some of the activities currently undertaken in the core to sub-centres could alleviate congestion and reduce commuting distances. Paris and Tokyo have been building new towns and "business core cities" such as Marne-la-Vallée and Omiya respectively which are well connected to the public transport networks. London has progressed the redevelopment of its disused docks by the river Thames linked by the new automated Docklands Light Railway. New York might consider incentives to attract further development to rail-based business sub-centres and enlarged towns. This is particularly so for Zone 2 in New York, which has a low ratio of jobs to population compared to the other cities' Zone 2 and compared to New York's other Zones.

Clustering development

- As Tokyo and Paris have done, London and New York might consider withholding approval of developments that can only be reached by car. Existing out-of-town retail, leisure and office developments could be curtailed and new ones not be given planning permits.

- New York might consider seeking more clustering of jobs, services, retailing, higher education and housing within walking distance of railway stations in Zones 3 & 4 in the way Tokyo encourages and plans for new urban development together with its needed public transport infrastructure.

Regional planning

- Paris and Tokyo have regional structure plans that conform to national plans with clear mechanisms for implementation. Regional plans in London and New York could be directed to promoting high density urban areas and discouraging car-based developments.

- In Paris and Tokyo land-use policies strongly contribute to transport goals. Amongst the four regions, New York is the only that has paid no official attention to formulating a coherent regional land-use structure plan related to transport policies. New York also possesses no institutional structures for the elaboration and implementation of a regional plan. The south-east of England, although it has planning guidance from central government, does not

have a clear regional plan or vision. Furthermore, there is no regional government able to implement planning guidance uniformly. In London, the proposals for a new Greater London Authority do not extend to giving it powers outside the metropolitan area (Zones 1 & 2).

Encourage walking and cycling

- Part of living in a city that offers a high quality of life, is the ability to walk freely without the fear of traffic to offices, shops and services. All four cities might pay more attention to land-use patterns that encourage trips on foot rather than by car.

- London has set accident reduction targets and adopted specific measures to achieve these, with reduction rates of around 50% in a decade. All cities could consider further measures to improve the safety and quality of walking and cycling.

5.3 Maximising efficiency in the transport systems

All four cities have mature public transport systems composed of metros, regional rail and buses. The systems have their problems with performance in all the cities, with inevitable congestion on the roads in the city centre, and often in the suburbs and surrounding towns. Public transport services may also be heavily overcrowded and unreliable, especially at peak hours. The cities are seeking measures to make car travel less onerous or at least to keep rush-hour travel from becoming worse as jobs and population increase.

The main transport issues and challenges are how to discourage car use, improve the public transport system and maximise the efficiency of the entire transport

Conclusions

system. The main policy instruments other than land-use planning are:

- pricing structures for public transport, car use and parking

- investing in and improving the quality of public transport
- improving the management and planning of the transport systems

- restraining the use of the car.

5.3.1 Tackling congestion on the road and public transport networks

Several conditions contribute to whether travellers choose public transport in competition with the car, but journey time, comfort, dependability and the cost of public transport are dominant.

In large and dense urban areas, there is a huge level of "suppressed demand", a large pool of public transport users ready to switch to driving when more road space becomes available. So after road space is added, congestion returns to the roads as new drivers clog up the new roads. Generally, experience indicates that new roads in a large urban environment do not reduce congestion.

The beneficiaries of the large expense of additional road building are the people who can undertake a more direct journey. For instance, orbital roads such as the M25 in London or the A96 in Paris permit travel between distant parts of the region without having to go through the city centre.

Transport policy professionals in all four cities recognise now that building more motorways will not eliminate peak period traffic congestion or improve rush-hour travel. In London the government, instead of planning new roads, is studying whether a re-allocation of road-

space may lead to improved traffic flow. Current policies in London consist of improving the flow of traffic through traffic management measures and enforcement of parking restrictions, especially on main roads, now designated as priority "red" routes.

Congestion is not just an issue of roads. Crowding can reach a painful state on Tokyo's peak period metro and regional rail and on several tracks of London's, Paris' and New York's metro lines. Measures of crowding vary among the metro systems so comparisons are somewhat subjective. Tokyo measures metro and rail car capacity by how many seats and holding-on places there are. In peak hours, trains carry nearly twice that number and the most crowded lines carry two and a half times the standard.

Both Tokyo and Paris are working on measures to reduce overcrowding. In the past 30 years, overcrowding has been reduced on nearly all of the most congested lines in Tokyo, but, still leaving them twice over capacity. And at least a half-dozen lines remain so crowded that whenever the train jolts, "passengers are forced to assume a slanting position, unable to move their body and even their hands". Tokyo regional rail has nearly doubled its capacity since 1965 but still most trains carry twice the set limits. The Japanese term these conditions "commuter hell".

London's metro has overcrowded sections and is alleviating some via new rolling stock with fewer seats (increasing the number of standing passengers) and a process of upgrading signalling to allow more trains on the tracks at peak times.

To combat crowding and to permit easier cross-city journeys, Paris developed the Réseau Express Régional, an express regional rail system that crosses the city centre and links regional rail routes at either end. The system has four existing lines and a new one is being built. Paris is also introducing new technologies with on-board signalling systems to increase the number of trains that can be accommodated during peak hours.

Both in London and New York a tight funding situation has meant that schemes to introduce the Réseau Express Régional concept, such as London's "Crossrail" or New York's Regional Plan Association's "Regional Express", have been either shelved or are not on the agenda. In New York a squeeze on metro operating funds has already had the effect of reducing the number of peak-period trains below the number that could be run, despite overcrowding. Combating crowding does not seem to be a major New York City Transit policy target.

In Tokyo, where combating overcrowding on the trains is a priority, many regional rail trains run through the city on metro tracks at peak hours (individual arrangements being made between metro operators and the regional rail operators). This has had the effect of improving travel times by cutting out a change between rail and metro.

Another way of improving the efficiency of the transport system is by improving "intermodality", aiding and encouraging transfers between modes to make quicker and more direct journeys. All four cities are concentrating on improving transfers, making them easier, cheaper and faster. Paris' most recent long-range plan emphasises inter-modal connections and extending "the web" of public transport throughout the metropolitan area. In the London region, local authorities applying to the national government for transport funds have been encouraged to take a more active strategic and multi-modal role in relation to transport in their areas, including integrating pedestrian, cycling and public transport facilities.

For passengers intermodality can be encouraged through multi-modal tickets. London's "travelcard" and Paris' "carte orange" are season tickets that allow access to nearly all of the cities' transport systems. New York has been moving in this direction by eliminating the extra fare for transferring from bus to metro, using a magnetic "farecard". Tokyo could study the effect of introducing multi-modal ticketing.

Tokyo provides the convenience of inter-rail transfers via an orbital rail line outside Zone 1, the Yamanote Loop line, connecting radial lines and new business centres. It is one of the most heavily used lines. Tokyo sees the promotion of orbital transport as a priority for its decentralisation strategy. Paris' regional structure plan also considers the possibility of building an orbital light rail line. New York's Regional Plan Association proposed orbital rail in 1929, like Tokyo's connected to new business centres where radial and orbital lines join, but the depression of the 1930s killed the idea. The success of Tokyo's orbital rail suggests that London and New York could seriously consider developing orbital rail links, co-ordinating them with business centre developments outside the central area.

5.3.2 Improving public transport

One of the main criteria for passengers in choosing public transport is its frequency and dependability. Passengers ask the following important questions: How much time is there to wait for the next train or bus? Has the next service been cancelled? Is the service running late and if so by how much? If passengers are to be wooed from their cars they need a frequent and reliable public transport system with good quality real-time information readily available.

Tokyo's rail services demonstrate that it is possible to run a frequent service and achieve high levels of reliability and punctuality - to the minute for both metros and regional rail, despite overcrowding that makes boarding difficult. The rail systems in the other cities do not even measure lateness to the minute.

New York's metro lags far behind in punctuality and Paris and London metros are only a little better, nowhere near Tokyo's performance. Tokyo's metro system has also fewer cancellations than the other three cities' metro systems. London, New York and Paris can learn from Tokyo's experience.

Conclusions

New York's regional rail is slightly more punctual than Paris', which is slightly more punctual than London's. All three cities could take measures to improve performance of their regional railways, especially London, which has a poor punctuality record. Although New York has a poor performance measure for the service offered on its metro services, it must be remembered that it has the highest density of metro stations (offset by the lack of regional rail stations in the metropolitan area - Zones 1 & 2). For the entire region, Tokyo not only has the best performing metro and regional rail network but also by far the highest number and density of stations.

In all four cities, buses that share the road with other vehicles are subject to delays and cancellations. London, New York and Paris have been taking some measures to improve the reliability of bus services. In London, to increase reliability, London Transport has been cutting the length of routes. It is also introducing real-time information at bus stops to indicate the likely length of the wait for the next bus, a measure which is popular with bus users.

London Transport is working with local authorities to introduce more bus lanes and bus priorities at signalised junctions. In New York, buses have their own lanes on two main avenues in Zone 1 and, more importantly, on river crossings into Zone 1 from both the east and the west. Under these conditions, buses offer a reasonable substitute for commuter rail from sectors without rail stations. Paris has built a segregated bus-way of 13 kilometres. Although bus use is high in Tokyo's outer suburbs, only 1% of travellers use the bus to enter the central area and bus travel accounts for only 6% of journeys within Zones 1& 2. There are few bus priority measures in Tokyo.

Because many households in Zones 1 & 2 do not own cars and since many of the cars they do own are used to go to work, the bus plays an important role outside of peak hours. In London's metropolitan area (Zones 1 & 2), buses carry 1.8 million people throughout the day, as many as the metro. New Yorkers are also heavy users of buses, also with 1.8 million trips.

The efficiency of the transport system can also be improved by promoting other transport modes such as river-buses as well as by encouraging walking and cycling. Both London and New York are returning to once almost abandoned modes, ferries and trams. In New York a private company has found ferry services profitable and is actively seeking new routes. London's Secretary of State in charge of transport is proposing a series of ferry stops along the Thames, some connected to other forms of transport. A light rail line is under construction along the New Jersey Hudson river-front, and London is close to completing a tram system in Croydon (Zone 2) that will operate both on the street and use existing rail rights-of-way.

Currently the use of the great majority of roads is free, both in the centre and the periphery of the four regions. There are some tolls on bridges, mainly to enter Manhattan, and on the use of some motorways in New York, Paris and Tokyo. The United Kingdom government is planning to introduce legislation to allow local authorities to experiment with road pricing measures.

5.3.3   Transport management and planning

Good management and planning is another way to obtain a high level and quality of transport provision. Integrating transport with land-use planning is one such important measure.

Paris and Tokyo closely relate land-use and transport planning. London recently combined responsibility for land-use and transport in a new national government ministry, the Department of the Environment, Transport and the Regions. Tokyo and Paris sponsor transport and land development together or promote development that fits with transport improvements. But in New York land-use is controlled by 780 separate municipal governments while transport planning is in the hands of the three state Departments of Transportation and the Metropolitan Planning Organisations, with little contribution from the municipalities, though the national transport law requires transport plans be related to land-use. Most local land-use policies preclude walking or public transport by encouraging the spread and scatter of housing, employment and services. National transport law encourages planning for more public transport, walking and cycling, but has no relationship to the land-use policies which would be required to achieve this.

Keeping up transport supply with new development presents all four cities with a problem. Tokyo invested heavily in infrastructure, including new transport systems, for planned new development in its waterfront area. But rising costs and an economic slow-down stalled private investment so the infrastructure investment is only partially used. On the other hand, London developed its old dock areas (Docklands) with the private sector taking the lead. Adequate public transport was not originally provided, making the area comparatively inaccessible although it is a short distance from central London. With the recession of the late 1980s, the effect was that Canary Wharf, the major developer, went into receivership. Now the Jubilee metro line is being extended to Docklands and the Docklands Light Rail is being upgraded to provide the much needed public transport improvement. This experience emphasises the need for public and private investment to be committed concurrently.

All four cities have a mixture of private and public operators for both bus and rail.

In Great Britain most public transport services, including the national railways, have been privatised. In London, all regional rail services and bus operations are run by the private sector. The government is also planning to sell and lease-back from the privatise sector the fixed infrastructure of the "Underground", London's metro. The privatisation of regional rail services has not

led to an increase in quality of provision or a diminution of costs to the users, but it is expected that public subsidies will diminish over the next five years. In New York, a light rail line in New Jersey, developed with public funds, will be implemented through a "design, build and operate" contract with a consortium of firms. Many commuter coach services and suburban bus systems are operated by private companies with national subsidies administered by municipalities.

In Paris, both regional rail and metro services are run by national government corporations. Many bus services in the suburbs are provided by private companies, closely supervised by the regional transport planning agency.

In Tokyo, all the regional rail services are privately operated (but are closely monitored by the national government and the Tokyo Metropolitan Government) as are the buses outside the Yamanote Loop line.

Relations between national and local governments in the metropolitan areas also affect efficiency. The national governments of Britain, France and Japan are heavily involved in the land-use and transport programmes of their national capitals. In Tokyo, the Tokyo Metropolitan Government works closely with the national government and its railway and road improvement plans must comply with national policy set out in the National Capital Region Development Plan.

In London the absence of a strategic metropolitan or regional local authority has meant that planning has been uncoordinated and made through a number of disparate bodies taking on specific responsibilities.

In Paris, the national government in partnership with a strong regional government is the recipe for providing some stability, greater land-use controls and national funds for transport. Paris continues to debate decentralisation of more authority to the Regional Council. On the one hand, the Region is the main funder of transport operations and infrastructure in the capital. On the other hand, the government (through its dominant position on the Syndicat des Transports Parisiens which establishes transport programmes) decides policies and priorities. The Region is not even represented on the Syndicat.

In the United States, the national government enforces regulations supposed to govern state-local actions by threatening to withhold the funds it allocates to transport projects, though there is often flexibility such as in extended deadlines on air quality standards. But the related land-use decisions remain steadfastly in the hands of 780 municipal governments. New York is the only one of the four cities that is not the national capital and has no special relationship with the national government.

5.3.4   Controlling the growth of car use

Despite the efforts of all four cities to minimise car travel, the appeal of the car is universal. All four cities' Zones 3 & 4 saw an increase in household car ownership in the 1980s. Car ownership and use keeps rising throughout the world in part because the driver does not pay the full social costs of car use, such as traffic congestion, air pollution, noise, traffic accidents, land-use costs (locating shopping, education and entertainment in out-of-town developments away from where people live), promoting sprawl, aesthetically degrading the landscape and reducing the mobility of those without cars by greatly increasing the costs of providing public transport.

The national governments in all four cities are trying to discipline the transport decisions we make as individuals to achieve a settlement pattern most people seem to favour as a community. Generally, the public supports efforts to discipline car use; for instance, there is usually strong local support for traffic calming measures in neighbourhoods. But as individuals, we continue to buy more cars and drive them more.

Unchecked growth in car traffic would result in further degradation of the environment in the four cities. It

would lead to an increase in traffic congestion, an increase in carbon dioxide emissions (the fastest growing contributor to climatic change) and local air pollution, endangering health. All four countries have pledged to restrain or reduce emissions that cause global warming. And in all four cities, governments require environmental impact statements before major transport projects can go ahead. Although improved technologies can substantially cut vehicle emissions, the long term trends are still upwards.

Accidents are a substantial public and private cost of driving. The European Commission's Green Paper estimated that the cost of traffic accidents is equivalent to 1.5% of Europe's Gross Domestic Product. In 1994 over one and half thousand people were killed in traffic accidents in the metropolitan areas of the four cities (Zones 1 & 2): 321 in London, 529 in New York, 499 in Paris and 280 in Tokyo. London has energetically campaigned to reduce motor vehicle accidents, by taking traffic safety measures and reducing speeds through traffic calming. London's road fatalities have dropped over the past 15 years, by about 50%. The other three cities might consider emulating London's prioritisation of road safety.

Controls on parking are a major tool for reducing car use in specific places. New York City has a tax on off-street parking charges and in the central area requires cars parked on the street to be moved almost every day.

In Tokyo a parking space is a prerequisite for purchasing a car.

Charges for illegal parking in the metropolitan areas of London and New York are high and rigorously enforced but enforcement is more lax in many areas of Paris where double parking can often be seen. There are charges for on-street parking in most of Paris' neighbourhoods.

Orbital roads keep unnecessary traffic out of a region's centre, but often have the effect of dispersing jobs and population outward, particularly at the junctions of radial and orbital motorways. Both Paris and Tokyo remain compact in their development despite heavily used orbital highways and are continuing to build motorways, especially orbital ones. New York and London could consider whether there may be a way to get the efficiency of an orbital road without the land-use liabilities. But Tokyo and Paris also should recognise New York's experience and be vigilant in controlling development along the new motorways.

5.3.5 *Measures the cities might consider to improve transport provision*

There are two basic areas for improving the efficiency of the transport system and improving the quality of life in the four metropolises: tackling congestion and providing high quality public transport. The construction of new roads will have little impact on the overall traffic congestion faced by the four metropolises.

Tackling congestion

- Traffic congestion and overcrowding on public transport affects all four cities. Through a combination of land-use policies and targeted investment this could be reduced.

- Paris' express regional rail services, the Réseau Express Régional network, is a model for improving through-passenger flows. Tokyo has some through-running of regional rail trains on metro tracks. London and New York could learn from Paris' and Tokyo's experiences by planning and implementing their own express regional metro systems.

- Tokyo's orbital Yamanote Loop rail line permits easy transfer to most of the regional rail and metro network. The other cities could consider orbital rail links of their own.

- New York could consider increasing regional rail provision in Zone 2 to relieve congestion on the metro.

- All four cities could consider further priority measures for buses, even at the expense of cars.

Improving quality

- It is important that the cities provide dependable, high quality public transport systems. Tokyo offers an example of a frequent, reliable and punctual system which attracts users throughout the region.

- The scheduled frequency of regional rail services in Paris is far below the other cities. It could be worth studying what would be the effects of improving the frequencies of suburban trains. New York and Paris could also look at providing enhanced off-peak regional rail services. New York would also need to provide more parking at stations.

- 98% of Tokyo's metro trains arrive within 1 minute of their schedule. London (85% within 5 minutes) and New York (80% within 5 minutes) need seriously to address their metros' punctuality record. London should also consider measures to improve punctuality on its regional rail system, which is the poorest of the four cities.

- New York and London have high public transport fares compared to the other cities. They could consider the impact of reducing fares on public transport to make it more affordable. Tokyo could consider multi-modal ticketing.

Bibliography

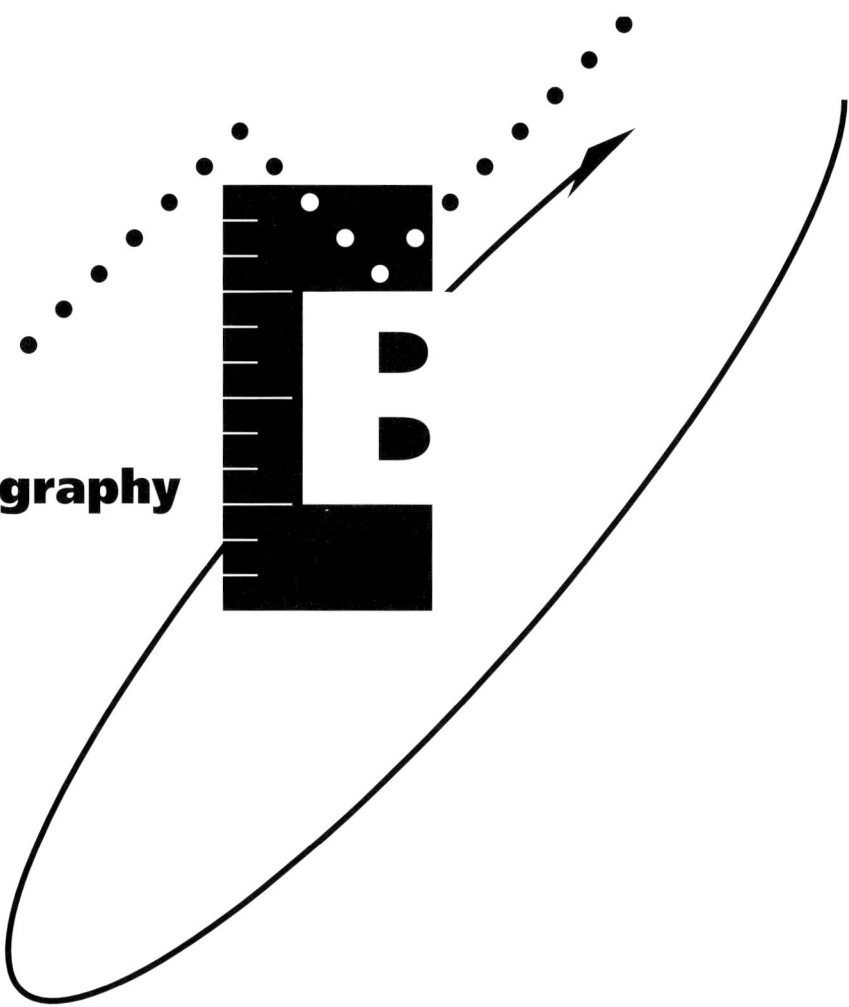

Bibliography

Abe Hitoshi et al., *The Government and Politics of Japan*, University of Tokyo Press, Tokyo 1994

Association of London Government/London Planning Advisory Committee, *An Integrated Transport Programme for London*, London Planning Advisory Committee, 1996

Benson Bobrick, *Labyrinths of iron: Subways in history, myth, art, technology, & war*, Henry Holt, New York 1994

Calvino Italo, *Invisible Cities*, Picador, London 1979

Chaudry Arfan, *Cycling in London*, London Research Centre, London 1997

Commission of the European Communities, *Towards Fair and Efficient Pricing in Transport: Policy Options for Internalising the External Costs of Transport in the European Union*, Commission of the European Communities, Brussels 1995

Commission of the European Communities, *The Citizens' Network: Fulfilling the Potential of Public Passenger Transport in Europe*, Commission of the European Communities, Brussels & Luxembourg 1996

Commission of the European Communities, Expert Group on the Urban Environment, *European Sustainable Cities*, Commission of the European Communities: Directorate General XI, Brussels 1996

Commission of the European Communities, *Fair Payment for Infrastructure Use: a Phased Approach to a Common Transport Infrastructure Charging Framework in the European Union*, Commission of the European Communities, Brussels 1998

Conseil Régional Ile-de-France, *La Charte de líIle-de-France*, Conseil Régional Ile-de-France, Paris 1991a

Conseil Régional Ile-de-France, *The Ile-de-France Planning Strategy*, Conseil Régional Ile-de-France, Paris 1991b

Conseil Régional Ile-de-France, *Smoother Traffic in the Ile-de-France*, Conseil Régional Ile-de-France, Paris 1995

Council of Local Authorities for International Relations, *Local Government in Japan*, Council of Local Authorities for International Relations, Tokyo 1994

Cudahy Brian J., *Under the sidewalks of New York*, Fordham University Press, New York 1995

Department of Environment/London Planning Advisory Committee, *Strategic Planning Guidance for the River Thames (RPG3 B/9B)*, The Stationery Office, London 1997

Department of the Environment, *Planning and Policy Guidance 6: Town Centres and Retail Developments*, Her Majesty's Stationery Office, London 1996

Department of the Environment, *The United Kingdom Air Quality Strategy*, The Stationery Office, London 1997

Department of the Environment, Transport and the Regions, *New Leadership for London*, The Stationery Office, London 1997a

Department of the Environment, Transport and the Regions, *Transport Statistics for London 1997*, The Stationery Office, London 1997b

Department of the Environment, Transport and the Regions, *New Deal for Transport: Better for Everyone: the Government's White Paper on the Future of Transport*, The Stationery Office, London 1998

Department of the Environment and Department of Transport, *Planning Policy Guidance 13: Transport*, Her Majesty's Stationery Office, London 1994

Department of Transport, *Transport: The Government's Expenditure Plans 1995-96 to 1997-98* Her Majesty's Stationery Office, London 1995

Department of Transport, *Travel by London's Men and Women: Why do Women Travel less than Men?*, London Research Centre, London 1995

Department of Transport, *Transport: The Way Forward*, Her Majesty's Stationery Office, London 1996

Department of Transport and Government Office for London, *A Transport Strategy for London*, Her Majesty's Stationery Office, London 1997

Edwards Philip & Flatley John, *The Capital Divided: Mapping Poverty and Social Exclusion in London*, London Research Centre, London 1996

Federal Transit Administration, *1996 Report,* Federal Transit Administration, Washington DC 1996a

Federal Transit Administration, *Impact of Mass Transit Investments: Selected Urbanised Areas*, Federal Transit Administration, Washington DC 1996b

Fischler Stan, *The subway: A trip through time of New York's rapid transit*, H & M Productions II Inc., New York 1997

Focas Caralampo & Brown Nigel, *Fares Compared: an International Comparison of Public Transport Fares (Summary Document, Volume 1 & Volume 2)*, London Research Centre, London 1995

Focas Caralampo & Navarre Danièle, *Paris-London: A Comparison of Transport Systems*, London Research Centre (Her Majesty's Stationery Office), London 1995

Focas Caralampo(in Grieco et al, 1989), *A Survey of Women's Travel Needs in London*, London Research Centre, London 1989

Focas Caralampo et al., *"Will Passengers Please Note..": a Survey of British Rail, London Underground and Docklands Light Railway Stations in London*, London Research Centre, London 1993

Focas Caralampo et al., *Shopping: an Increasingly Motorised Activity*, London Research Centre, London 1995

Government Office for London, *Strategic Guidance for London Planning Authorities*, Her Majesty's Stationery Office, London 1996

Government Office for London, *Strategic Guidance for London Planning Authorities (Regional Planning Guidance 3)*, Her Majesty's Stationery Office, 1996

Granick Harry Granick, *Underneath New York*, Fordham University Press, New York 1991

Grieco Margaret et al., *Gender Transport and Employment*, Avebury, Aldershot, 1989

Group for European Metropolitan Area Comparative Analysis, *North-West European Metropolitan Regions: Geographical Boundaries and Economic Structures*, Institut d'Aménagement et d'Urbanisme de la Région d'Ile-de-France, Paris 1996

Hall Peter, *London 2001*, Unwin Hyman, London 1989

Howes Eileen, *London's Workers: From the 1991 Census*, London Research Centre, London 1997

Ishizuka Hiromichi & Ishida Yorifusa eds., *Tokyo: Urban Growth and Planning 1968-1988*, Tokyo Metropolitan University, Tokyo 1988

Japan Transport Economics Research Centre, *Transportation Outlook in Japan: '95*, Japan Transport Economics Research Centre, Tokyo 1995

Bibliography

Kasai Masaaki, *Tokyo: The Making of a Metropolis*, Tokyo Metropolitan Government, Tokyo 1993

Land Transport Administration, *Urban Public Transport in France: Institutional Organisation*, Land Transport Directorate, Paris 1995

Llewelyn-Davies et al., *Four World Cities: a Comparative Study of London, Paris, New York and Tokyo*, Llewelyn-Davies, London 1996

London First, *London The Millennium City*, London First, London 1997

London First Transport Initiative, *London's Action Programme for Transport: 1996 – 2010*, London First, London 1995

London Planning Advisory Committee, *Strategic Planning Advice for London*, London Planning Advisory Committee, London 1988

London Planning Advisory Committee, *London: World City*, Her Majesty's Stationery Office, London 1991

London Planning Advisory Committee, *Advice on Strategic Planning Guidance for London*, London Planning Advisory Committee, London 1994

London Planning Advisory Committee, *Advice on a Strategy for Walking in London (1997 Walking Advice)*, London Planning Advisory Committee, London 1997a

London Planning Advisory Committee, *Revised Advice on a Parking Strategy for London (1997 Parking Advice)*, London Planning Advisory Committee, London 1997b

London Regional Passengers Committee, *Major Rail Construction Schemes in London*, London Regional Passengers Committee, London 1997

London Research Centre, *Women's Travel*, London Research Centre, London 1998

London Research Centre, *London Accident Analysis Unit Annual Report 1997*, London Research Centre, London 1998

London Research Centre & Department of Transport, *Travel in London*, Her Majesty's Stationery Office, London 1994

London Research Centre et. al., *Focus on London 97*, The Stationery Office, London 1997

London Transport, *Planning London's Transport*, London Transport, London 1995

London Transport, *Planning London's Transport: to Win as a World City*, London Transport, London 1996a

London Transport, *The Impact of New Rail Schemes: A Review of How Major Schemes Affect Passenger Movement in Central London*, London Transport, London 1996b

London Transport, *Statement of Strategy*, London Transport, London 1997

London Transport Marketing, *Market Report*, London Transport, London 1996

London Transport Planning, *Interchange in London: Patterns of Access and Interchange at Rail Stations Outside Central London*, London Transport, London 1997

London Transport Planning, *Bus service in London: A comparison with the rest of Great Britain*, London Transport Planning, London 1998

Macket Roger et. al., *Transport, Land-Use and the Environment in London and Tokyo: Problems, Policies and Lessons*, 8th World Conference on Transport Research, Antwerp 1998

Mairie de Paris, *Paris en Chiffres*, Mairie de Paris, Paris 1996

Mammen David, *Making Tokyo a World City*, Kodansha International, Tokyo 1989

Midgley Peter, *Urban Transport in Asia: An Operational Agenda for the 1990s*, The World Bank, Washington DC 1994

Ministry of Transport, *Annual Report on the Transport Economy: Summary*, Ministry of Transport, Tokyo 1995

Ministry of Transport, Transport Policy Bureau and Information and Research Department, *National Transportation Handbook*, Japan Transport Economics Research Centre, Tokyo 1997

Mizutani Fumitoshi, *Japanese Urban Railways: A Private-Public Comparison*, Avebury, Brookfield 1994

Mogridge Martin, *The Rejuvenation of Inner London*, Mogridge Martin Associates, London 1996

Murray Lesley, *Transport in London: Whose Decision?*, London Research Centre, London 1997

MVA Consultancy and Government Office for London, *The London Congestion Charging Research Programme - Principal Findings*, Her Majesty's Stationery Office, London 1990

Nakagawa, D. and Matsunaka, R., *Funding Transport Systems: A Comparison among Developed Countries*, Pergamon, Oxford 1997

Nakano Minoru, *The Policy-Making Process in Contemporary Japan*, Macmillan Press, London 1997

New Jersey State, *Communities of Place, The New Jersey State Development and Redevelopment Plan*, Threnton 1997

New York City Transit, *New York City Transit's Facts & Figures*, New York City Transit, New York 1996

New York Metropolitan Transportation Council, *Hub-Bound Travel 1993*, New York Metropolitan Transportation Council, New York 1995a

New York Metropolitan Transportation Council, *Regional Transport Status 1993: New York Metropolitan Region and Environs*, New York Metropolitan Transportation Council, New York 1995b

New York Metropolitan Transportation Council, *Critical Issues - Critical Choices: a Mobility Plan for the New York Region Through the Year 2015*, New York Metropolitan Transportation Council, New York 1997a

New York Metropolitan Transportation Council, *Regional Transportation Statistical Report 1995*, New York Metropolitan Transportation Council, New York 1997b

Newman Peter & Kenworthy Jeffrey, *Cities and Automobile Dependence: an Interactive Source-book*, Gower, Aldershot 1989

Newman Peter & Kenworthy Jeffrey, *Sustainability and Cities*, Island Press, Washington DC (forthcoming)

Pucher John & Lefèvre Christian, *The Urban Transport Crisis in Europe and North America*, Macmillan, London 1996

Ravelli Robert J., *Car-Free in New York City: The regional public transit guide*, Camino Books Inc., Pennsylvania 1994

Bibliography

Reyes Joseph, *Hub-bound Travel: 1995, New York Metropolitan Transportation Council (Information Compendium: PT 1275801)*, New York 1997

Samuels Richard J., *The Politics of Regional Policy in Japan: Localities Incorporated?*, Princeton University Press, Princeton 1983

Sansone Gene, *Evolution of New York City Subways*. New York Transit Museum Press, New York 1997

Sassen Saskia, *The Global City: New York, London, Tokyo*, Princeton University Press, Princeton 1991

Seidensticker Edward, *Tokyo Rising: The City since the Great Earthquake*, Alfred A. Knopf, New York 1990

Sharman K. et al., *Changing Patterns of Travel in the London Area (1971-1991)*, Transport Research Laboratory, Crowthorne (unpublished) 1996

Sharpe L. J., *The Government of World Cities: the Future of the Metro Model*, John Wiley & Sons, Chichester 1995

Shore, William B., *The Renaissance of Rail Transit in America*, Regional Plan Association & American Public Transit Association, New York 1996

Storkey et al., , *Cosmopolitan London: Past, Present and Future*, London Research Centre, London 1997

Teito Rapid Transit Authority, *Tokyo Teito Rapid Transit Authority Subways: Developments Over the Past 50 Years*, Teito Rapid Transit Authority, Tokyo 1993

Togo Hisatake in L. J. Sharpe ed., *The Metropolitan Strategies of Tokyo: Toward the Restoration of Balanced Growth*, John Wiley & Sons, Chichester 1995

Tokyo Metropolitan Government, *Bureau of City Planning, Planning of Tokyo Metropolitan Government*, Tokyo Metropolitan Government, Tokyo 1994

Travers Tony & Jones Georg, *The New Government of London*, Joseph Rowntree Foundation, York 1997e

Tri-State Transportation Campaign, *Citizens Action Plan: a 21st Century Transportation System: a Vision of Our Region's Land, Cities and Communities*, Tri-State Transportation Campaign, New York 1995

Truelove Paul, *Decision-making in Transport Planning*, Longman Scientific & Technical, London1992

United States Department of Transportation, Federal Highway Administration, *1990 Nation-wide Personal Transportation Survey: Urban Travel Patterns*, United States Department of Transportation, Washington DC 1994

United States Department of Transportation, Federal Highway Administration, *Journey-to-Work Trends in the United States and its Major Metropolitan Areas 1960-1990*, United States Department of Transportation, Washington DC 1993

United States Department of Transportation, Federal Highway Administration, *Highway Statistics 1995*, United States Department of Transportation, Washington DC 1996a

United States Department of Transportation, Federal Transit Administration, *Transit Profiles: Agencies in Urbanised Areas Exceeding 200,000 Population (for the 1995 National Transit Database Report Year)*, United States Department of Transportation, Washington DC 1996b

Yamamoto Hirofumi, *Technological Innovation and the Development of Transportation in Japan*, The United Nations University, Tokyo 1993

Yaro Robert D. & Hiss Tony, *A Region at Risk: The Third Regional plan for the New York-New Jersey-Connecticut Metropolitan Area*, Regional Plan Association (Island Press), Washington D. C. & Covelo Ca. 1996

Printed in the United Kingdom for the Stationery Office by
Commercial Colour Press, Plc.
J0064557, C10, 12/98.